Brand Culture

Brands occupy an increasingly prominent place in the managerial mind as well as in the cultural landscape. Recent research has shown that brands are interpreted in multiple ways, prompting an important and illuminating reconsideration of how branding 'works', and shifting attention from brand producers toward consumer response to understand how branding interacts with consumers to create meaning. Largely missing from these insights, however, is an awareness of basic cultural processes that affect contemporary brands, including historical context, ethical concerns, and consumer response. Neither managers nor consumers completely control brand image and corporate identity – cultural codes constrain how brands work to produce meaning. *Brand Culture* places brands firmly within culture to look at the complex underpinnings of branding processes.

The reader will find case studies of iconic global brands like Benetton, LEGO, and Ryanair, practical managerial advice, as well as thoughtful analyses of brand concepts and strategic brand management by leading brand researchers, including John M. T. Balmer, Stephen Brown, Mary Jo Hatch, Jean-Noël Kapferer, Majken Schultz, and Richard Elliott.

Topics covered include:

- the role of consumption
- brand management
- corporate branding
- branding ethics
- the role of advertising.

Brand Culture offers a thoughtful update on brands from a cultural and managerial perspective for all students and scholars interested in brands, consumers, and the broader cultural domain that surrounds them.

Jonathan E. Schroeder is Professor of Marketing at the University of Exeter, UK, and Visiting Professor in Marketing Semiotics at Bocconi University, Milan. His research focuses on the production and consumption of images.

Miriam Salzer-Mörling is Associate Professor at the School of Business, Stockholm University. As a branding consultant she has specialized in the development of the 'corporate soul' and communicative strategies for both public and commercial organizations.

Brand Culture

Edited by

Jonathan E. Schroeder and Miriam Salzer-Mörling

with Søren Askegaard, John M. T. Balmer,
Anders Bengtsson, Sven Bergvall,
Janet L. Borgerson, Arianna Brioschi,
Stephen Brown, Fabian Faurholt Csaba,
Andrea Davies, Richard Elliott, Martin
Escudero Magnusson, Mary Jo Hatch,
Benoît Heilbrunn, Ulla Johansson, Jean-Noël
Kapferer, Frank Magnusson, Majken Schultz,
Lisbeth Svengren Holm and Henrik Uggla

Routledge
Taylor & Francis Group

LONDON AND NEW YORK

First published 2006
by Routledge
2 Park Square, Milton Park, Abingdon, Oxon OX14 4RN

Simultaneously published in the USA and Canada
by Routledge
270 Madison Ave, New York, NY 10016

Transferred to Digital Printing 2006

Routledge is an imprint of the Taylor & Francis Group, an informa business

Typeset in Perpetua and Bell Gothic
by Keystroke, Jacaranda Lodge, Wolverhampton
Printed and bound in Great Britain by TJI Digital, Padstow, Cornwall

British Library Cataloguing in Publication Data
A catalogue record for this book is available from the British Library

Library of Congress Cataloging in Publication Data
A catalog record for this book has been requested

ISBN10: 0–415–35598–2   ISBN13: 9–78–0–415–35598–8 (hbk)
ISBN10: 0–415–35599–0   ISBN13: 9–78–0–415–35599–5 (pbk)

Contents

Illustrations

FIGURES

TABLES

Contributors

Søren Askegaard is Professor of Marketing at the University of Southern Denmark. He has a Masters degree in Social Sciences from Odense University, a postgraduate diploma in Communication Studies from the Sorbonne University, Paris and a PhD in Business Studies from Odense University. His research interests generally lie in the field of consumer behaviour analysis from a cultural perspective, including such topics as lifestyles, consumer motivations, food consumption, product-origin imagery, globalization and branding. He has received two major Danish research awards. He is the co-author of the best-selling textbook on consumer behaviour in the European market. He has published in numerous anthologies as well as in journals such as the *Journal of Consumer Research*, *International Business Review*, *European Journal of Marketing*, *Psychology and Marketing*, *Advances in Consumer Research* and *Consumption, Markets, and Culture*. In 2003, he co-founded the business–university collaboration project 'Brand Base', and he is also its leader.

John M. T. Balmer is Professor of Corporate Identity at Bradford School of Management, UK. His appointment is believed to be unique. Prior to this, he was the founder/director of the International Centre for Corporate Identity Studies at Strathclyde Business School in Scotland. He has organized numerous conferences on identity and corporate funding where leading scholars and captains of industry have spoken (including the Chairman of British Airways, the Group CEO of BP and the Chairman of Barclays Bank). He has acted as a special adviser to the BBC and has also been involved with projects for the branding consultancies Landor and Enterprise, and with Mercedes Benz. He leads the corporate brand and identity electives for the company MBA programmes of the BBC and for Emirate Airways. Along with Professor Greyser (Harvard Business School) he is the author of *Revealing the Corporation* which explores corporate brands and identity, reputation, image and corporate level marketing (Routledge, 2003). His articles have appeared in *California Management Review*, *Long Range Planning*, *International Studies of Management and Organizations*, *European Journal of Marketing*, *Journal of Marketing Management*, and the *International Journal of Bank Marketing*, among others. He has given seminars at a number of leading business schools including Harvard, Oxford, Copenhagen and

Stockholm. Currently, he is involved with leading scholars from Harvard Business School and Lund University (Sweden) on a major project on Monarchies as Corporate Brands where unprecedented access was given to Senior Court Officials and to Their Majesties the King and Queen of Sweden. He has served as a guest editor for several leading journals and is on the editorial board of four journals. He received his PhD from the University of Strathclyde, his MBA from the University of Durham and his first degree from the University of Reading. Before his academic career he was a senior manager at the Dome Concert Hall complex in Brighton and Assistant Administrator to Lord Menuhin's concert agency 'Live Music Now'.

Anders Bengtsson is Assistant Professor of Marketing at Suffolk University, USA. He received his doctorate in marketing from Lund University in 2002. Previously he has held appointments at the University of Southern Denmark and Lund University. His research focuses on the production and consumption of brand cultures. This interest has brought him to study topics such as the use of brands in tattooing and the roles brands play in consumers' everyday lives across cultures. His articles have been published in *Consumption, Markets and Culture* and *Advances in Consumer Research*.

Sven Bergvall is a Doctoral Researcher in Marketing at the Royal Institute of Technology in Stockholm. His research focuses on branding in the information technology sector, with particular emphasis on Sony Ericsson. He has conducted research in new product introduction for Ericsson Corporation.

Janet L. Borgerson is a Philosopher at the School of Business and Economics, University of Exeter, UK. She received her PhD in Philosophy from the University of Wisconsin-Madison, followed by postdoctoral studies at Brown University. She has been awarded a Harvard University School of Public Health Scholarship and a Fellowship from the Marketing Technology Center, Stockholm. Recent research has appeared in the *European Journal of Marketing*, *International Marketing Review*, *Organization Studies*, *Consumption, Markets and Culture*, *Journal of Knowledge Management*, *Feminist Theory*, *Journal of Philosophical Research*, *Gender Work and Organization*, *Culture and Organization*, *Radical Philosophy Review*, *Journal of Consumer Affairs* and *Advances in Consumer Research*, among others.

Arianna Brioschi received her doctorate from L. Bocconi University in Milan, where she is currently a Lecturer. She has also been working as a researcher and trainer at the Bocconi University Business School since 1995, where she is part of the Marketing Studies department.

Stephen Brown is Professor of Marketing Research at the University of Ulster, Northern Ireland. Best known for *Postmodern Marketing* (Routledge, 1995), he has written or co-edited twelve other books, including *Marketing Apocalypse* (Routledge, 1996), *Time, Space, and the Market* (Sharpe, 2003), *Marketing: The Retro Revolution* (Sage, 2001) and *Free Gift Inside!!* (Capstone, 2003). His articles have been published in the *Journal of Marketing*, *Harvard Business Review*, *Journal of Advertising*, *Business Horizons*, *Journal of Retailing*, *European Management Journal*, and more besides. In addition to receiving diverse awards, such as the *Irish Times*' coveted 'Book of the Week' accolade, Stephen has held Visiting Professor positions at Northwestern University, University of California-Irvine and University of Utah, amongst others.

Fabian Faurholt Csaba is Assistant Professor at the Department of Intercultural Communication and Management at the Copenhagen Business School. He received his PhD from University of Southern Denmark and has taught at Bilkent University in Turkey. His research addresses marketing and consumption across cultures, investigating phenomena as diverse as American shopping malls, oriental carpets and the branding of cola in Denmark.

Andrea Davies is a Senior Lecturer in Marketing at the University of Leicester, UK. She received her PhD from the Open University. Her research interests focus on contemporary and historical aspects of consumer behaviour as they inform brand theory, advances in marketing research methodology and cultures of consumption. Recent publications attend to symbolic, experiential and tribal consumption practices, persuasion knowledge in advertising, consumer research methodology and cross-cultural consumer behaviour. With a recent ESRC (Economic and Social Research Council, UK) research grant award she will examine the evolution of brand consciousness. Her work has been published in the *European Journal of Marketing*, *Advances in Consumer Research*, *Journal of Consumer Behaviour*, *Journal of Tourism Management*, and the *International Journal of Museum Management and Curatorship*.

Richard Elliott is a Fellow of St Anne's College, Oxford and Professor of Marketing and Consumer Research at Warwick Business School. He is a Visiting Professor at ESCP-EAP Paris, ESSEC Paris, Université Paris II, and Thammasat University Bangkok. He is Associate Editor of the *British Journal of Management* and European Editor of the *Journal of Product and Brand Management*. He has published books on 'Strategic Advertising Management' and 'Interpretive Consumer Research' and over 100 research papers in such journals as the *Journal of Consumer Research*, *Consumption, Markets, and Culture*, *Human Relations*, *International Journal of Advertising*, *European Journal of Marketing*, *International Journal of Research in Marketing*, *Journal of Marketing Management*, *Advances in Consumer Research*, *Journal of Consumer Policy*, *International Journal of Market Research*, *Journal of Product and Brand Management*, *Psychology & Marketing* and *Journal of Consumer Behaviour*. His research focuses on the symbolic meaning of brands, consumer culture and identity, and the dynamics of brand ecology.

xi

Martin Escudero Magnusson completed his Masters degree in Marketing from Stockholm University and a postgraduate degree as International Trade Specialist from the Swedish Trade Council. He currently works for the Sendoline Corporation, covering the Latin American, South European, and Scandinavian markets. He is also a successful hip-hop performer and producer.

Mary Jo Hatch (PhD, Stanford 1985) is Professor of Commerce at the McIntire School of Commerce, University of Virginia and Adjunct Professor at the Copenhagen Business School. She has published numerous articles on organizational culture, corporate branding and organizational identity in academic journals such as the *Academy of Management Review*, *Harvard Business Review*, *Human Relations*, *Journal of Management Inquiry* and the *European Journal of Marketing*. Other research papers on the humour and aesthetics of management and organization as well as her work on jazz as a metaphor for organizing can be found in *Organization*, *Organization Science* and *Organization Studies*. Hatch's textbook *Organization Theory: Modern, Symbolic and Postmodern Perspectives* (1997) is available from Oxford University Press, which also published *The Expressive Organization: Linking Identity, Reputation and the Corporate Brand* (2000, co-edited with Majken Schultz and Mogens Holten Larsen) and her latest book *Organizational Identity: A Reader* (2004, co-edited with Majken Schultz).

Benoît Heilbrunn is Assistant Professor of Marketing at ESCP-EAP in Paris. Trained as a semiologist and philosopher, he teaches and researches in the areas of brand management, consumer behaviour and design management. He has co-edited *European Perspectives on Consumer Behaviour* (Prentice-Hall, 1998) and written books such as *Le logo* (PUF, 2001) and *ABCdaire du design* (Flammarion, 2003). He is also a consultant for many fast-moving consumer goods (FMCG) brands.

Ulla Johansson is a former architect who now holds a PhD in Management. She works as a researcher and teacher at Växjö University, Sweden. In her teaching, she covers a broad range of courses at different levels, including methodology, organization theory, feminism and design management at all levels. She is also active in a platform for entrepreneurial research and design. Her dissertation focused on the concept of responsibility and how corporate employees respond when their employers claim to have delegated responsibility to them. Together with Lisbeth Svengren Holm, she directs a long-range research project in design management, focusing on the relationship between industrial designers, marketers and engineers. She is also working on a book about irony as a platform for academic critical thinking.

Jean-Noël Kapferer is an internationally recognized authority on brands and brand management. A Professor of Marketing Strategy at HEC Graduate School of Management in France, he holds a PhD from Northwestern University (USA) and is an active consultant to many European and US corporations. His articles have been published in *Marketing Science*, *Journal of Marketing Research*, *Journal of International Marketing*, *Journal of Advertising Research*, *Public Opinion Quarterly*, *Ivey Business Journal*, *Journal of Brand Management*, as well as in the *Financial Times*. He is the author of eleven books, including the international best-seller *Strategic Brand Management: Re-inventing the Brand* (Kogan Page, 1992) and, the very latest, *The New Strategic Brand Management* (Kogan Page, 2004).

Frank Magnusson received his Masters degree in Business Administration and Economics from Stockholm University, and is currently working for Selecta First Class, Inc., managing their North American operations.

Miriam Salzer-Mörling is Associate Professor at the School of Business, Stockholm University. She received her PhD in 1994 with a cultural study on organizational identity in the IKEA-world. Her current research centres on story-telling, brands, culture and expressive leadership and she has published various articles on these topics in, for example, the *European Journal of Marketing* and *Scandinavian Journal of Management*. Among her most recent publications is a co-edited book on the new economy, *Stuck in the Future* (BookHouse, 2002). Salzer-Mörling has been a lecturer at Linköping University and senior researcher at the Centre for Advanced Studies in Leadership at Stockholm School of Economics. As a consultant and adviser to a number of Scandinavian companies she has specialized in the development of the 'corporate soul' and communicative strategies in a branded world.

Jonathan E. Schroeder is Professor of Marketing at the University of Exeter, UK. He is a Visiting Professor in Marketing Semiotics at Bocconi University in Milan, where he lectures in the Masters Program in Fashion, Experience and Design Management. He has taught at the University of California, Berkeley, the University of Rhode Island, Novgorod State University, Russia and the Royal Institute of Technology, Stockholm. He is an editor of the journal *Consumption Markets and Culture*. His research focuses on the production and consumption of images and has been published widely in marketing, psychology, design and anthropology journals. His book *Visual Consumption* (Routledge, 2002) introduced an interdisciplinary, image-based approach to understanding consumer behaviour. He received his PhD from the University of California, Berkeley, and pursued postdoctoral work in visual studies at the Rhode Island School of Design.

Majken Schultz (PhD, Copenhagen Business School 1988) has been Professor of Organization at the Department of Intercultural Communication and Leadership at the Copenhagen Business School since 1996. Majken's research interests include the relations between organizational identity, organizational culture and image. She also takes an interest in corporate branding and reputation management, drawing on insights from marketing and strategy. She has published articles on these topics in

xiii

Academy of Management Review, Human Relations, Harvard Business Review, Organization Studies, Journal of Management Inquiry, Studies in Cultures, Organizations and Societies, European Journal of Marketing, Corporate Reputation Review and *International Studies of Management and Organization*. She is the first editor of *The Expressive Organization: Linking Identity, Reputation and the Corporate Brand*, co-edited with Mary Jo Hatch and Mogens Holten Larsen (Oxford University Press, 2000). Majken also serves as a board member of several Danish companies, including Danske Bank, one of the largest financial institutions in Scandinavia.

Lisbeth Svengren Holm is Head of the Marketing Department at Stockholm University School of Business. She is Project Co-Leader (together with Ulla Johansson) of the research programme Managing Design Processes. She is participating in a multidisciplinary research programme: Design in the Niche Society (Dennis) and in the international research programmes: Design Drivers and Design Against Crime. Her research focuses on the integration of industrial design as a strategic resource in a corporate context. She is editor of *Designjournalen* (the Design Journal) published by the Swedish Industrial Design Foundation.

Henrik Uggla is a Postdoctoral Researcher in Brand Management at the Royal Institute of Technology, Stockholm. Henrik received his BA in Cognitive Psychology and doctorate in Strategic Brand Management at Stockholm University. Henrik is particularly involved with issues related to the handling of mature brands. He has published several books on brand architecture, co-branding and brand extensions, and is an active branding consultant for Scandinavian industry.

Acknowledgements

Thanks to Pierre Guillet de Monthoux, Mats Alvesson, Barbara Czarniawska, Inga-Lill Holmberg, Donatella Depperu, Stefano Puntoni, Peter Dobers, Detlev Zwick, Markus Geisler, Hervé Mathe, T. C. Melewar, Tony Apéria, Karin Ekström, Craig Thompson, John Sherry, Doug Holt, Barbara Stern, Pierre McDonagh, Andy Prothero, Frank Piller, Tom O'Guinn, Mali Pohlmann and David Musson for encouragement of and interest in this project. We also appreciated the comments of our anonymous reviewers, and Avi Shankar read parts of the manuscript. At Routledge, Francesca Helsop and Emma Joyes have been enthusiastically supportive of *Brand Culture* and thanks to Victoria Lincoln and David Armstrong in Marketing, and Liz Dawn and Colin Morgan on the production team. Thanks to the Department of Industrial Economics and Management, Royal Institute of Technology, Stockholm, the Centre for Advanced Studies in Leadership, Stockholm School of Economics, the School of Business and Economics, University of Exeter, the School of Business, Stockholm University and Bocconi University in Milan for institutional support. We also acknowledge financial support from the Jan Wallanders and Tom Hedelius Foundation and the Bank of Sweden Tercentenary Foundation. Thanks also to the dynamic brand researchers affiliated with the research project 'Brands, Companies, and Consumers: A Dynamic Perspective': Søren Askegaard, Anders Bengtsson, Sven Bergvall, Jon Bertilsson, Clara Gustafsson, Henrik Uggla and Jacob Östberg; and to the staff at Handelsbanken research foundation, Inga-Lill Göransson, Ingmarie Severien and Karin Påhlson.

Jonathan E. Schroeder and Miriam Salzer-Mörling
Exeter, UK and Stockholm, Sweden

Introduction

The cultural codes of branding

Jonathan E. Schroeder and Miriam Salzer-Mörling

Brands occupy an increasingly prominent place in the managerial mind as well as the cultural landscape. Recent research has shown that brands are interpreted or read in multiple ways, prompting an important and illuminating reconsideration of how branding 'works', and shifting attention from brand producers toward consumer response to understand how branding creates meaning (e.g. Fournier 1998; Hirschman and Thompson 1997; Holt 2004; Muñiz and O'Guinn 2001; Ritson and Elliott 1999; Scott 1994). Cultural codes, ideological discourse, consumers' background knowledge, and rhetorical processes have been cited as influences in branding and consumers' relationships to advertising, brands, and mass media. Consumers are seen to construct and perform identities and self-concepts, trying out new roles and creating their identity within, and in collaboration with, brand culture (e.g. Borgerson and Schroeder 2002; Solomon *et al.* 2002; Wikström 1996).

Largely missing from these insights, however, is an awareness of basic cultural processes that affect contemporary brands, including historical context, ethical concerns, and consumer response. In other words, neither managers nor consumers completely control branding processes – cultural codes constrain how brands work to produce meaning. This collection of articles reveals how branding has opened up to include cultural, sociological, and philosophical enquiry, that both complements and complicates economic and managerial analysis.

If brands exist as cultural, ideological, and political objects, then brand researchers require tools developed to understand culture, politics, and ideology, in conjunction with more typical branding concepts, such as equity, strategy, and value. Brand culture refers to the cultural influences and implications of brands in two ways. First, we live in a branded world: brands infuse culture with meaning, and brand management exerts a profound influence on contemporary society. Second, brand culture provides a third leg for brand theory – in conjunction with brand identity and brand image, brand culture provides the necessary cultural, historical, and political grounding to understand brands in context. *Brand Culture* places brands firmly within culture to look at the complex underpinnings of the branding process. We concur with Doug Holt's assessment in *Harvard Business Review*:

[brand] knowledge doesn't come from focus groups or ethnography or trend reports – the marketer's usual means for 'getting close to the customer'. Rather, it comes from a cultural historian's understanding of ideology as it waxes and wanes, a sociologist's charting of the topography of contradictions the ideology produces, and a literary critic's expedition into the culture that engages these contradictions.

(Holt 2003: 49)

To which we would add, a brand researcher's engagement with the cultural codes of branding.

AIM OF THE BOOK

Brand Culture explores current issues in brand management, including brand building, corporate identity management, marketing communication, and brand theory, from a unifying perspective on what we call brand culture. This volume fills a niche in the burgeoning branding literature with a distinctive managerially and theoretically informed perspective on the cultural dimensions of branding. We present sophisticated, informative, and focused brand research, drawing from cutting edge work on brands and their multiple roles in organizational practices and cultural processes. We are not content merely to offer strategic advice, for we believe researchers and managers alike must understand brands at a deeper cultural level. *Brand Culture* dwells between checklist-type managerial models on one hand and studies of consumer behaviour on the other. We introduce the brand culture concept as the theoretical space between strategic concepts of brand identity and consumer interpretations of brand image, and draw out implications for brand management and research. *Brand Culture* sheds light on the gap often seen between managerial intention and market response.

We believe that understanding brands requires integrative thinking, drawing from management strategy, organization theory, and consumer behaviour, and that understanding brands requires theoretical work. Brand management has grown to challenge traditional models of product management and industrial production; and branding has emerged as an interdisciplinary research area, drawing from management, marketing, and allied fields. Reflecting the growth of brand research, the book presents innovative cultural perspectives on branding, including several case-based studies of well-known companies such as Benetton, LEGO, and Ryanair. Together, this group of researchers maintains that managing, researching, and understanding brands requires understanding how meaning and aesthetic expression function in the marketplace.

Although there are numerous brand management books, most of the branding literature has a somewhat limited scope, often treating brands as a corporate prerogative, removed from culture and consumers. Some textbooks present branding as a strategic communication problem, to be solved by 'integrated marketing communications', 'top down' branding, or 'brand champions'. Branding, however, is a far more complex issue that cannot be understood as a mere communications campaign. Rather, branding represents a cultural process, performed in an interplay between art and business, production and consumption, images and stories, design and communication (see Salzer-Mörling and Strannegård 2004; and Schroeder 2005).

Brand Culture includes contributions by marketing, management, consumer research, and communication researchers, and provides a handy guide to the latest thinking about brands. The book is designed as a supplemental text in many business and management courses at both graduate, including MBA, and advanced undergraduate levels. Each chapter includes a key point and several questions for discussion for classroom use. The book will be of interest to researchers and students in brand management, strategic marketing, organization theory, marketing communications, and international marketing. In particular, courses in product design, marketing strategy, marketing communication, and consumer behaviour – and, certainly, brand management – should find this collection a convenient, lucid, and thought-provoking overview of current brand thinking. Advertising and communication researchers will also deem this book of tremendous interest, specifically those who are studying corporate identity and international management. *Brand Culture* is designed to appeal to managers in the areas of consumer research, branding, and advertising and corporate identity who want a convenient, stimulating overview of some of the best recent brand research.

THE BURGEONING BRAND BOOKCASE

There are many, many books on brands. However, most take a practical, checklist approach to branding, perhaps best illustrated by Aaker's growing brand library, including *Managing Brand Equity* (1991), *Building Strong Brands* (1996), and, with Joachimsthaler, *Brand Leadership* (2000). Keller's *Strategic Brand Management* (2003) follows this approach, whilst a more popular version of this general trend is available in *Brand Asset Management* by Davis (2000), replete with remedial suggestions and retro strategies.

Strategic Brand Management by Kapferer (2004) has become a standard text in the brand literature, one that exemplifies a European approach in its emphasis on the meaning of brands and its semiotically informed brand model. As a monograph, however, its focus is somewhat narrow, and it often neglects the cultural processes that inform both corporate branding efforts and consumer response – the cultural codes of branding. Kapferer has a chance to refute this claim – he is one of the book's contributors.

Revealing the Corporation edited by Balmer and Greyser (2003) provides a compelling historical account of the field of corporate identity. Its subtitle, *Perspectives on Identity, Image, Reputation, Corporate Branding, and Corporate-level Marketing*, signals its ambition and scope. However, this anthology draws primarily from previously published work, stretching back to the 1950s, mostly American, and mainly covers practical applications, reprinting several articles from the managerially oriented *Harvard Business Review*.

3

Creating Powerful Brands: The Strategic Route to Success in Consumer, Industrial and Service Markets by de Chernatony and McDonald (1992) and *From Brand Vision to Brand Evaluation* by de Chernatony (2001) are other contenders for *the* European brand book. These are aimed at the practical side of the market, slightly to the expense of theoretical work. *Brand Management: A Theoretical and Practical Approach* (2003) by Riezebos represents more of a standard text, aimed at marketing students.

Brand Culture is different from these offerings – we write for researchers, scholars, and students who are interested in new currents of brand research, as well as managers who want a thoughtful update on brands from a cultural, yet managerially relevant, perspective. The reader will find case studies of iconic brands like Benetton, LEGO, and Ryanair, practical managerial advice, as well as thoughtful analyses of brand concepts and strategic brand management. Our authors present state-of-the-art thinking about brands, and many draw upon theoretical developments from other fields. The book moves beyond simplistic notions of brands as managerial assets, and presents a more multi-faceted understanding of brands and brand management, grounded in interdisciplinary perspectives on the cultural codes of brands.

THE CULTURAL LIBRARY

As Stephen Brown discusses in Chapter 3, few concepts are as complicated as culture. Writers have discussed myriad ways that culture interacts with commerce: advertising culture (e.g. Nixon 2003); brand culture (Pettinger 2004); corporate culture (e.g. Deal and Kennedy 1988); engineering culture (Kunda 1992); and organizational culture (e.g. Martin 1992; Parker 1999). However, marketing has trailed other disciplines in adopting a cultural perspective. Brands form part of culture, mediating between organizations and consumers, yet branding scholars have seemed reluctant to embrace the cultural world's potential contributions to branding knowledge. This book is part of a larger call for inclusion of cultural issues within the management and marketing research canon, joining in the contention that culture and history can provide a necessary contextualizing counterpoint to managerial and information processing views of branding's interaction with consumers (cf. Holt 2004).

How do brands interact with culture? From a cultural perspective, brands can be understood as communicative objects that the brand manager wants consumers to buy into a symbolic universe as defined by, in part, the brand identity (cf. Lury 2004). In theory, brand management is about communicating a message interpreted in line with the brand owner's intention. This perspective fails to take into account consumers' active negotiation of brand meaning (Elliott 1994), contextual effects, such as time (cf. Aaker *et al.* 2004), space, and personal history, and cultural processes (Holt 2004; Schroeder 2002, 2003). Consumer choice is critical to understand why certain brands become more successful than others (see Aaker 1996). The meanings consumers ascribe to brands are not only the result of a projected brand identity – a process of negotiation also takes place in and between a marketing environment, a cultural environment, and a social environment. Managing brands successfully mandates managing the brand's meaning in the marketplace – the brand image. Yet, the brand meaning is not wholly derived from the market. Culture, aesthetics, and history interact to inject brands into the global flow of images.

We have assembled a dynamic group of brand researchers – including well-known, established experts and up-and-coming newcomers – that takes brand culture seriously from both a theoretical and managerial point of view. We offer a unique contribution to the branding literature by joining together several research disciplines – including marketing, management, organizational, and semiotics – in an enlightening collection that helps clarify the brand's role in organizations, marketing strategy, and culture.

OVERVIEW

The book is organized into three parts, that move generally from corporate perspectives, through culture and on to the consumer. In Part I, 'Corporate perspectives on brand culture', several of the leading lights of branding, corporate identity, and marketing management research present compelling and comprehensive analyses of contemporary brand management. In Chapter 1, 'A cultural perspective on corporate branding: the case of LEGO Group', productive corporate identity researchers Majken Schultz and Mary Jo Hatch describe the activities that comprised LEGO's brand strategy process in the early 2000s, providing empirical data for their influential conceptual model of brand cycles. LEGO Group, the iconic Danish manufacturer of play materials, has been moving from a product to a corporate brand strategy, confronting all the obstacles and challenges that such a process involves. Schultz and Hatch show how LEGO's dual challenge generated a comprehensive top management effort to revisit LEGO's cultural brand heritage and integrate the company via the implementation of a strategy that focused on the corporate brand but was rooted in its cultural heritage. They present a 'toolkit' model that outlines how the cycles of corporate branding interact with cultural processes.

John M. T. Balmer has been sounding the call for a separate arena for corporate brands for awhile now, and in Chapter 2, 'Corporate brand cultures and communities', he argues that corporate brands and their cultures and communities are stronger, wider, and of greater consequence when compared to product brands and product brand culture. Balmer points out that many of the world's biggest companies – and most highly valued brands – are seen as corporate *brands* rather than corporate entities – think of McDonald's, Nike, and BMW. These corporate brands are an increasingly important, powerful, and visible part of culture, and demand distinctive management and research programmes.

Stephen Brown has nearly single-handedly produced a sophisticated and rather cultured branch of marketing scholarship with his trenchant analyses of everything from marketing research to the new retro Mini. In Chapter 3, 'Ambi-brand culture: on a wing

5

and a swear with Ryanair', Brown challenges branding dogma, overturning a few sacred branding concepts along the way. With his customary penetrating insight and searing wit, Brown skewers the old idea that individual brands stand for one thing and one thing only. He points to *Ambi-brands* – those 'inherently ambiguous, enigmatic, polymorphic, plurivalent brands' – that pose problems for traditional branding theory. He suggests, in his characteristically mild manner, that not only are brand cultures co-created with consumers – who often ignore or subvert the messages and meanings that managers try to convey – but also that ambiguity is central to the magical aura that surrounds allegedly legendary brands like Apple, Nike, and Harley. Brown shows how Ryanair, whose CEO Michael O'Leary notoriously disdains, mistreats, and cusses out consumers, tells a quite different story than most brand strategists would recommend – a tale of betrayal and mistrust – all the while enjoying financial and critical success in the low-cost airline industry segment they all but created. Ryanair appears to be a case study in *brand arrogance*. According to Brown, contradiction, inconsistency, uncertainty, and dissensus offer illumination of the conquest of brand culture.

At the other end of the spectrum, the luxury brand sector – encompassing jewellery, cosmetics, fashion, automobiles, along with a growing number of luxury lifestyle products – has boomed recently, despite economic downturns, Internet pricing information, increased competition, and a growing market of counterfeits. Jean-Noël Kapferer, one of the world's leading brand researchers, asks: What role does culture play in the highly competitive luxury goods sector? In Chapter 4, 'The two business cultures of luxury brands', he argues that two different models – based upon opposing cultural assumptions – of luxury brands coexist: one rooted in history, rarity, and craftsmanship, often associated with European luxury goods, and another based upon stories, image, and marketing strategy, generally connected to US brands. Drawing upon a wide range of examples from around the world, Kapferer suggests that authenticity remains critical for luxury brands, hinting that some well-known American designers may be in for a surprise.

Henrik Uggla is obsessed with meaning. His savvy approach to brand management blends strategy and semiotics in a way that will please both managers and marketing researchers who share his obsession. Chapter 5, 'Managing leader and partner brands: the brand association base', provides a theoretical overview of brand leveraging, and identifies some problems related to brand boundaries and the popular notion of fit. He describes the *brand association base* model that connects brands in the surrounding environment to a leader brand, drawing upon several well-known brands, such as illy coffee, Gore-Tex, and Peak Performance. Uggla carefully outlines implications for brand leveraging research and semiotic research, pointing to the cultural influences in co-branding, ingredient branding, strategic alliances, and partner brands.

In Part II, 'Clarifying brand concepts', more brand ideas come up for scrutiny. How does brand management interact with related fields, such as corporate identity, design management, leadership, or marketing strategy? What intellectual resources are useful – or misleading – for understanding brands? What role does identity play in brand culture? These are some of the issues that this section will develop, introducing new and emerging insights into a relatively recent intellectual and managerial arena.

In Chapter 6, 'Brands as a global ideoscape', leading consumer researcher Søren Askegaard takes up a central issue in brand management – whether to employ a global, standardized strategy, or adapt to local markets. He offers useful insights that move the discussion about brands and globalization beyond the standardization vs. adaptation debate. He argues that brands are not only strong mediators of cultural meaning but also that the brand itself becomes a strong ideological referent shaping economic activities among consumers and producers. Using social theorist Arjun Appadurai's 'scape' metaphors, Askegaard introduces a promising way to think about brands as part of a modern global *ideoscape* – strong motivating ideas that may fundamentally reshape the way consumers and producers regard the world of goods. He concludes that brands and branding can be seen as a central historical and cultural force with profound impacts on the perception of the marketplace and the consumer.

In Chapter 7, 'Brave new brands: cultural branding between Utopia and A-topia', Benoît Heilbrunn explores these historical and cultural forces, opening up brand analysis to ideology and the concept of Utopia. In an illuminating and closely argued account, Heilbrunn declares that brands now pre-empt cultural spheres which used to be the privilege of either religion or the political, and that strong brands occupy symbolic places left empty by the retreat of the divine. Furthermore, the ideology promoted both explicitly and implicitly by brands is thus closely related to a theological and political model which equates consumption with happiness – a classic advertising proposition. Strong brands constantly develop prescriptive models as regard the way we talk, the way we think, and the way we behave. Based on these assumptions, the chapter attempts to show how strong brands promote a utopian model based on a series of inherent contradictions and paradoxes, which brands are able to reconcile through a narrative programme. In Heilbrunn's hands, a turn to literature and semiotics identifies a typology of transcultural values which are constantly promoted by brands and which helps their discourses to cross cultures and frontiers. Through numerous examples, such as McDonald's, Club Med, and Disney, he exposes the power of brand culture.

Identity enjoys high value in brand circles. Companies, organizations, and brand managers are all exhorted to create, maintain, and express a coherent and compelling identity. In Chapter 8, 'Rethinking identity in brand management', Fabian Faurholt Csaba and Anders Bengtsson take aim at identity as it informs brand management theory. They argue that the literature is fraught with inconsistent and taken-for-granted notions of identity, and has been adapted from work on corporate identity without sufficient consideration of its applicability to branding. Furthermore, they question the very notion of utilizing an anthropomorphic concept of identity at all. Informed by recent theory of consumer–brand relationships, they argue that brand identity – to the extent that brands can have an identity at all – must be understood in terms of broader questions of social and cultural identity in modern society. Faurholt Csaba and Bengtsson conclude that we

7

need to rethink central tenets of brand management, and provide a useful starter kit focused on brand identity.

Design marks another keyword in branding strategy. In Chapter 9, 'Brand management and design management: a nice couple or false friends?', Ulla Johansson and Lisbeth Svengren Holm discuss the relationship between design management and brand management, placing them in historical context, and showing how they relate to different professional communities. This causes trouble when managers apply one or the other – or a poorly operationalized combination of the two. Their case study of a Scandinavian flooring company shows how – when properly applied – design can enhance competitive advantage, by increasing product value and brand identity. However, design and branding occupy separate, if overlapping, cultural and managerial realms, which may lead to problems. They review how these problems arise, discuss their strategic and theoretical implications, and offer guidelines for implementing design within brand management.

Part III, 'Consuming brand culture', gathers four chapters that focus on consumers and how they experience brand culture, providing useful perspectives that brand management often neglects. In Chapter 10, 'Symbolic brands and authenticity of identity performance', Richard Elliott and Andrea Davies study identity from a consumer perspective as they explore authentic and inauthentic identity performance in an empirical study of young consumers' brand communities and their consumption of fashion, music, and club culture. They invoke the concept of 'the performing self' (Featherstone 1991) to investigate how brand culture expresses appearance, display, and impression management. In their informants' lives, style defines, communicates, and helps maintain group membership. In this way, subcultures produce their own recognizable social practices – particular ways of dancing, walking, talking, and consuming. Elliott and Davies discuss how subcultural group members negotiate brands and their meanings in the context of their own lives, illuminating key concepts in consumer-focused brand research such as brand communities, neo-tribes, subcultures, and authenticating acts.

Authenticity also figures in Chapter 11, 'Branding ethics: negotiating Benetton's identity and image' by Janet L. Borgerson, Martin Escudero Magnusson, and Frank Magnusson. To differentiate their brand identity, Benetton has connected to global issues with ethical import, attempting to associate the company's business with ethical behaviour and project an authentically responsible image to consumers. How can we understand the infamous *gap* between Benetton's brand identity and consumers' brand image of Benetton, in this case a gap between Benetton's so-called corporate values and purchase behaviour? They found that consumers say they do value ethics and think that companies should communicate their ethical values in everything they do, but found little bottom-line evidence – these same consumers reported not being too concerned about ethical values when out shopping for Benetton clothes. They examine several possible explanations for this paradox, and then discuss the provocative idea that authentic corporate identity is ephemeral. Extending Stephen Brown's claim that brands need not be consistent, Borgerson, Escudero Magnusson, and Magnusson entertain the notion that corporate identity and values may not be real at all, rather corporate identity relies upon performative acts and gestures. Drawing upon semiotic analysis and empirical data of actual outcomes in consumer and retail environments, they report that when consumers seek, or call out for, an ethical response, they receive only an echo, provoking the impression that there is something missing behind the brand image's ethical message. They ask, can Benetton, the company and site of identity, control this brand? Or can it be seen as a Frankenstein, a creation no longer controlled by the forces that apparently created it?

In Chapter 12, 'Brand ecosystems: multilevel brand interaction', Sven Bergvall borrows a metaphor from the natural world to understand some of the complexities of brand culture. For example, airports constitute a site where town planners, airlines, architects, government regulators, consumers, and style and progress coalesce, with brand management co-mingling with planning processes, progress, and public debate (see Leslie 2005). Bergvall is concerned with the multiple influences upon brands, beyond corporate strategists and consumer response, and considers a number of branding arrangements, such as Sony Ericsson's joint venture in the mobile phone market, in which various cultural forces play prominent, if understudied, roles. He introduces the conceptual framework 'multilevel brand interaction' to characterize the various forces that create and maintain brand meanings.

Among the many players that interact with brand meaning, advertising maintains a dominant role. In the final chapter, 'Selling dreams: the role of advertising in shaping luxury brand meaning', Arianna Brioschi turns to her native Italy's most successful export (if we exclude pizza) – luxury brands such as Armani, Gucci, and Prada. She presents a study of how advertising helps build luxury brands and develops a model of the two-way value creating relationship that links the firm and the consumer. Her framework complements the general approach to brand culture – as she argues that the firm-designed brand identity is driven by the cultural codes of luxury branding. She identifies consumer-related luxury brand meanings – brand values from the firm's point of view – that can be effectively incorporated into luxury brand communication strategies to shorten the gap between brand identity and brand image. Finally, she presents a typology of luxury good marketing communication strategy and offers suggestions for research and practice.

TOWARD BRAND CULTURE

Brands have become a contested managerial, academic, and cultural arena. Management models struggle over the relative importance of branding vs. customer relationship management, branding vs. innovation, and brand identity vs. corporate identity. Scholars from different disciplines squabble over who owns the brand management literature, with marketing, management, corporate identity, and advertising academics squaring off for dominance. Sociologists, anthropologists, historians, and even literary scholars have joined the brand brigade and have set about to deconstruct brands and their relationships with consumers, citizens, and culture. Furthermore, branding issues exacerbate cultural differences – with Americans often at odds with Europeans, Anglos arguing with their Latin colleagues, and quantitative modellers fighting with qualitative researchers over how to measure brands, what research techniques are most important, and how brands should be conceptualized.

In short, the cultural landscape has been profoundly transformed into a commercial brandscape in which the production and consumption of signs rivals the production and consumption of physical products. This shift has been called an attention economy, an experience economy, a dream society, and an image economy (cf. Guillet de Monthoux 2004; Pine and Gilmore 1999; Schroeder 2002). These various labels each emphasize the expressive dimensions of production and consumption. What does this transformation imply for branding and consumer culture? Constructing and expressing emotional, aesthetic, and symbolic values assume centre stage. Blurring the borders between economy and culture, brand culture and our designed existence signals something created and consumed in the interface between art and industry, production and consumption, creativity and commerce.

In brand culture, organizations are increasingly competing on the basis of their ability to communicate who they are and what they stand for, and organizations are therefore in many aspects becoming more 'expressive' (Salzer-Mörling 2002; Schultz *et al.* 2000). When production and consumption are no longer just a matter of function, aesthetic, emotional, and symbolic values seem to be central to organizations. To better understand how brands engage culture, and how culture envelops brands, we turn to this collection of chapters, whose authors clarify the brand concept, even as they struggle with the complex underpinnings of brand culture.

REFERENCES

Aaker, D. A. (1991) *Managing Brand Equity: Capitalizing on the Value of a Brand Name*, New York: The Free Press.

Aaker, D. A. (1996) *Building Strong Brands*, New York: The Free Press.

Aaker, D. A. and Joachimsthaler, E. (2000) *Brand Leadership*, New York: The Free Press.

Aaker, J., Fournier, S., and Brasel, S. A. (2004) 'When good brands do bad', *Journal of Consumer Research* 31, 2: 1–16.

Balmer, J. M. T. and Greyser, S. A. (eds) (2003) *Revealing the Corporation: Perspectives on Identity, Image, Reputation, Corporate Branding, and Corporate-level Marketing*, London: Routledge.

Borgerson, J. L. and Schroeder, J. E. (2002) 'Ethical issues in global marketing: avoiding bad faith in visual representation', *European Journal of Marketing* 36, 5/6: 570–594.

Davis, S. M. (2000) *Brand Asset Management*, San Francisco, CA: Jossey-Bass.

Deal, T. and Kennedy, A. (1988) *Corporate Cultures*, Harmondsworth: Penguin.

de Chernatony, L. (2001) *From Brand Vision to Brand Evaluation*, Oxford: Butterworth-Heinemann.

de Chernatony, L. and McDonald, M. H. B. (1992) *Creating Powerful Brands: The Strategic Route to Success in Consumer, Industrial and Service Markets*, Oxford: Butterworth-Heinemann.

Elliott, R. (1994) 'Exploring the symbolic meaning of brands', *British Journal of Management* 5: 3–19.

Featherstone, M. (1991) 'The body in consumer culture', in M. Featherstone, M. Hepworth, and B. Turner (eds) *The Body: Social Process and Cultural Theory*, London: Sage.

Fournier, S. (1998) 'Consumers and their brands: developing relationship theory in consumer research', *Journal of Consumer Research* 24: 343–373.

Guillet de Monthoux, P. (2004) *The Art Firm: Aesthetic Management and Metaphysical Marketing from Wagner to Wilson*, Stanford, CA: Stanford Business Books.

Hirschman, E. and Thompson, C. J. (1997) 'Why media matter: advertising and consumers in contemporary communication', *Journal of Advertising* 26: 43–60.

Holt, D. B. (2003) 'What becomes an icon most?', *Harvard Business Review* 80 (March): 43–49.

Holt, D. B. (2004) *How Brands Become Icons: The Principles of Cultural Branding*, Boston, MA: Harvard Business School Press.

Kapferer, J.-N. (2004) *Strategic Brand Management: Creating and Sustaining Brand Equity Long Term*, London: Kogan Page.

Keller, K. L. (2003) *Strategic Brand Management*, Upper Saddle River, NJ: Prentice Hall.

Kunda, G. (1992) *Engineering Culture*, Philadelphia: University of Pennsylvania Press.

Leslie, T. (2005) 'The Pan Am terminal at Idlewild/Kennedy airport and the transition from jet age to space age', *Design Issues* 21, 1: 63–80.

Lury, C. (2004) *Brands: The Logos of the Global Economy*, London: Routledge.

Martin, J. (1992) *Culture in Organizations: Three Perspectives*, Oxford: Oxford University Press.

Muñiz, A. M. J. and O'Guinn, T. C. (2001) 'Brand community', *Journal of Consumer Research* 27 (March): 412–432.

Nixon, S. (2003) *Advertising Cultures: Gender, Commerce, Creativity*, London: Sage.

Parker, M. (1999) *Organizational Culture and Identity*, London: Sage.

Pettinger, L. (2004) 'Brand culture and branded workers: service work and aesthetic labour in fashion retail', *Consumption, Markets and Culture* 7, 2: 165–184.

Pine, B. J. II and Gilmore, J. (1999) *The Experience Economy: Work is a Theatre and Every Business a Stage*, Boston, MA: Harvard Business School Press.

Riezebos, R. (2003) *Brand Management: A Theoretical and Practical Approach*, Harlow: Prentice Hall.

Ritson, M. and Elliott, R. (1999) 'The social uses of advertising: an ethnographic study of adolescent advertising audiences', *Journal of Consumer Research* 26, 3: 260–277.

Salzer-Mörling, M. (2002) 'Changing corporate landscapes', in I. Holmberg, M. Salzer-Mörling, and L. Strannegård (eds) *Stuck in the Future: Tracing the New Economy*, Stockholm: BookHouse.

Salzer-Mörling, M. and Strannegård, L. (2004) 'Silence of the brands', *European Journal of Marketing* 38, 1/2: 224–238.

Schroeder, J. E. (2002) *Visual Consumption*, London and New York: Routledge.

Schroeder, J. E. (2003) 'Building brands: architectural expression in the electronic age', in L. Scott and R. Batra (eds) *Persuasive Imagery: A Consumer Response Perspective*, Mahwah, NJ: Lawrence Erlbaum: 349–382.

Schroeder, J. E. (2005) 'The artist and the brand', *European Journal of Marketing*, in press.

Schultz, M., Hatch, M. J., and Larsen, M. (2000) *The Expressive Organization*, Oxford: Oxford University Press.

Scott, L. A. (1994) 'The bridge from text to mind: adapting reader-response theory to consumer research', *Journal of Consumer Research* 21 (December): 461–480.

Solomon, M., Bamossy, G., and Askegaard, S. (2002) *Consumer Behaviour: A European Perspective*, Harlow: Prentice Hall.

Wikström, S. (1996) 'The customer as co-producer', *European Journal of Marketing* 30: 6–19.

Part I

Corporate perspectives on brand culture

Chapter 1

A cultural perspective on corporate branding

The case of LEGO Group

Majken Schultz and Mary Jo Hatch

We argue that moving away from product to corporate branding means moving from a communication/marketing driven activity towards adapting a brand-based strategy for managing the organization. Corporate branding implies that the whole organization serves as the foundation for brand positioning and entails that the organization is able to make specific choices, design organizational processes and execute activities in ways that are distinct to the organization compared with competitors and mainstream trends. As opposed to product branding, corporate branding highlights the important role employees play in brand practice, making how employees engage with and enact the values and vision of the brand more profound and strategically important to corporate brands (see also Aaker 2004; Ind 2001; Schultz and de Chernatony 2002; Olins 2003). Accordingly, the values, beliefs and aesthetic sensitivity held by organizational members become key elements in differentiation strategies, as the company itself moves centre stage in the branding effort. Issues like credibility and relevance of the brand to external stakeholders rest heavily on the shoulders of employees, whose cultural behaviour supports – or damages – the company's claims to brand uniqueness and attraction. In short, employees are crucial for the ability of the company to practise what it preaches. That is why we see more and more companies engaged in making the brand understandable, relevant and engaging to their employees through a host of different internal activities, such as internal marketing, employee communication campaigns, brand programmes, company intranet websites, corporate merchandise, staged events – often conceived in terms of 'Living the Brand' or 'Being the Brand' (Aaker 2004; Ind 2001; Schultz and de Chernatony 2002).

Based in our conceptual framing of corporate branding, we focus on the role of employees and thus organizational culture in constituting a corporate brand. In our opinion, organizational culture has been the most underestimated element in corporate branding, and yet represents the most important difference from product branding. This is because culture manifests itself in the ways employees interpret and emotionally engage with the brand and its stakeholders. In this chapter, we offer an illustration of how a

15

cultural perspective can be applied in the managerial effort to shift from product branding to corporate branding. We argue that the corporate brand implementation process moves through different stages, each creating a distinct paradoxical challenge for brand management and each posing different opportunities and limitations for involvement of employees in the corporate brand. We illustrate our conceptual framework with a description of the branding process taking place in LEGO Group, the Danish producer of play materials. This chapter is based on extensive experience working with LEGO, which we also discuss in articles from *Harvard Business Review* (Hatch and Schulz 2001) and *California Management Review* (Schultz and Hatch 2003).

A FRAMEWORK FOR CORPORATE BRANDING

In previous articles we have emphasized that successful corporate branding resides in the alignment of strategic vision, organizational culture and stakeholder images (Hatch and Schultz 2001, 2003; Schultz and Hatch 2003). These were defined as:

1 *Strategic vision* – the central idea behind the company that embodies and expresses *top management's* aspiration for what the company will achieve in the future.
2 *Organizational culture* – the internal values, beliefs and basic assumptions that embody the heritage of the company and manifests in the ways *employees* feel about the company they are working for.
3 *Stakeholder images* – views of the organization developed by its *external stakeholders*; the outside world's overall impression of the company including the views of customers, shareholders, the media, the general public, and so on (Hatch and Schultz 2001).

Together these key elements of corporate branding underpin the Corporate Brand Toolkit (Hatch and Schultz 2001, 2003). To enhance or maintain corporate brand alignment, we have argued that companies must pay attention to all three elements of corporate branding simultaneously. It is important to remember that corporate branding is not only about differentiation in the marketplace; it is also about belonging.

Based on our continuing research on corporate branding and organizational identity, we add identity as the conceptual anchor for the simultaneous differentiation and belonging, as identity articulates who the organization is and what it stands for compared with others (Hatch and Schultz 2002; Albert and Whetten 1985; Gioia *et al.* 2000). Contrary to strategic vision, which embodies future aspirations for the company (Collins and Porras 1994), identity is comprised of claims about who the company is as an organization, which many companies explicitly express when they espouse organizational values or core beliefs (Whetten and Mackey 2002; Olins 2000, 2003; Balmer and Greyser 2003). In practice, however, there may be little difference between vision and identity, as identity claims sometimes express desired future identity rather than describe actual organizational behaviour, just as vision, mission and values rhetorics in companies are often intertwined. Comparing image and identity, identity is a privileged claim of self among organizational members, whereas images reside among multiple (other) stakeholders engaged in different interpretations of the company who together produce a multiplicity of images that feed into the continuous development – or fragmentation – of the brand (e.g. Dutton and Dukerich 1991; Gioia *et al*. 2000). Particularly in the case of well-established and well-known brands, such as the LEGO brand, the brand image is important in the marketplace, but also as an influence on the commitment and loyalty of employees (Dutton *et al*. 1994).

Organizational culture, in contrast, emerges from the taken-for-granted assumptions and tacit webs of meaning that lie behind everyday employee behaviour. Cultural assumptions and meanings are manifested in numerous cultural forms, such as rites and rituals, symbols, espoused values, myths, stories, etc. (Martin 1992, 2002; Hatch 1993; Schein 1992). In that regard, organizational culture serves as a contextual reference and conceptual backdrop for the collective reflections of 'who we are' as an organization. The notion of culture also includes espoused values, which may be similar to identity claims to the extent that these values focus on the official definition of an organizational self rather than being, for example, more general codes of conduct for organizational behaviour. Adding identity as the fourth element of corporate branding completes the Corporate Branding Toolkit (see Table 1.1):

Table 1.1   *The cycles of corporate branding*

Cycles of corporate branding	Cycle 1 Stating	Cycle 2 Organizing	Cycle 3 Involving	Cycle 4 Integrating
Key process	Stating the identity for the corporate brand and linking it to corporate vision	Linking vision to culture and image	Involving stakeholders through culture and image	Integrating vision, culture and image around a new identity
Key question	Who are we as an organization? What do we want to stand for?	How can we reorganize behind our corporate brand?	How can we involve internal and external stakeholders in the corporate brand?	How can we integrate vision, culture and image for the corporate brand?
Change mode	Decentralized	Centralized	Decentralized	Centralized
Key concerns	Company wide-audit of brand expression Revisiting brand cultural heritage Analysing brand images among key stakeholders	Create a coherent brand organization and provide managerial foundation for implementation processes	Does the company have a shared cultural mindset? Active inclusion of global stakeholder perceptions	Integrate the brand across markets and business areas

17

4 *Identity* – organizational claims about who we are as an organization, which serve as the foundation for defining what the corporate brand stands for compared with others and are often stated as core values, central ideas or core beliefs.

We claim that organizations whose managers attend to the dynamics of vision, culture and image – centring on identity – will outperform those whose managers either ignore these issues or do not understand the interrelations between them.

JOURNEY TOWARDS CORPORATE BRANDING: LESSONS FROM LEGO

This section of the chapter provides examples of some cultural dimensions of the managerial and organizational challenges that faced the top managers of LEGO Group when they moved to corporate branding in their strategy formulation process. Using the Corporate Branding Toolkit as the analytical framework, the LEGO Group case shows how their branding effort expanded from its initial marketing focus into a company-wide reorganization that involved several change management programmes and an ongoing initiative to create a global brand based in the LEGO Group company culture and unique heritage.

The LEGO Group corporate brand was created in 1932 when Ole Kirk Christiansen, a carpenter from rural Denmark, created a company for the manufacture of wooden toys. For decades it acted as a strong umbrella brand, guiding the company through extensive international growth as well as numerous product innovations. The LEGO brand has obtained an iconic status (Holt 2003) and has been among the world's most admired brands among families with children, along with Disney, Kellogg's and Coke according to Young and Rubicam's Brand Asset Evaluator. However, in the late 1980s, and particularly in the mid-1990s, brand extensions into software, lifestyle products, new licences, parks and television fragmented the LEGO brand. Combined with fluctuating financial performance and an ever more competitive and rapidly changing marketplace, brand fragmentation presented top management with the dual challenges of maintaining a focus on the substance and distinction of LEGO Group heritage, while allowing for continuous innovation and expansion into new businesses. At the same time, top management had the overall challenge of changing the severe financial fluctuation with sustainable profitable growth. In response, LEGO top managers decided to reintegrate the company via a corporate brand strategy that was tied into the deep roots of LEGO's cultural heritage and unique global stature as a brand in children's development.

In 2001, top management created an internal task force with the purpose of crafting a concrete strategy for shifting to corporate branding. The task force included 12 organizational members from different functions and different parts of the world. Its brief was to define key challenges facing the LEGO brand and provide the outline for a future identity for the brand. Midway through their process, the task force expanded the scope of analysis, when it became apparent that the fragmented character of the LEGO brand was partly due to the organizational processes involved in managing the brand. It was at this point that Hatch and Schultz's Corporate Branding Toolkit (see Table 1.1) was introduced as an addition to the more classic branding models (e.g. Aaker and Joachimsthaler 2000) and produced a second round of analysis that identified organizational challenges to the LEGO brand related to vision, culture and image.

Introducing the Corporate Branding Toolkit focused LEGO's corporate branding effort, not only on strategic alignment, but also on alignment between consumers' and employees' understanding of the brand. Keeping in mind that the end goal of the brand strategy was a strong and coherent global position for the LEGO brand in the eyes of all stakeholders, the Toolkit model reinforced the need to attend to existing organizational cultures and images held by stakeholders and compare them with the aspired redefinition of the identity for the LEGO Group corporate brand. In retrospect, we see that the managerial and organizational process of aligning vision, culture and image behind the LEGO brand identity developed through successive approximations to the ideal presented by the Toolkit. Below we first describe the main activities that comprised these successive approximations as four cycles through the corporate branding process (summarized in Table 1.1). Table 1.2 summarizes the processes that are related in particular to a cultural perspective on corporate branding.

Cycle 1   Stating who we are

The first cycle focused on the high fragmentation of brand expressions across different product lines, sub-brands and businesses. We characterize the changes within this cycle as decentralized in the sense that stating a credible vision for the corporate brand identity required the managers to combine multiple insights derived from assessing the strengths and weaknesses of the company's cultural heritage with data describing global consumer images of the brand. For instance, using insights from different methodologies (e.g. Millward Brown's Brand Tracking, Young and Rubicam's Brand Asset Evaluator), market research showed that: (1) few consumers were able to distinguish between LEGO's sub-brands, and (2) although LEGO was highly regarded for its devotion to development and learning (particularly by mothers), it lacked 'coolness and street cred[ibility]' among children. Also, the taskforce conducted thorough comparisons with the core values of competitors, mapping the distinctiveness of the LEGO brand identity in the global marketplace in order to see how the unique heritage of the LEGO culture could be better used to create a sustainable differentiation and in this way better leverage the uniqueness of the organizational culture in a future global brand culture among all stakeholders.

However, although LEGO had a long heritage as a value-driven company, it had lost track of its numerous value expressions during a long period of brand fragmentation and increasingly overlapping value propositions. The corporate branding process therefore began with a return to LEGO core values as the foundation for redefining the brand identity. As the most important part of this process, the task force engaged in a series of

Table 1.2 *The cultural dimensions of the shift to corporate branding*

Cycles of corporate branding	Cycle 1 Stating	Cycle 2 Organizing	Cycle 3 Involving	Cycle 4 Integrating
Key managerial challenge	Select values for the redefinition of the corporate brand and make them relevant to own managerial practices	Set priorities and implications of redefined brand values for cultural practices	Listening to the organizational culture in order to enhance cultural change towards a more coherent culture	Build awareness of national cultural differences and estimate their importance for brand execution
Key cultural activities	Creating a range of new cultural symbols, redefining espoused values; renewed reflections about strengths and weaknesses of basic assumptions	Shift in relations between subcultures; inserting new competencies and cultural mindset. Overcoming cultural conflicts	Dialogue workshops with top management. Development of LEGO Brand School; involving new group of brand champions	Dialogue with regional markets; cascading processes to involve local employees; exploring the limits of a one-company culture.
Key cultural paradox	Balance the promises the company wants to make to stakeholders and what stakeholders want to hear from the company	Balance the central policing of cultural values and key symbols and the need to empower employess to enact the brand decentrally	Balance the respect for past cultural heritage and the need to make the culture relevant and emotionally appealing to current and future employees	Balance the vision for a global one-company culture and adaptation to national cultures; business subcultures and local markets

workshops, conversations with the family owner (the founder's grandson) and archival studies of LEGO Group's previous value statements in order to gain a deeper understanding of the LEGO organization culture – both as it has unfolded over time, but also as it has generated new subcultures within new business areas by attracting people with different competencies and mindsets to LEGO Group. These people were recruited for example in LEGO Software in computer games and in LEGO Direct dealing with e-business and online development. For these people, the attraction of the LEGO brand image had served as a significant draw to the company and created expectations of playfulness and youthfulness, which were not always found in the organizational culture (Karmark 2002). In order to obtain a deeper understanding of why previous attempts to redirect the LEGO brand had been incomplete and not fully executed, the task force conducted a series of interviews with employees involved in the creation and execution of such attempts. These interviews revealed that one of the cultural challenges of LEGO Group was to link espoused values or identity claims to business processes and to leverage the emotional commitment among employees to the LEGO values in their everyday application of those values across different business areas and subcultures.

Based on these insights about organizational culture and stakeholder images, the task force reformulated the traditional LEGO values for the aspired brand identity giving them a contemporary feel and making the generic values based in the cultural heritage more distinctive to LEGO Group and potentially more relevant for the brand execution. Figure 1.1 shows how this sharpening of the brand identity was visualized in this cycle of the corporate branding process.

Along with the redefinition of the brand identity values, LEGO Group reshaped and redefined its brand architecture based on the play experiences that consumers obtain by engaging in LEGO play (e.g. the functional, emotional and self-expressive benefits, i.e. Aaker and Joachimsthaler 2000). This allowed for the potential development of a new and more efficient brand portfolio management system, revitalizing the LEGO core in open-ended construction, while at the same time seeking to tighten the company's expanding involvement in story concepts and licensed properties.

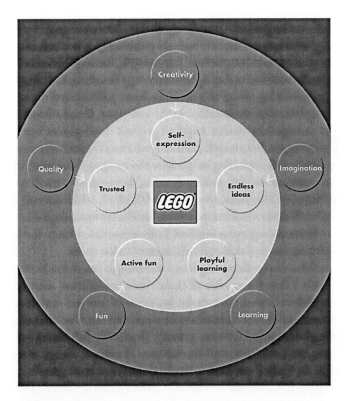

Figure 1.1 *Making brand identity values more LEGO specific (reproduced with permission of Lego Group).*

Cycle 2   Organizing behind the brand

The second cycle focused on adapting organizational and managerial processes (including business systems) to the demands of corporate branding. Key issues that received management attention in Cycle 2 included: the lack of a coherent brand organization, redefinition of roles and responsibilities for managing the brand, and a clear need to link top management's vision for the brand to both its organizational culture and its external stakeholders. One result of actions taken during this cycle was centralization of the corporate branding process

While still heavily involved in communicating the brand vision to stakeholders, top management reorganized the company to support the implementation of the brand strategy developed in Cycle 1. Based on their past experiences, top managers did not take the organization's ability to implement the new strategy for granted. Their dominant concern was to provide infrastructure to ensure strategic brand leadership, realizing that past managerial processes had been more concerned with tactical product-by-product decisions than with creating and monitoring the long-term development of the corporate brand. The organization-wide reorganization included both the corporate level and the establishment of new interfaces between the functions of corporate communication, marketing, innovation and global business support.

Of course these changes in the overall organizational structure (e.g. creation of a new global branding function) and the new business processes (e.g. new role of marketing in the innovation process) were intertwined. For example, the establishment of a company-wide brand function entailed reshaping brand strategy functions, including for instance changes in the advertising set-up to a focus on fewer partners and the establishment of a new global public relations function. At the same time, the new brand architecture and portfolio management system required product development teams to accept new campaign managers. For example, the composition of the innovation teams changed by including people with marketing insight (the new campaign managers) much earlier in the development process than previously. Also, the company started to build a new international brand relation function out of the UK office, which not only implied the hiring of people with a new set of competencies, but also created a range of new interfaces in the culture between employees involved in the communication to the local Danish audiences and those involved in the global communication effort.

As expected in such significant organizational changes and redistributions of power and status, Cycle 2 caused a number of clashes between different subcultures as well as a rather explicit resistance towards the inclusion of new and deviant subcultures. Cycle 2 demonstrated the interrelatedness between structural and cultural dimensions of organizational change and between primary (leadership behaviour) and secondary (infrastructure, etc.) reinforcement mechanisms of cultural change as suggested by Schein (1992). As Cycle 2 unfolded it involved more and more people inside LEGO Group who engaged in presentations and discussions about the brand. This expanding internal involvement continued into Cycle 3 and marked the transition back to a decentralized mode of managing the corporate brand.

Cycle 3   Involving stakeholders

During Cycle 3, LEGO's corporate branding process moved most noticeably from a marketing-led branding effort to an integrated effort involving almost all of the company. Through employee involvement activities and additional market research, organizational culture and images were given a more decentralized role than in previous cycles. Here, we only address the internal involvement, but want to make it clear that Cycle 3 included an equal effort to engage external stakeholders.

The first step in creating internal involvement with the brand was an attempt to enhance employee commitment to the new brand strategy and plant the seeds for a cultural change. Change initiatives took the form of strengthening cross-functional relations, creating dialogue, and developing specific culture-oriented programmes and activities, such as the LEGO Brand School. The goal of the LEGO Brand School was to introduce the vision to employees and create opportunities for them to make the new LEGO brand identity relevant to their various responsibilities and challenges. The Brand School was founded in 2002 and consisted of 1- to 3-day workshops facilitated by a team of internal coaches supported by top management talks. So far, the LEGO Brand School has involved 1,500 participants.

The first round of brand schools focused on generating increased awareness of company values and brand strategy by communicating and debating the identity claims of the LEGO brand (e.g. value statements, aspired brand personality and core beliefs). As it turned out, people had difficulties making these values relevant to their ongoing work and connecting them to the LEGO everyday behaviour. These experiences influenced the second round of the brand school, which was more concerned with 'living the brand' by creating role models among LEGO managers for how the LEGO brand values should be enacted on an everyday basis. When developing the second brand school, the people responsible teamed up with the LEGO Learning Institute, which is a network dedicated to understanding children's learning and play. This generated new ideas about how knowledge of playful learning can contribute to the interpretation process of LEGO company values along with creating stronger consumer understanding. In its own explanation, the renewal of the brand school was based on the ambition to combine a deeper understanding of the core beliefs of the company, stating that 'Children are our role models', with a stronger insight into the unique capabilities and mindset of children. Learning from how children engage in playful learning and creative self-expressions, the brand school sought to facilitate similar processes among the participants in making company values relevant to their everyday culture.

This ambition inspired the construction of a range of new expressions with strong symbolic meanings, such as exercises and working methods, wherein the brand school participants turned abstract values into tangible symbols. In this process, the use of the brick as the core artefact rooted in the culture was particularly important, and spurred several creative applications of the brick, as the participants were invited to create their own expressions of the brand, e.g. playing with giant bricks made of soft material and

23

engaging in self-expressive building exercises such as building company values and discussing their symbolic meanings with others afterwards. Here, the brand school deliberately used the strength of the LEGO brand image to spur enthusiasm and creativity among employees. The brand school also constructed new cultural forms, which took on new symbolic meanings; e.g. a 'value gallery', which is a game where pictures are used to help the participants articulate their associations with company values. In this cycle, the corporate branding activities seeking to involve and transform the organizational culture were given sense both by referring to the revised brand identity that emerged in Cycle 1 and the emotional attraction of the brand image (construed external image, see Dutton and Dukerich 1991; Gioia and Chittipeddi 1991).

Cycle 4   Integrating the brand across cultural boundaries

Cycle 4 got under way when top management's vision for the global corporate brand was again challenged, this time to clarify the boundaries for the LEGO corporate brand in terms of how far the brand values could be stretched, and to what extent individual product propositions should drive the LEGO brand expression. Also, the limitations and obstacles in turning LEGO into a global corporate brand were addressed during this cycle, coping with the difficulties of holding significantly different positions in global markets (e.g. in Europe LEGO is associated with strong and highly differentiated values of playful learning, whereas in the USA it is at risk of being associated with a generic construction play). In contrast to the decentralizing that occurred during Cycle 3, Cycle 4 marked a return to centralization where aspirations to have one global corporate brand based in a 'one-company culture' were vigorously renewed.

By participating in local workshops run by visiting senior executives from LEGO headquarters, all regions and business areas were engaged in the process of establishing what the brand strategy meant in their local context and how it should be implemented in their various markets. Each workshop addressed local organizations' concerns, such as the balance between long-term brand building and short-term earnings, and the future marketing mix including new retailing strategies, increased community activity, etc. In these sessions local managers were encouraged to articulate the brand in ways that made it relevant to their employees and other stakeholders. Through means of cascading, such as involving seminars and follow-up on LEGO Pulse (the human resource tracking system), management was seeking to initiate a culture change process with the overall ambition to create the foundation for a more shared organizational culture. This effort was expected to broaden managerial responsibility for using the brand vision to influence LEGO culture by encouraging regional managers to become leaders of change processes aimed at developing a corporate branding mindset among LEGO Group employees. If continued, this activity might have generated additional local cycles similar to those of Cycles 1–3 within each of the company's five global regions. However, this cycle was complicated by an additional setback in the financial performance of the company and thus the full integration of all markets in the corporate branding process was delayed.

24

PARADOXES OF CORPORATE BRAND MANAGEMENT

The LEGO Group example shows some of the cultural dimensions of the managerial and organizational processes as the organization started the journey from fragmented, product-led branding to integrative corporate branding. Specifically, we observed that LEGO Group moved through four cycles of change in its corporate brand implementation process (see Figure 1.2). Each cycle represented a shift in the way LEGO Group orchestrated corporate branding and the different managerial challenges most significant to each cycle: (1) stating – incorporating cultural values and current consumer images into a new vision, (2) organizing – restructuring LEGO company to support the new corporate brand vision and reshaping managerial processes to better connect the brand with LEGO Group's organizational culture and corporate images, (3) involving – creating activities to directly involve employees and consumers in the LEGO brand, and (4) integrating – aligning the concerns and resources of all stakeholders including managers and employees behind the brand on a global scale.

Table 1.2 highlights the challenges and activities that were particularly related to organizational culture and summarizes the managerial efforts to align organizational culture(s) with the renewed identity. Furthermore, as we studied LEGO Group's corporate branding process we became aware of several recurring themes that are similar to experiences other companies report having had in their corporate brand strategy implementation and related cultural change processes. We began to see these themes in terms of paradoxes that may be present in all corporate brand management process, although in this chapter we stress the cultural interpretation of this paradoxical balancing act. By paradox we mean a seeming contradiction, both poles of which are necessary for

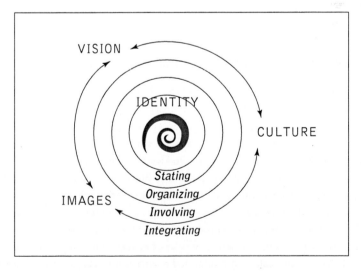

Figure 1.2 *Visualizing the cycles of corporate branding.*

25

maintaining a strong corporate brand (Quinn 1991; Van de Ven and Scott Poole 1989). The reason we believe these paradoxes are essential to the management of corporate brands is that resolving any of them in either direction appears to involve some unpleasant results. These cultural paradoxes are summarized in Table 1.2.

Paradox of stating: culture driven and image driven

A statement made by LEGO Group's former global brand manager Francesco Ciccolella provided an early hint of the paradox created by the simultaneous influences of culture and images in the corporate branding process. This senior LEGO manager expressed the need he felt to avoid both being a 'headless chicken' (enslaved by consumer trends, i.e. image driven) and an 'arrogant bastard' (enmeshed in an inwardly focused, the-company-knows-best culture, i.e. culture driven). His comment reflected the constant pressure corporate brand managers face to adapt to shifting market developments and stakeholder preferences balanced against an equal need to preserve the uniqueness of the LEGO brand in a coherent and credible brand communication over time. This simultaneous need to look outward and inward creates the paradox to which Ciccolella referred.

The inside-out/outside-in paradox can also be seen in a company such as Bang & Olufsen whose managers must balance coherent strategic visions for their brand (the vision of 'combined technological excellence and emotional appeal') against shifting consumer images and demands in a trend-driven and highly competitive marketplace. Bang & Olufsen has oscillated between trying to adapt to the shifting consumer images in the luxury goods market and revisiting its Bauhaus values of simplicity, functionality and poetry of design, deeply embedded in its organizational culture. A top manager of the company remarked about these oscillations: 'For periods we have become exclusive with too much gold and empty marble palaces. We want to be excellent based in simplicity and modesty. Aluminium is excellence.'

Paradox of organizing: centralization and decentralization

As we pointed out throughout the case analysis, LEGO managers struggled to maintain the right balance between centralization and decentralization. While this is another common paradox for international companies, corporate branding places this paradox squarely on the shoulders of the brand manager, which is particularly challenging in a cultural context with multiple subcultures and a strong headquarter culture. In LEGO Group's case, management's need to lead the branding process in order to achieve global coherence was continuously offset by the need to involve employees and other stakeholders and to build the brand upon their activities and interests. LEGO management balanced the risk of too much brand policing versus total chaos by continually shifting between centralizing and decentralizing modes of managing its corporate brand.

Given the scope and scale of the intended changes, it is little wonder that LEGO's corporate branding effort met internal resistance. However, this resistance was most articulated in relation to the organizing cycle, where the primary reinforcement mechanisms of culture management were used (Schein 1992), such as redistribution of power, status and scarce resources; shifts in leadership attention; and the promotion and recruitment of people new to the existing culture. However, rather than overcoming resistance at a particular stage in the change process, LEGO Group faced an ongoing dynamic between resistance and engagement as the process shifted from centralizing integration efforts (Organizing and Integrating) to decentralized adaptive processes (Stating and Involving). Thus, LEGO's corporate brand management maintained the flexibility to shift between making explicit demands about the direction branding would take, and being willing to decentralize the branding process to accommodate local concerns expressed by employees and other stakeholder groups around the world.

Other companies have managed the paradox between centralization and decentralization differently. This is illustrated by the various models of brand leadership suggested by Aaker and Joachimsthaler (2000), who argue that global branding involves centralized brand leadership, but not necessarily a single global brand. For many companies, pursuing a corporate brand strategy requires centralization of the brand vision and brand management process at the risk of causing severe resistance from employees in local markets and loosing local brand equity. For example, the healthcare company Novo Nordisk has institutionalized a value-driven brand management process, in which local business units are carefully assessed by a team of 'culture facilitators' who evaluate whether they are living the brand according to corporate values and business principles. Although this process at first created resistance, the company has found ways of including local perceptions in the assessment and feedback process, which has made this a highly successful way of executing and empowering the culture directed by the vision for the brand (see www.novonordisk.com).

Paradox of involving: cultural heritage and contemporary relevance

Finding the right balance between respecting the cultural heritage of the brand and making this heritage relevant to current and future stakeholders is an ongoing concern for any company pursuing a corporate brand strategy, particularly in a time of increasing stakeholder involvement. For example, LEGO Group managers continually struggled to find the right mix of respect for long-standing corporate values and the desire to draw new stakeholders closer to the brand. This struggle resulted in early efforts to restate LEGO's traditional values in more contemporary and forceful language, and later led to initiatives to make these values more relevant to organizational members via its brand school and internal dialogue processes. Through this heritage/relevance paradox the involved employees were simultaneously looking back to their proud, but distant, cultural past and looking forward, seeking to revitalize this heritage in contributing to a global brand culture for the LEGO brand.

27

There are examples of companies that have almost lost sight of their cultural heritage in their eagerness to adapt to current market needs, which illustrates the difficulty of revitalization for companies with a strong heritage. For example, Swedish Volvo nearly lost its image for being a safe family car in order to become a more mainstream up-scale brand. Hewlett-Packard, under the guidance of CEO Carly Fiorina, attempted to recover the company's past, with ads showing images of the garage in which the founders invented their first products, while, at the same time, working feverishly to redefine HP as not just a technology company but a valuable business partner that is consumer friendly.

Paradox of integrating: global and local

We found a fourth paradox in the company's ongoing effort to balance between global coherence and local adaptation. This paradox is a classic dilemma of international strategy. LEGO Group has long practised local adaptation in their market communication, and this contributed to the brand fragmentation and the strong internal subcultures that the new brand strategy was inaugurated to overcome. However, the risk of imposed coherence is that the brand becomes isolated from market needs and local cultural preferences, just as internal subcultures may lead to obstructive and countercultural behaviour. Although this is a common challenge for companies pursuing international strategies, the emotional and expressive dimensions that corporate branding add to the strategic process, combined with a highly transparent global environment, made LEGO Group more vulnerable to this paradox.

Companies have dealt with these subcultural tensions in multiple ways, allowing for different degrees of local autonomy in everything from expressing the symbolism of the brand to the leadership culture. Increasingly, companies turn to organizational culture as an importance source of coherence despite local and national difference. For example, a company like Johnson & Johnson supports independence in the brand expressions for its multiple businesses, whereas it maintains a profound global cultural coherence through its relentless adherence to its 'Credo' and its strong cultural values (see the Credo at www.jnj.com).

GAPS IN DYNAMIC BRAND MANAGEMENT

Our longitudinal study of LEGO Group showed that each of the four paradoxes of brand management took centre stage during different branding cycles. Mastering the paradox in each cycle allowed the company to move forward to the next stage of managing its corporate brand. Based on our analysis, we hypothesize that successful corporate brand management depends upon balancing the paradoxes that corporate branding generates and that timing the shifts between the poles of those paradoxes during the different cycles of the corporate branding process becomes management's key contribution.

The LEGO Group example also showed that corporate branding processes are rarely as coherent and aligned as the simple model represented by the Corporate Branding Toolkit suggests. The toolkit can be applied as a framework for revealing major gaps in the constitution of a corporate brand at a given moment in time (e.g. the gap between culture and vision; or between culture and image); but to obtain a more realistic view of corporate branding requires repeated analysis that ultimately shows how gaps unfold and transform during the brand management process (such an application of the model to British Airways was offered in Hatch and Schultz 2003). We argue that a dynamic analysis of how the elements of the corporate brand get aligned or misaligned during the corporate branding process will enable management to be more responsive and proactive in their effort to guide the organization through the shifting set of challenges and obstacles entailed in full-scale corporate brand management.

Table 1.3 summarizes examples of gaps from the corporate branding process in LEGO Group that emerged from analysis using the Corporate Brand Toolkit. Here, we emphasize branding gaps seen from the organizational culture perspective, which involves focusing on employee perceptions and in particular the different ways in which the

Table 1.3 *Gaps in corporate brand management and their relations to brand cycles*

Corporate branding gaps	Example of gap challenge	Managerial attempt to close gap	Most significant to brand cycles
Culture–identity gap	To make the cultural heritage based in construction and playful learning relevant to the renewed brand identity	Revise the brand identity based on extensive historical culture research and observations of the actual enactment of LEGO values	Stating: examining gap between the claimed LEGO values and everyday culture behaviour among all employees
Culture–vision gap	To better involve different internal subcultures (emerging from functions, location, nationality) actively in the new brand strategy	Support and initiate stronger collaboration between different functions (e.g. marketing, innovation, HRM) to create a coherent corporate brand	*Involving and organizing*: aligning subcultures with strategic vision by organizing and creating motivation for such employee involvement
Culture–image gap	To better engage employees in consumer interaction to create more 'street credibility' and reduce dusty image	Make stronger internal distribution of knowledge of consumer images and ensure that those images are communicated to employees in innovation and product development	*Organizing and involving*: creating organizational infrastructure to facilitate distribution of insights from consumer images to everyday culture behaviour in product development

29

Table 1.3 *continued*

Corporate branding gaps	Example of gap challenge	Managerial attempt to close gap	Most significant to brand cycles
Image–vision gap	To align differences in global images particularly between USA and Europe with new aspirations for a global brand and to engage employees in this global venture	Build stronger awareness of growing competition in the marketplace and different image challenges in key markets (the fragmentation of the global LEGO brand culture)	*Integrating:* supporting a managerial process which enables the company to find the balance between global brand management processes and local brand adaptation

corporate branding process involves or disengages employees. A strong interest in consumer behaviour would involve analysing gaps from a different angle.

Although it is not possible to argue a mutually exclusive relationship between corporate branding gaps and the different cycles of the brand management process, we find that the need for management to address some gaps is more profound in specific cycles; e.g. the stating cycle is most concerned with how the redefined identity related to existing cultures (culture–identity gap), whereas the culture–vision gap is most explicitly present in the involving cycle, but also serves as an important contextualization for the organizing cycle. The particular order in which the various elements of corporate branding became interrelated during the journey from product branding to corporate branding is unique to LEGO Group. Corporate brands emerge from relationships over time, engaging a multiplicity of different stakeholders, and therefore critical challenges and obstacles may emerge in different orders for individual companies. However, based on our studies of other corporate branding processes, we argue that corporate brand management conducted with the ambition to align the whole organization behind the brand will face challenges similar to those of LEGO Group.

CONCLUSION

In this chapter we have suggested that corporate brand management can be conceived as shifting dynamics between the corporate branding elements in the Corporate Brand Toolkit, i.e. organizational culture, strategic vision, stakeholder images and brand identity; and that the challenges entailed in creating alignment between those elements can be analysed as different cycles of the corporate branding process. We have further argued that each branding cycle is particularly sensitized to a set of managerial and organizational paradoxes, where the corporate brand is balanced and rebalanced rather than resolved. Furthermore, we have argued that a cultural perspective on corporate branding places special emphasis on employees, whose roles are critical but different in each of the corporate branding cycles. On the one hand, employees represent the cultural heritage of the brand in the sense that their everyday sense-making and behaviour are manifestations of brand values and traditions in the company; and, on the other hand, employees are seismographs for the shifting brand images in the global marketplace, as their attraction and commitment to the company is fuelled and inspired by the brand images. By the same token, the active and loyal involvement of employees in the corporate branding process is crucial for a successful – and meaningful – implementation of the vision and identity of the brand, while at the same time employees need to deepen their knowledge of the cultural trends surrounding the corporate brand and stay aligned with shifting brand culture contextualizing it.

Taking a cultural perspective on corporate branding involves much more than 'living the brand' in the sense that employees represent both the brand culture (in terms of the knowledge, style and tacit assumptions that have built the brand), and future brand images (in their ability to listen, adapt and challenge customers and other stakeholders in seeing what the brand could be and making it happen). A culture perspective on brand management expands the agenda of corporate branding from one of executing top management's vision to involving employees in the creation and enactment of the brand and its promises, at the same time deepening their relations with stakeholders and using their passion for the brand to help align the culture, image and vision for the brand.

KEY POINT

■ Corporate branding is a cross-disciplinary construct building on marketing (image), strategy (vision) and organization theory (culture and identity). What are the theoretical and managerial implications of this cross-disciplinary content?

QUESTIONS FOR DISCUSSION

1   What is your image of LEGO brand and how do you expect the organizational culture to be compared with the brand image?
2   How can the LEGO company use its brand image to involve employees in the branding process?
3   How can ideas and concepts from organizational culture theory inspire the implementation of corporate brands, e.g. the works of Edgar Schein and Joanne Martin?
4   Looking at other companies, are there additional paradoxes in implementing global corporate brands?
5   Can you think of other examples of gaps in corporate brands (between vision, culture, image and identity) and how companies have overcome those gaps?

REFERENCES

Aaker, D. A. (2004) 'Leveraging the corporate brand', *California Management Review* 46, 3: 6–18.

Aaker, D. A. and Joachimsthaler, E. (2000) *Brand Leadership,* New York: The Free Press.

Albert, S. and Whetten, D. A. (1985) 'Organizational identity', in L. L. Cummings and M. M. Staw (eds) *Research in Organizational Behavior* 7: 263–295.

Balmer, J. M. T. and Greyser, S. (eds) (2003) *Revealing the Corporation,* London: Routledge.

Collins, J. C. and Porras, J. (1994) *Built to Last,* New York: Harper Business.

Dutton, J. and Dukerich, J. (1991) 'Keeping an eye on the mirror: image and identity in organizational adaptation', *Academy of Management Journal* 34: 517–554.

Dutton, J., Dukerich, J. and Harquail, C. (1994) 'Organizational images and member identification', *Administrative Science Quarterly* 39: 239–263.

Gioia, D. A. and Chittipeddi, K. (1991) 'Sensemaking and sensegiving in strategic change initiation', *Strategic Management Journal* 12: 433–448.

Gioia, D. A., Schultz, M. and Corley, K. (2000) 'Organizational identity, image and adaptive instability', *Academy of Management Review* 25: 63–82.

Hatch, M. J. (1993) 'The dynamics of organizational culture', *Academy of Management Review* 18: 657–663.

Hatch, M. J. and Schultz, M. (2001) 'Are the strategic stars aligned for your corporate brand?', *Harvard Business Review* 44: 128–134.

Hatch, M. J. and Schultz, M. (2002) 'Organizational identity dynamics', *Human Relations* 55: 989–1018.

Hatch, M. J. and Schultz, M. (2003) 'Bringing the corporation into corporate branding', *European Journal of Marketing* 7/8: 1041–1064.

Holt, D. (2003) 'What becomes an icon most?', *Harvard Business Review* 83 (March): 43–49.

Ind, N. (2001) *Living the Brand*, London: Kogan Page.

Karmark, E. (2002) *Organizational Identity – A Dualistic Subculture*, Copenhagen: Copenhagen Business School.

Martin, J. (1992) *Cultures in Organizations. Three Perspectives*, Oxford: Oxford University Press.

Martin, J. (2002) *Organizational Culture: Mapping the Terrain*, Thousand Oaks, CA: Sage.

Olins, W. (2000) 'Why brands are taking over the corporation', in M. Schultz, M. J. Hatch and M. H. Larsen (eds) *The Expressive Organization: Linking Identity, Reputation, and the Corporate Brand*, Oxford: Oxford University Press: 51–65.

Olins, W. (2003) *On Brand*, London: Thames & Hudson.

Quinn, R. (1991) *Beyond Rational Management*, San Francisco, CA: Jossey-Bass.

Schein, E. H. (1992) *Organizational Culture and Leadership*, second edition, San Francisco, CA: Jossey-Bass.

Schultz, M. and de Chernatony, L. (2002) 'Special issue on corporate branding', *Corporate Reputation Review* 5.

Schultz, M. and Hatch, M. J. (2003) 'The cycles of corporate branding; the case of the LEGO Group', *California Management Review* 46, 1: 6–24.

Van de Ven, A. and Scott Poole, M. (1989) 'Using paradox to build organization and management theories', *Academy of Management Review* 15, 3: 562–578.

Whetten, D.A. and Mackey, A. (2002) 'A social actor conception of organizational identity and its implications for the study of organizational reputation', *Business and Society* 41, 4: 393–414.

Chapter 2

Corporate brand cultures and communities

John M. T. Balmer

INTRODUCTION

Brands, in their various guises, are integral to our everyday existence. As argued by the anthropologist John Sherry, the corporate landscape has become a brandscape (1998). I argue that it has increasingly become a *corporate brand*scape. Consider your most favourite brands or look at the brand valuation lists produced by organizations such as Interbrand and you are likely to discover that they are *corporate* rather than product brands. Increasingly, many of the world's biggest companies – Coca-Cola, Microsoft and IBM – are seen as corporate brands rather than corporate entities (Davies 2004); corporate brands are increasingly being viewed as a vital component for organizational success and survival.

In the context of this chapter, I wish to make the simple point that corporate brands and their cultures and communities are stronger, wider and of greater consequence when compared to product brands and product brand cultures: consider BMW (a corporate brand) *vis-à-vis* KitKat (a product brand) in this regard. Clearly, corporate brands are worthy of scrutiny as a branding category *of their own*.

Of course, a world without brands would be almost unthinkable, as would a world devoid of cultural associations. As marketing scholars have realized for some time the spheres of culture and of branding are inextricably linked. Culture can help us to comprehend brands whereas brands can provide a powerful lens by which to comprehend organizational-related cultures. This helps to explain the utility of the phrase 'brand culture'. It is a notion that is of considerable value to brand managers and scholars alike. As such, brand culture provides a window through which some of the quintessential attributes of brands may be discerned. No more so is this the case than with corporate brands where brand culture is three-dimensional in that it is found not only within and outside the organization but also across organizations.

What is exciting in terms of corporate brand culture is that unlike product brands its importance is tangible, incontrovertible but also challenging. This is because corporate brands, unlike product brands, are 'consumed' by *different groups* in *different ways*. As such, corporate brand culture can be compared to a crucible: a crucible that subsumes different stakeholder groups and networks that feed in to, and benefit from, membership of a brand's cultural community.

Membership of a corporate brand culture is varied. It can be realized by a variety of stakeholder groups through a multitude of means:

- consumer consumption (the preference accorded to a corporate brand in relation to consumer buyer behaviour: a preference to shop at Tesco rather than at Sainsbury's);
- employment (the status accorded to a newly minted marketing graduate employed as a brand manager at Unilever);
- endorsement (the prestige accorded by being awarded a Royal Warrant by HM King Carl XVI Gustaf of Sweden);
- association (the 'prestige' accorded to a spouse whose partner is head of a Cambridge college);
- acquisition (the ownership of the *QE2* and of the Cunard brand *and brand culture* by a US company); and
- aspiration (shoppers at Harrods whose current financial status mean that they can only afford a branded heavy-duty carrier bag).

It has been argued that corporate brands serve as a powerful navigational tool to a variety of stakeholders (and not just customers) for a miscellany of purposes including employment, investment and for the creation of individual identities. This helps to explain why corporate brands are adored, venerated and coveted by customers and organizations alike (Balmer and Gray 2003).

Corporate brands have a wide utility. They not only relate to corporations (Ford, HSBC Bank, Telia) but also to subsidiaries (Jaguar, Volvo and Aston Martin being subsidiaries of Ford). They are also applicable to sovereign states (Denmark, Eire), nations and semi-autonomous states (Greenland, the Faroes, Scotland and Wales), regions (Campania in Italy, and Tyrol in Austria) and cities (Bergen, Edinburgh, Exeter, Naples, Paris); to the 'ancient' universities of Bologna, Cambridge, Le Sorbonne, Oxford and St Andrews; to the Catholic church and its various religious orders such as the Augustinians, Benedictines, Carthusians, Dominicans, Franciscans, Oratorians, Premonstratensians and Jesuits. At the supra-national level certain institutions have brand-like qualities such as the Commonwealth, European Union, Le Francophone and NATO and at the supra-organizational level business context the oneworld and star airline alliances may be viewed as corporate brands (albeit in their infancy). All of the above have attendant brand communities.

Before returning to the issue of brand culture at the organizational level, I will briefly explain some of the principal characteristics of the *corporate brand*scape.

CORPORATE BRANDSCAPE

In my discussion of corporate brands I (a) discuss the literature, (b) the schools of thought relating to corporate brands, (c) the worth of corporate brands, (d) the inseparability between corporate brands and corporate identity, (e) the corporate brand covenant, and lastly (f) explain why corporate brands have 'a life of their own'.

The nascent literature on corporate brands

Currently, corporate branding is generating considerable ardour from marketing scholars (see Balmer 2003; Knox and Bickerton 2003; Schultz and de Chernatony 2002; Hatch and Schultz 2003; Kapferer 2002; Aaker 2004) and consultants (Ind 1997; Olins 2004). Account is being taken of the protestations of King (1991), Balmer (1995, 2001) and Balmer and Greyser (2003) to face up to the challenges in terms relating to the comprehension and management of corporate brands.

Table 2.1 compares corporate brands with product brands.

Corporate brands: schools of thought

The five schools of thought relating to corporate brands as identified by Balmer (see Balmer and Gray 2003) illustrate the various ways in which corporate brands have been characterized. They are as follows:

1 *Marks denoting ownership* At its simplest, a brand denotes a name, logotype or trademark signifying ownership (Barwise *et al.* 2000). However, other identifiers that draw on the non-visual senses can also be marshalled. Consider the consistent use of the music from Delibes' opera *Lakmé* by British Airways (BA) has resulted in this having the status of the signature tune for BA. In 2000 the Carlson Market Group established a new division to communicate corporate brands through sensory means and to address such questions as 'What would Vodafone smell like?' (Brayfield 2000).

2 *Image-building devices* This school of thought focuses on the consumer and, in communications terms, on the 'receiver-end' of the equation. As noted by Kapferer (2002), metaphors and animate objects are used to convey an image. Consider Jaguar, Johnnie Walker and Sarah Lee in this regard.

3 *Symbols associated with key values* The recent literature on corporate branding observes that key values can characterize corporate brands (see de Chernatony 1999 and Urde 2003). The BBC brand, for instance, is associated with quality broadcasting and authoritative and impartial news coverage.

4 *A means by which to construct individual identities* Brands are appropriated by consumers as a means of defining who they are, wish to be and/or wish to be seen as (Elliot and Wattanasuwan 1998; Newman 2001) and as a means of creating

Table 2.1 *A comparison between product and corporate brands*

	Product brands	Corporate brands
Management responsibility	Brand manager	Chief executive
Functional responsibility	Marketing	Most/all departments
General responsibility	Marketing personnel	All personnel
Disciplinary roots	Marketing	Multidisciplinary
Brand gestation	Short	Medium to long
Stakeholder focus	Consumers	Multiple stakeholders
Values	Contrived	Real
Communications channels	The marketing communications mix	Total corporate commuciations
		Primary communication: *performance of products and services; organizational policies; behaviour of CEO and senior management; experience of Personnel and discourse by personnel*
		Secondary communication: *Marketing and other forms of controlled communication*
		Tertiary communication: *Word of mouth*
Dimensions requiring alignment	Brand values (*covenant*) Product performance	Brand values (*covenant*) Identity (*corporate attributes/subcultures*) Corporate strategy Vision (as held by the CEO and senior management)
	Communication Experience/image and reputation Consumer commitment	Communication Experience/image and reputation Stakeholders' commitment (*internal and external constituencies*)
	Environment (*political, economic, ethical, social, technological*)	Environment (*political, economic, ethical, social, technological*)

Source: adapted from Balmer (2001)

individual identities. A Jaguar can connote power and prestige, a Volvo can confirm a person's credentials as 'good parent' owing to the brand's focus on safety, whereas an Aston Martin might confirm a man's self-perception as someone who is a distinctive, stylish, sporty individual and having, perhaps, the savoir-faire of James Bond 007.

5 *A conduit by which pleasurable experiences may be consumed* It has been argued that corporate brands can be closely associated with pleasurable experiences (Schmitt 1999). The Disneyland brand and the city brand of Venice are two obvious examples.

The value of corporate brands

The value of brands has long been recognized by corporations. Established corporate brands are a guarantee of quality, and an insurance against poor performance or financial risk. They provide a conduit by which the organizations' values and culture/s may be communicated, identified and comprehended and the brand cultures that often emerge as a consequence can be of immense value.

Brands are *not* made in the factory but *in people's minds* as the astute founder of the US graphic design agency Landor once remarked. I argue that whereas *legal ownership* of a corporate brand resides with one or more corporations, *emotional ownership* resides with stakeholders. It is these perceptions that give a corporate brand a good deal of its value and this also helps to explain the importance of corporate brand cultures and communities, as well as the high financial values that are often apportioned to corporate brands. Consider the $12.6 billion buyout of Kraft by Philip Morris, six times its book value (Newman 2001) and the fact that 59 per cent of Coca-Cola's, 61 per cent of Disney's and 64 per cent of McDonald's capitalization is attributable directly to the value associated with the corporate brand (Barwise *et al.* 2000).

Research has also revealed that managers saw corporate brands as having distinct benefits in terms of increased profile, customer attractiveness, product support, visual recognition, investor confidence, as well as in encapsulating organizational values and providing staff motivation (Lewis 2000). They are seen to afford benefits also in terms of the recruitment and retention of employees. Virgin Atlantic (Mitchell 1999: 32) and Waterstone's (a leading UK retail book outlet) selects personnel that mirror corporate brand values (Ind 1997).

Corporate brands and corporate identity

Corporate identity provides the grit around which a corporate brand is formed.

(Balmer 2001)

The Latin phrase *Vultus est index animi* captures the awesome nature of corporate brands. Translated, the literal meaning of the phrase is: 'The expression on one's face is a sign of the soul.' It takes only a small leap of imagination to realize that for many organizations the corporate brand is *the face* of the organization and is also an icon of the culture that customers, employees and others have an affinity to. As such, when we regard a thriving corporate brand that has stood the test of time, we also see important elements of the parent *corporate identity* and by this means the brand cultures that characterize corporate brands.

As such, the identity perspective informs my comprehension of corporate brands and notions of brand culture. You can no more take oxygen out of the atmosphere or remove identity when examining brands without catastrophic effect in both instances. In other words, corporate identities provide the bedrock of corporate brand building. Interestingly, there appears to be a symbiosis of thought among marketing scholars who adopt an identity perspective, such as Balmer (2003: 281), and those who adopt a branding perspective, such as Kapferer (2002: 176), both of whom conclude that corporate brands are underpinned by corporate identities.

Although corporate identities and corporate brands are closely related, I argue that they are distinct for the following reasons:

- corporate brands have a value, portability and longevity that corporate identities may not have;
- every entity has a corporate identity but may not necessarily have a corporate brand;
- corporate brand culture tends to be explicit whereas culture, when discussed in corporate identity contexts, is more complex and opaque;
- the focus of corporate brands has an important external focus: customers are critical. Identity has an important internal focus: employees are critical;
- corporate brands draw on the emotional and intangible to a greater degree compared to corporate identities;
- corporate brands can be marshalled by other entities in ways that corporate identities cannot (franchise arrangements for example).

Table 2.2 compares corporate identities with corporate brands.

The corporate brand covenant: evangelists and terrorists

Corporate brands often engender a loyalty that is not so dissimilar from that found in various faith groups. As such, a corporate brand (the faith) and the corporate brand community (the faithful) are mutually dependent. The notion of the corporate brand as representing an explicit covenant between an organization and its key stakeholder groups and vice versa has been used to describe this relationship (Balmer 2001, 2003). Some corporate brand covenants are expressed in terms of a brand mantra such as Nike's 'authentic athletic performance', GE's 'imagination at work' and Nokia's 'connecting people'. A corporate brand can be viewed as an informal contract between an

Table 2.2 *A comparison between corporate identities and corporate brands*

	Corporate identity	*Corporate brands*
Necessary or contingent?	Necessary	Contingent
Applicable to all organizations?	Yes	No
Stability or attributes	Constantly evolving	Relatively stable
Applicability	Normally a single entity	Normally a single identity *but* can be multiple
Management responsibility	CEO	CEO
Functional responsibility	All functions	All Functions
Disciplinary roots	Multidisciplinary	Multidisciplinary
Principal drivers	Strategy, culture, vision	Branding covenant, culture
Gestation	Short	Medium/long
Stakeholder focus	Mainly internal. External stakeholders vary in importance depending on strategy	Mainly external. Internal stakeholders also important
Desired profile among internal and external stakeholder groups	Variable: low to high	Normally high
Importance of controlled communication	Variable	Normally crucial
Importance of advertising and visual identity	Variable	Normally crucial
Key elements	Culture (subcultures), strategy, structure, communication, performance, perception	The branding covenant, communication plus other identity elements such as (see below)
Key dimensions requiring alignment	Organizational attributes – (including subcultures) Communication/perception	Corporate brand Covenant/communication Plus other identity elements (including subcultures)
Portability	Normally difficult	Variable
Financial goodwill	Variable	Can be very high indeed

organization and its stakeholders: contracts that are underpinned by emotion rather than by law.

In 'corporate faith communities' emotions can be negative as well as positive. Corporate brands engender strong emotions. There are not only corporate brand *evangelists*: there are also corporate brand *terrorists*. A good example of corporate *brand evangelism* can be found in team sports such as football where supporters show their brand affiliation by wearing the team colour and emblem, by chanting certain songs and chants and by referring (in a way not dissimilar to British Army regiments) to successful campaigns of the past against a particular team. Football stadiums are the shrines of such communities.

For their part *brand terrorists* abhor the belief systems and manifestations of those who do not share 'their faith and belief system'. Football teams are cases in point. For the most part there is good-humoured rivalry and ribaldry between supporters from different football teams. Occasionally, however, supporters react in acutely negative terms to football fans of other teams with actions that are violent and, sometimes, fatal. Then there are those who find certain corporate brands repulsive. For instance, in the UK, some ethnic communities resent 'Coca-Colonization' and Muslim shopkeepers have responded by offering Islamic alternatives to Coca-Cola such as Mecca Cola, Qibla Cola and Zanzam Cola (*The Economist* 2004). Interestingly, research undertaken by *Marketing* magazine in September 2004 supports the above proposition by its identification of the UK's most hated brands. Among the most hated corporate brands were Manchester United, McDonald's and the supermarket chain Lidl.

Corporate brands: a life of their own?

However, once established, a corporate brand can have a life, a meaning and a set of expectations of its own that, although derived from its founding identity, with the passage of time, let it *have a life of its own*; it is an organism that is separate and divisible from the corporate identity that gave it existence. This is because the values and cultures that underpin the various subcultures of the organization may, over time, be distilled to form a corporate brand with a clearly defined, communicated, understood and experienced set of values and may not only be owned by other entities but can be used as a template in the creation of new identities (such as when Rolls-Royce moved to the south of England).

The fact that corporate brands can have a life of their own can be seen in the fact that corporate brands have a *portability* that a corporate identity does not have. In such instances the corporate brand becomes the embryo in the creation of a new identity or the reformation of an existing identity so that the resulting corporate identity will be in alignment with corporate brand values and culture.

Most corporate brand cultures are historically rooted in a particular identity type. Consider these well-known British brands: Bentley, Clydesdale Bank, Cunard, Harrods, Jaguar, *The Times*, Tetley, Thomas Cook and Yorkshire Bank. All are now in foreign ownership, but these examples illustrate why corporate brands can have 'a life of their own'. All are still fundamentally concerned with the values associated with their historical roots as independent entities: in addition to their associations with the brand culture of an entity they are also associated with the brand culture of a nation. As such, to deny the cultural associations of these brands (British, Scottish, Yorkshire) would undermine their value and viability.

Corporate brands can, of course, be *bought, borrowed, sold* and, in certain circum-stances, be *shared* among a variety of organizations: Virgin, Rolls-Royce and Hilton being

41

cases in point. *Established* corporate brands can serve as a genetic template on which identities can be moulded. Consider the Rolls-Royce car marque. Today, Rolls-Royce cars are made/assembled in rural Sussex, in a state-of-the-art assembly plant where many of the workers have not previously worked for Rolls-Royce. The original Rolls-Royce factory in Coventry and most of its original employees there now make and work for Bentley. The numerous companies and identities that underpin the franchise operations of the Body Shop have been honed to provide a homogeneous promise, style and service that are in alignment with the corporate brand. Again, this illustrates why corporate brands can 'have a life of their own' in that the brand can be owned by one entity and marshalled by many as in the case of franchise arrangements.

CORPORATE BRAND CULTURE

Corporate brand culture is important in several regards: it needs to underpin the communicated corporate brand values, its covenant and, importantly, its activities and behaviour. Adherents to a corporate brand, whether they are customers, employers, investors, etc. are, de facto, members of a brand community or network: a community that encapsulates the values of a brand and a community whose actions also help to define a brand community.

Culture in context

The notion of a single company culture is a very attractive one. It is based on the notion that organizational members have a similar comprehension of the organization's mission and ethos (Deshpande and Webster 1989). However, there is a growing realization that organizations consist of multiple subcultures. Such subcultures may be corporate but may also be professional or 'national'. They can be in the ascendant, descendant and may be moribund (Balmer and Wilson 1998). Just as issues of complexity and multiplicity characterize the identity literature the same appears to be true for issues associated with brand culture as the following section illustrates.

Cultures and identities

Organizations are typically underpinned by a number of identities each of which has an attendant 'culture'. The following is a representative rather than a comprehensive list of the sources of various identity types that may be present within organizations:

- identity reflecting the values of the company founder (Richard Branson *vis-à-vis* Virgin and Bill Gates *vis-à-vis* Microsoft)
- identity derived from the original corporate philosophy (the BBC's public service remit 'to educate, inform and entertain')

- identity reflecting a key corporate competency (Volvo's impeccable credentials *vis-à-vis* safety)
- identity reflecting homogenous industries (undertakers/funeral parlours, oil companies and building societies)
- identity reflecting national norms and precepts (Italian style of Alfa Romeo, Swiss precision of Rolex and high service standards of Singapore's national airline)
- other identity types drawing on corporate social responsibility (Ben & Jerry's and the Co-operative Bank), feminine allure and sexuality (Ann Summers) and associations with human celebrations and sadness and emotions (Hallmark cards and Hallmark television).

Examples of corporate brand communities

The power of brand communities is expressed in a multiplicity of ways. A key aspect of brand culture and community is that it transcends the traditional internal/external divide of organizations and may even span groups of organizations. Brand culture is therefore not only a relevant notion for customers but also employees, prospective employees, investors, business partners and may also accommodate governments and the media. A good example of this is Marks & Spencer which, until quite recently, eschewed advertising: it did not need to. Not only were customers and employees proud advocates of the corporate brand but so were its suppliers and a former British Prime Minister (Margaret Thatcher). A similar phenomenon can be found in relation to the Harley Davidson brand in the USA. Clearly, an organization such as Marks & Spencer derived real benefit from having such a strong brand culture which manifested itself not only in terms of loyalty from customers and staff but also resulted in considerable savings in terms of marketing and corporate communications. Amazingly, the company did not accept credit cards and thereby saved on the commission paid to companies such as Visa and MasterCard; for many years this did not seem to concern customers.

One important aspect of corporate brand culture is how it has a value to multiple stakeholder groups. This can be seen with regard to a number of well-known British corporate brands that were built on philanthropic and Quaker foundations such as Cadbury and Rowntree. The wholesome family values of these brands not only had meaning to customers in terms of product brand messages built around health and goodness but also to employees with such corporations emphasizing worker welfare and education, health and temperance (Pavitt 2000).

Not all 'brand cultures' benefit the organization in ways that are tangible or, indeed, financial. Consider the world famous football club of Manchester United. Although it enjoys a phenomenally large international following it does, all the same, find it difficult to leverage financial benefit from its supporter base. Contrast this with the Prime Minister of Thailand's acquisition of a significant shareholding of Liverpool Football Club (LFC) which de facto means that the Kingdom of Thailand will be inextricably linked to LFC (see Berger 2003; Smith 2003). This gives a quite new meaning to brand culture

43

and reminds us that while *legal ownership* of a corporate brand is vested within one or more corporations, *emotional ownership* transcends not only the internal/external organizational divide, but transcends stakeholder groups and even nations. In the case of Thailand, that Kingdom's strong emotional attachment to the brand will be formalized in that country acquiring a substantial ownership stake in the brand. Although UK supporters feel that this is incongruous, they fail to realize that some of the club's most ardent supporters are to be found outside the UK. You don't have to be British to drive a Jaguar, to wrap yourself in Burberry or travel with British Airways. What the above examples show, is that you don't need to be from Liverpool to have an attachment to Liverpool Football Club, the Beatles or to the Royal Liverpool Philharmonic Orchestra! Brand communities challenge traditional notions of organizational boundaries.

Consider, Coca-Cola's corporate brand, which is as much about Americana as it is about fun refreshing beverages and, even, Christmas. It is a mix of corporate as well as national cultures. The Danish monarchy (as a corporate brand) would appear to be a fusion of national culture as well as the generic (and international) identity of royalty. The Virgin brand is a fusion not only of contemporary and youthful notions of British identity but also is imbued with the identity of its founder, whereas British Airways appears to draw on more traditional and timeless notions of Britishness.

Of course, some corporate brands are a fusion of *several* national cultures. In Europe, the Anglo-Dutch behemoths of Royal Dutch/Shell Transport and Unilever are cases in point. For the main, it is the 'corporate' mix of cultures that predominates but as the Brent Spar example revealed national cultural differences came to the fore and as such there were serious divisions between the UK's Shell Transport and Royal Dutch of the Netherlands and led to divergent policies being followed by each part of the Shell/Royal Dutch Group: whereas the UK wing of Shell (Shell Transport) advocated the sinking of the Brent Spar oil rig in the North Sea, the Dutch wing (Royal Dutch Shell) and vehemently opposed to the sinking of the rig.

Orchestrating the mix of cultures that suffuse a corporate brand so as to form a coherent whole can be a far from easy task, however. In the Netherlands, Philips placed great store on its technological prowess but this aspect of its culture was not mediated by a sufficiently strong customer focus (something that has also characterized Marks & Spencer in the UK). In the USA when Coca-Cola changed the taste of Coca-Cola this seemed to reflect its strong consumer credentials: exhaustive testing revealed that customers preferred the new taste. However, senior managers had failed to realize that such a change was seen in terms of assault on a quintessential American icon and this explained the public backlash (and the eventual reintroduction of the original Coca-Cola formula).

Something similar happened when British Airways adopted symbols of the world in the late 1990s as part of its new complex system of visual identification that was introduced by the airline's senior management in an attempt to position BA as more of an international rather than a British brand. The scheme was eventually abandoned and the airline's British credentials were reasserted. Senior executives at BA appeared to have made a number of cardinal errors *vis-à-vis* the management of their corporate brand in that they confused corporate/legal ownership of the brand with emotional/stakeholder ownership of the brand; undue emphasis was accorded to visual identity and to management fiat as a means of changing BA's corporate brand culture; the iconic status of BA as a British brand was not recognized; BA's brand community was narrowly conceived and the new corporate covenant was not authentic: there had been a change of face but not a change of heart

Brand architecture, culture and custodianship

Complexity reveals itself in the myriad of relationships in terms of ownership and use of the corporate brand. Such associations are more complicated than is sometimes realized. Consider corporate brand ownership and custodianship in the cultural values associated with nationality and lifestyle of the following corporate brands: Hilton (US/a quality hotel marque); Volvo (Sweden with an emphasis on safety); Rolls-Royce (British, high quality and aristocratic); Brooks Brothers (US, Ivy League and preppy); Ben & Jerry's (US with strong environmental credentials). Now ponder the following:

- *Hilton* brand is used both by a US as well as a British corporation.
- *Volvo* is not only an independent engineering and commercial vehicles corporation but also a corporate brand that is owned by Ford, which exclusively manufactures Volvo cars.
- *Rolls-Royce* refers to the huge, British-owned, aero-engines group as well as to the famous car marque which is owned by Germany's BMW.
- *Brooks Brothers* is a quintessential preppy and East-Coast (US) outfitter that was acquired by the UK's Marks & Spencer (a brand that was long-associated with middle-of-the-range clothes that offered value and quality; it was especially noted for the durability of its underwear).
- *Ben & Jerry's*, which is known for its environmental and ethical values, is now owned by the Anglo-Dutch Unilever corporation, which does not have such a strong pedigree in terms of these concerns.

In this context it is no surprise that there is increased interest in questions relating to corporate brand architecture (LaForet and Saunders 1994; Kapferer 2004; Aaker and Joachimsthaler 2000; Balmer and Gray 2003). Brand architecture refers to the relationships between a corporation and its subsidiary companies. What has become apparent however is that such relationships are no longer restricted within the confines of a single corporation but can boundary-span organizations and industries. The tripartite characterization of brands as monolithic, endorsed or branded is simplistic in the extreme when account is taken of the myriad types of relationships that characterize the branding domain.

Therefore, the notion of brand culture may be seen in terms of pan-corporate as well as pan-industrial relationships. I have identified a further six categories in addition to the

45

monolithic, endorsed and branded categories identified by Olins (2004): familial, shared, surrogate, supra, multiplex and federal (see Balmer 2003).

- *Familial*: where two organizations in the same industry sector share the same corporate brand, such as Hilton, where there is common ownership of the corporate brand by two entities: one in the UK and the other in the USA.
- *Shared*: where two or more organizations share the same brand but operate in different sectors, such as Rolls-Royce car/aero-engine companies.
- *Surrogate*: where the corporate brand is licensed through franchise arrangements, as with McDonald's and the Body Shop.
- *Supra*: a corporate brand as pertaining to such entities as the United Nations, the Commonwealth or to a business alliance.
- *Multiplex*: a corporate brand that is used in multifarious sectors and where there can be shared ownership, such as in the case of Virgin.
- *Federal*: a distinct business entity and corporate brand that is underpinned by a federal business arrangement, as with Airbus.

The incidence of multiple entities sharing the same corporate brand is more common than is sometimes appreciated. Such relationships have existed for some time and some can be quite complex, as in the case of the *keiretsu* notion in Japan, which, incidentally, is the model that underpins the Virgin family of brands. It can also be found in relation to non-business contexts such as the 'British' monarchy. This is because Queen Elizabeth is separately and divisibly queen of no less than sixteen autonomous monarchies of which the United Kingdom is one; others include Canada, New Zealand and Jamaica. Constitutional scholars describe this in terms of one monarch but different monarchies. In a branding context I view such a phenomenon in terms of one corporate brand and one brand culture but different ownership and constitutional roles.

CONCLUSION

This chapter examines corporate brand cultures and communities. Such cultures and communities are stronger, wider and of greater consequence than product brand cultures. I argue that a corporate brand culture has its roots in the identity (and the myriad of subcultures) of the organization from which it evolved. However, once established, a corporate brand can have a life that is separate and divisible from its parent identity and this helps to explain why corporate brands can be viewed as valuable and portable assets: they can be bought, sold, shared and borrowed. Whereas legal ownership of a corporate brand resides with one or more entities, its real power comes from its emotional ownership, which resides within the corporate brand community. Membership of a corporate brand community can be varied via means of consumption, employment, endorsement, association, acquisition and aspiration (there can be, so to speak, multiple membership of the above). Just as there are corporate brand advocates, so there are corporate brand terrorists: those who dissociated themselves from or who abhor certain corporate brands, their values and their cultural communities. Rival football teams are cases in point. What I hope has become clear is that notions of corporate brand culture affords a powerful new lens through which to comprehend the vibrancy of corporate brands and their role as strategic resources.

KEY POINT

■ Corporate brand culture and communities are important in the comprehension and management of corporate brands.

QUESTIONS FOR DISCUSSION

1 What are the differences between corporate brand cultures and corporate brand communities?
2 What is the importance of corporate brand culture from the perspective of a customer, employee, prospective employee, business partner and the local community where the corporate brand is based?
3 How does a corporate brand culture manifest itself?
4 How does corporate brand management differ from product brand management?
5 Why (or why not) are corporate brands and corporate identities inextricably linked?

ACKNOWLEDGEMENT

Material contained in this chapter originally appeared in the following publication: Balmer, J. M. T. (2004) 'Initial reflections on the notion of corporate brand cultures and communities', Bradford University School of Management, Working Paper Series No. 04/44.

REFERENCES

Aaker, D. A. (2004) 'Leveraging the corporate brand', *California Management Review* 46: 6–18.

Aaker, D. A. and Joachimsthaler, E. A. (2000) 'The brand relationship spectrum: the key to the brand architecture challenge', *California Management Review* 42: 8–23.

Balmer, J. M. T. (1995) 'Corporate branding and connoisseurship', *Journal of General Management* 21: 22–46.

Balmer, J. M. T. (2001) 'Corporate identity, corporate branding and corporate marketing: seeing through the fog', *European Journal of Marketing* 35: 248–291.

Balmer, J. M. T. (2003) 'The three ventures and the seven deadly sins of corporate brand management', in J. M. T. Balmer and S. A. Greyser (eds) *Revealing the Corporation: Perspectives on Corporate Identity, Image, Reputation, Corporate Branding and Corporate-level Marketing*, London: Routledge: 299–316.

Balmer, J. M. T. and Wilson, A. (1998) 'Corporate identity: there is more to it than meets the eye', *International Studies of Management and Organizations* 28: 12–31.

Balmer, J. M. T. and Gray, E. R. (2003) 'Corporate brands: what are they? what of them?', *European Journal of Marketing* 37: 972–997.

Balmer, J. M. T. and Greyser, S. A. (eds (2003) *Revealing the Corporation: Perspectives on Corporate Identity, Image, Reputation, Corporate Branding and Corporate-level Marketing*, London: Routledge.

Balmer, J. M. T., Greyser, S. A. and Urde, M. (2004) 'Monarchies as corporate brands', Working Paper, Division of Research, Harvard Business School, Cambridge, MA.

Barwise, P., Dunham, A. and Ritson, M. (2000) 'Ties that bind: brands, consumers and businesses', in J. Pavitt (ed.) *Brand New*, London: V&A Pubications: 70–97.

Berger, S. (2003) 'Shinawatra scathing of opposition to Anfield investment', *Daily Telegraph* 12 May: 21.

Boulding, K. (1956) *The Image*, Ann Arbor: University of Michigan Press.

Brayfield, C. (2000) 'In the realm of the senses at the supermarket', *The Times* 6 November: 6.

Davies, P. (2004) 'Much more to Allianz than a big rebranding exercise', *Financial Times*: 3.

de Chernatony, L. (1999) 'Brand management through narrowing the gap between brand identity and brand reputation', *Journal of Marketing Management* 15: 157–180.

Deshpande, R. and Webster, F. (1989) 'Organizational culture and marketing: defining the research agenda', *Journal of Marketing* 53: 3–15.

The Economist (2004) 'Political food: Mullah moolah', 30 October: 37.

Elliott, R. and Wattanasuwan, K. (1998) 'Brands as symbolic resources for the construction of identity', *International Journal of Advertising* 17: 131–144.

Galbraith, J. K. (1986) *The Anatomy of Power*, London: Hamish Hamilton.

Hatch, M. J. and Schultz, M. (2003) 'Bringing the corporation into corporate branding,' *European Journal of Marketing* 37: 1041–1079.

Ind, N. (1997) *The Corporate Brand*, New York: New York University Press.

Kapferer, J. N. (2002) 'Corporate brand and organizational identity', in Moingeon, B. and Soenen, G. (eds) *Corporate and Organizational Identities*, London: Routledge.

Kapferer, J. N. (2004) *The New Strategic Brand Management*, London: Kogan Page.

King, S. (1991) 'Branding in the 1990s', *Journal of Marketing Management* 7: 3–13.

Knox, S. and Bickerton, D. (2003) 'The six conventions of corporate branding', *European Journal of Marketing* 37: 998–1016.

LaForet, S. and Saunders, J. (1994) 'Managing brand portfolios: how the leaders to it', *Journal of Advertising Research* 34, 5: 64–76.

Lewis, S. (2000) 'Let's get this in perspective'. Unpublished paper presented at the Confederation for British Industry Branding and Brand Identity Symposium at Bradford School of Management, Bradford University, 24 February.

Mitchell, A. (1999) 'Out of the shadows', *Journal of Marketing Management* 15: 25–42.

Newman, K. (2001) 'The sourcerer's apprentice? Alchemy, seduction and confusion in modern marketing', *International Journal of Advertising* 20: 409–429.

Olins, W. (2004) *On Brand*, London: Thames & Hudson.

Pavitt, J. (ed.) (2000) *Brand New*, London: V&A Publications.

Schmitt, B. (1999) 'Experimental marketing', *Journal of Marketing Management* 15: 53–67.

Schultz, M. and de Chernatony, L. (eds) (2002) 'Special issue on corporate branding', *Corporate Reputation Review* 5: 100–271.

Sherry, J. F. Jr (ed.) (1998) *Servicescapes: The Concept of Place in Contemporary Markets*, Chicago, IL: American Marketing Association.

Smith, G. (2003) 'Owen and co will have to hope it's not murder on the Orient Express', *The Times* 15 May: 33.

Urde, M. (2003) 'Core value-based corporate brand building', *European Journal of Marketing* 37: 1017–1040.

Chapter 3

Ambi-brand culture

On a wing and a swear with Ryanair

Stephen Brown

What part of no refund don't you understand? You are not getting a refund so fuck off.

(Michael O'Leary, CEO, Ryanair)

CHECK IN

Few words are more freighted with meaning than 'culture' (Jenks 1993). For those of an aesthetic disposition, it carries connotations of concert halls, art galleries, literary salons and analogous elitist pursuits. For those with anthropological inclinations, it refers to the rituals, customs, technologies, lifestyles, belief systems, social practices and material possessions of groups or gatherings of people. For those who walk in the Valley of the Shadow of Bourdieu, culture is akin to capital and, as such, is central to the ceaseless struggle between dominant and subordinate classes in society. So plurivalent is 'culture', indeed, that Raymond Williams (1983: 87) describes it as 'one of the two or three most complicated words in the English language'.[1]

Williams, sadly, doesn't tell us what the second (or third) most complicated word is, but 'brand' may well be a contender. The merest glance through the textbooks reveals that marketers can't agree on what brands are, exactly, much less what they mean. De Chernatony (2001), for example, maintains that at least fourteen definitions of 'brand' are extant, ranging from logocentrism ('brands are logos') to out-and-out imperialism ('branding is the management philosophy'). Simmons (2004), similarly, suggests that brand discourse is beset by logorrhoea, where the target word is becoming increasingly festooned with add-ons and modifiers – brand awareness, brand dilution, brand equity, brand focus, brand platform, brand positioning, brand relevance, brand resonance, brand strategy, brand synergy – a process he calls 'brand brand brand brand brand stretch'. Kotler (2003: 8), by contrast, is much more concise, if characteristically ambitious. 'Everything', he avers, 'is a brand: Coca-Cola, FedEx, Porsche, New York City, the United States, Madonna, and you – yes, you! A brand is any label that carries meaning and associations.'

50

If Kotler's final sentence is correct, 'Shrink to Fit', 'May Contain Nuts' and 'Do Not Exceed Stated Dose' presumably qualify as brands. No doubt they're being trademarked as I type. But, rather than disparage the disagreement surrounding both words – or engage in pointless attempts to pin the slippery suckers down – it is perhaps simpler to set semantics aside and openly acknowledge that, taken separately, 'brand' and 'culture' are terribly troublesome terms. In combination, however, 'brand culture' has an attractively oxymoronic quality. The expression carries intriguing connotations of high art meets base commerce, what White (2004), Seabrook (2000) and Collins (2002) call 'Middle Mind', 'NoBrow' and 'High-Pop' respectively. As such, it is very much in keeping with our purportedly postmodern times, where former barriers fall, sacrosanct boundaries dissolve, irreconcilable opposites are successfully reconciled, and irresistible forces reach accord with immovable objects (Brown 1995).

DEPARTURE LOUNGE

Brand culture, then, is in tune with the art-for-mart's-sake mindset that characterizes the postmodern condition, what Featherstone (1991) terms 'the aestheticization of everyday life'. It also strikes a chord with postmodern marketing and consumer researchers, many of whom maintain that cultural artefacts – art, literature and media representations generally – can provide more meaningful insights into contemporary consumer society than traditional tracking studies, questionnaire surveys or laboratory experiments. As Holt rightly observes,

> Knowledge doesn't come from focus groups or ethnography or trend reports – the marketer's usual means for 'getting close to the consumer'. Rather, it comes from a cultural historian's understanding of ideology as it waxes and wanes, a sociologist's charting of the topography of contradictions the ideology produces, and a literary critic's expedition into the culture that engages these contradictions.
>
> (2003: 49)

Viewed from this perspective, the aforementioned academic agonizing over 'brand' and 'culture' is not only unnecessary but nugatory. Contradiction, inconsistency, uncertainty and dissensus are not causes for concern. On the contrary, they help us comprehend the latter-day 'triumph of the brand concept' (Barwise 2003: xii). The old idea that individual brands stand for one thing and one thing only – the USP/share-of-mind ethos espoused by proselytes of positioning and suchlike – is giving way to an appreciation that brand culture is inherently ambiguous, enigmatic, polymorphic, plurivalent. Not only are brand cultures co-created with consumers, who often ignore or subvert the messages and meanings that managers try to convey (Fournier 1998), but it is arguable that ambiguity is central to the magical aura that surrounds allegedly legendary brands like Apple, Nike and Harley (Vincent 2002). Certainly, many exponents of storytelling

51

approaches to brand management stress that mystery, intrigue and dramatic tension are central to the development of meaningful marketing narratives (Simmons 2004). We live in a world of equivocation, a world of tergiversation, a wonderful world of ambi-brands.

This ambivalent ethos is cogently evoked in *The Savage Girl*, a novel by Alex Shakar (2001). Set in the cool-hunting department of a trendy research company, Tomorrow Inc., the novel posits that 'paradessence' is the key to successful branding in post-modernity. Paradessence, according to Chas Lacoutere, the CEO of Tomorrow Inc., invariably involves an irresolvable paradox. Products blessed with paradessence somehow combine two mutually exclusive states and satisfy both simultaneously. Ice cream melds eroticism and innocence. Air travel offers sanitized adventure. Amusement parks provide terror and reassurance. Automobiles render drivers reckless and safe. Sneakers grasp the earth and help consumers soar free. Muzak is a hybrid of transience and eternity:

> 'What's the paradessence of coffee?' Chas asks her.
>
> *Paradessence?* She came across the word *essence* in a couple of the marketing books she skimmed, usually attached to some glib distillation of the product's selling points. But *paradessence?* What could that mean? Something paradiselike, perhaps.
>
> She takes a shot. 'I guess something about how it wakes you up, maybe. Or the way it warms you up on a cold morning.'
>
> 'Waking and warming,' Chas says. 'Very close. Now think. Locate the magic. Locate the impossibility.'
>
> '"The impossibility"? I don't know. Being warm. That's kind of like being sleepy, I guess.'
>
> 'The paradessence of coffee is stimulation and relaxation. Every successful ad campaign for coffee will promise both of those mutually exclusive states.' Chas snaps his fingers in front of her face. 'That's what consumer motivation is about, Ursula. Every product has this paradoxical essence. Two opposing desires that it can promise to satisfy simultaneously. The job of the marketer is to cultivate this schismatic core, this broken soul, at the center of every product.'
>
> (Shakar 2001: 72–73)

BOARDING GATE

Although Shakar's paradessence premise owes much to Walter Benjamin, the interwar cultural critic who expatiated on the ambivalent pleasures of Parisian shopping arcades, as well as the religious aura of original artworks when reproduced by profane mechanical means like film and photography (Benjamin 1973, 1999), it captures something of the character of today's marketing- and brand-obsessed world. This is a world where 50 per cent of the US population has attended a marketing training course of some kind. It is a world where television channels and radio stations are chock-a-block with programmes and stories about marketing, consumption, shopper psychology and all the rest. It is a world where stand-up comics perform lengthy routines on supermarkets, shopping carts and stereotyped TV ads for shampoo, shaving foam or sanitary napkins. It is a world where glossy magazines routinely appraise their readers of the rationale behind retail store design and the rebranding exercise *du jour*. It is a world where Sunday newspaper supplements are replete with reflections on, and deconstructions of, breaking advertising campaigns, as well as industry gossip, impending pitches and account executive shenanigans (Brown 2003).

It is a world, in short, where consumers are wise to marketers' wiles. They are cognizant that the customer is always right. They are aware that customer satisfaction and loyalty are the drivers of corporate competitive strategy. They are fluent in Brandsperanto, Malltalk, Productpatter. They aren't so much Generation X, Y or Z, as Generation ®.

Marketers, of course, are wise to the fact that consumers are wise to them. This is reflected in the latter-day rise of ironic branding and anti-marketing marketing campaigns. Consider Sprite's Image-is-Nothing image, or Death brand cigarettes, or Aquafina's promise that there is no promise, or Comme des Garcons' anti-flagship stores, or Japanese apparel retailer Uniglo's claim, 'you are not what you wear!', or Baby Ruth candy bars, which cheekily urge calorie-counters to 'Eat half', or Mullet Shampoo, specially formulated for headbangers, has-beens and the terminally unhip, or the brilliantly brazen bid by Nike to recruit Ralph Nader as a celebrity sneakers spokesperson, or Pulmo cough medicine, whose unforgettable slogan boasts, 'Anything that tastes this bad must be good for you!', or indeed, those wonderfully wry brand names like *I Can't Believe It's Not Butter*, *Too Good to be True* and, doubtless coming soon to a supermarket shelf near you, *I Can't Believe It's Too Good to Be True*.

Sublime though it is, the basic problem with ironic or anti-marketing marketing is that the tongue-in-cheek anti-sellers are themselves involved in selling. They are part and parcel of the marketing system. They are complicit with the thing they're critiquing. They are engaged in commercial exchange and are seen as such by consumers. The selling may be soft, or subtle, or subversive, but it is still selling. They aren't so much anti-marketers as ambi-marketers. Their status is ambiguous, equivocal, conflicted.

There's an additional problem with anti-branding strategies, inasmuch as it opens the door to serial second-guessing, where savvy-consumers and savvy-marketers try to outsmart one another (Brown 2003). Indeed, the absurdity of this contrapuntal marketing minuet is admirably captured in *Mister Squishy*, an arresting short story by cult novelist David Foster Wallace (2004). Cognizant that today's consumers are marketing conscious, a focus group in a cutting-edge marketing research agency, Team Δy, is informed of the marketing thinking behind confectionary conglomerate Mister Squishy's latest anti-brand offering, *Felony!* A fat-filled, sugar-stuffed, chocolate-covered donut, *Felony!* is positioned as a permissible indulgence, a guilty pleasure, a temporary transgressive antidote to the lo-carb, lo-calorie, lo-cholesterol dietary discourse that dominates contemporary society. Every trend, the focus group moderator explains, is counterbalanced by a transverse or

53

shadow trend, which develops inside and against the larger trend or MCP (Metastatic Consumption Pattern).

But how, he goes on, to sell the shadow product? By a shadow ad campaign of course, one that incorporates the codes of advertising and marketing research into its ironic sales pitch:

> The concept of making some new product's actual marketers' strategies themselves a part of that product's essential Story . . . but with the added narrative twist or hook of, say for instance, advertising Mister Squishy's new *Felony!* line as a disastrously costly and labor-intensive ultra-gourmet snack cake which had to be marketed by beleaguered legions of nerdy admen under the thumb of, say, a tyrannical mullah-like CEO who was such a personal fiend for luxury-class chocolate that he was determined to push *Felonies!* into the US market no matter what the cost- or sales-projections, such that (in the proposed campaign's Story) Mister Squishy's advertisers has to force Team Δy to manipulate and cajole Focus Groups into producing just the sort of quote unquote 'objective' statistical data needed to greenlight the project and get *Felonies!* on the shelves, all in other words comprising just the sort of arch and tongue-in-cheek pseudo-behind-the-scenes Story designed to appeal to urban or younger consumers' self-imagined savvy about marketing tactics and 'objective' data and to flatter their sense that in this age of metastatic spin and trend and the complete commercialization of every last thing in their world they were unprecedentedly ad-savvy and discerning and canny and well nigh impossible to manipulate by any sort of clever multi-million dollar marketing campaign.
>
> (Wallace 2004: 60–61)

Foster Wallace's fictional focus group, in other words, is the fictional marketing-savvy focus group that's being manipulated for the fictional marketing-savvy storyline of the fictional marketing-savvy brand designed to appeal to fictional marketing-savvy consumers. Phew! A veritable marketing *mise en abyme*.

FASTEN SEATBELTS

There is, however, another even more Machiavellian marketing twist in the ambi-brand culture spiral. And that is the faux forthright format, one based on old-fashioned, no-nonsense, straight-to-the-point sales pitches, which may or may not be ironic (Brown 2003). These are epitomized by the recent UK television ads for Ronseal, a quick drying range of varnishes and wood stains, which boast the deathless slogan, 'It does exactly what it says on the tin'. The ingenuity of Ronseal's campaign is that it works on two levels. Not only does it work as a good old-fashioned, buy-this-product sales pitch, but for marketing-savvy audiences, it also works as a tongue-in-cheek take on old-fashioned, hard-selling, straight-to-camera sales pitches. It is impossible to tell whether it's flagrantly crude and naive or fiendishly pseudo-naive and cod-crude. It is ambiguous. It is oxy-moronic. It is both. It can be taken at face value or at two-faced value. It is a compelling example of sophisticated unsophistication or, at the very least, a refreshing change from the glossy, cinematic, self-referential advertising extravaganzas that are de rigueur nowadays.

The consequences of this back-to-basics ethos are again cogently captured by David Foster Wallace (1996). In his stupendous shaggy-dog novel, *Infinite Jest*, a low-rent advertising agency, V&V, develops a cheap 'n' nasty campaign for tongue scrapers – yes, tongue scrapers – which induces extreme advert-avoidance among grossed-out consumers, even as sales of the unspeakable product take off. Other advertisers avoid V&V's grisly tongue-scraper spots; the television networks see their advertising revenues plunge, making them ever more dependent on tongue-scraper income, which further alienates viewers and advertisers; and a spiral of decline quickly ensues. The Big Four networks flatline. Madison Avenue is devastated as agencies expire and suppliers of ancillary services sink without trace, all on account of a so-bad-it's-good ad for NoCoat own-brand tongue scrapers:

Stylistically reminiscent of those murderous mouthwash, deodorant, and dandruff-shampoo scenarios that had an anti-hero's chance encounter with a gorgeous desire-object ending in repulsion and shame because of an easily correctable hygiene deficiency, the NoCoat spots' chilling emotional force could be located in the exaggerated hideousness of the near-geologic layer of gray-white material coating the tongue of the otherwise handsome pedestrian who accepts a gorgeous meter maid's coquettish invitation to have a bit of a lick of the ice cream cone she's just bought from an avuncular sidewalk vendor. The lingering close-up on an extended tongue that must be seen to be believed, coat-wise. The slow-motion full-frontal shot of the maid's face going slack with disgust as she recoils, the returned cone falling unfelt from her repulsion-paralyzed fingers. The nightmarish slo-mo with which the mortified pedestrian reels away into street-traffic with his whole arm over his mouth, the avuncular vendor's kindly face now hateful and writhing as he hurls hygienic invectives.

These ads shook viewers to the existential core, apparently. It was partly a matter of plain old taste: ad-critics argued that the NoCoat spots were equivalent to like Preparation H filming a procto-exam, or a Depend Adult Undergarment camera panning for floor-puddles at a church social. But . . . V&V's NoCoat campaign was a case study in the eschatology of emotional appeals. It towered, a kind of Uberad, casting a shaggy shadow back across a whole century of broadcast persuasion. It did what all ads are supposed to do: create an anxiety relievable by purchase. It just did it way more well than wisely, given the vulnerable psyche of an increasingly hygiene-conscious USA in those times . . . when a nation became obsessed with the state of its tongue, when people would no sooner leave home without a tongue-scraper and an emergency backup tongue scraper than they'd fail to wash and brush and spray. The year when the sink-and-mirror areas of public restrooms were such grim places to be. The NoCoat co-op folks traded in their B'Gosh overalls and handwoven ponchos for Armani and Dior, then quickly disintegrated into various eight-figure litigations. But by this time everybody from Procter & Gamble to Tom's of Maine had its own brand's scraper out, some of them with baroque and potentially hazardous electronic extras.

(Wallace 1996: 413–414)

TAKE OFF

In a marketing-savvy world, in other words, no-marketing is the ultimate form of marketing. This is nowhere better illustrated than in the case of Ryanair, the lowest of the low-cost airlines, the no-frills carrier that every consumer loves to hate (Calder 2003). Established in 1985, as a one-plane, one-route operation, Ryanair was very much the runt of Tony Ryan's business litter. A legend in Ireland's commercial community, Tony Ryan made his fortune with Guinness Peat Aviation, a leading aircraft leasing company, and duly dabbled in all sorts of sidelines. Yet despite the benign neglect of its founder, the opposition of Aer Lingus, the Irish state airline, and the indifference of Aer Rianta, the Irish airports authority, Ryan's runt somehow survived and slowly struggled to its feet. By 1989, it was carrying 60,000 passengers per year, predominantly on the lucrative Dublin-to-London route. Although Ryanair was little more than a clone of the flag-carrier, its prices were slightly lower than Aer Lingus, it flew into Luton, which was convenient for an enclave of Irish expatriates in north London, and because it also operated flights to and from Knock, a holy shrine in the west of Ireland, Ryanair received the unofficial blessing of the Catholic church, which sang its praises incessantly (Creaton 2004).[2]

Ryanair, unfortunately, fell foul of an Act of God, the first Gulf War of 1991. Like many of the world's airlines, it suffered from the downturn in passenger traffic that accompanied the conflict and, because the company got caught up in Guinness Peat Aviation's disastrous IPO of 1992, Tony Ryan's tiny yet tidy sideline teetered on the brink of collapse. An unlikely saviour, however, existed in the shape of Michael O'Leary, the bagman, bean counter, bottom-line manager and all-purpose consigliere of the Ryan empire. A fixer first and foremost, O'Leary's Damascene moment occurred when he made a courtesy call to Southwest Airlines in Dallas, where he was taken under the wing of Herb Kelleher, the rambunctious renegade behind the low-cost, no-frills flying revolution that had taken the United States by storm in the years after airline deregulation (Freiberg and Freiberg 1996). O'Leary saw the light.

Convinced by Herb's low-cost credo, O'Leary returned to Ryanair with the born-again, brook-no-opposition belief of the recently converted. Appointed CEO in 1993, he set about rebuilding the company on the Southwest model. Aided and abetted by the admittedly glacial deregulation of the European airline industry – a consequence of the 1992 European Union Act – Ryanair rapidly rewrote the commercial aviation rulebook. Come the end of the decade, it was flying 6 million passengers to 32 European destinations, from Stanstead to Stockholm, and providing employment for 1,200 people. Two years later, in the aftermath of 9/11, its market capitalization exceeded that of high and mighty British Airways, as well as the erstwhile leader of the pack, American Airlines. The runt of the litter had become top dog, albeit a mangy mongrel that many in the industry regard as flea-ridden and distempered, and would like to see put down.

Actually, a better canine comparison is the Rottweiler. Ryanair has been nothing if not ferocious in its adherence to the Southwest template. If anything, it is even more Southwestern than Southwest, a rabid, attack-dog strain of the original breed. Kelleher may have trained, groomed and nourished the young pup, but O'Leary has made the low-cost bone his own. Compared to the latter, in fact, the former is a pussycat. Tomcat rather.

CRUISING ALTITUDE

Michael O'Leary is an accountant by training and he has no love lost for smarmy marketing types. On one occasion, when refreshing the Ryanair 'brand' came up for discussion, he promptly pronounced,

> We have no intention of changing the brand or redesigning the image or the rest of that old nonsense. In my thirteen years at this company, Aer Lingus has changed its branding three times, British Airways has changed it three times, we've changed it not once, and the virtue of what we've done has been proven.
>
> (Calder 2003: 114)

True, these comments are fairly mild compared to some of the CEO's choicer phrases, most of which are derivations of 'fucker', 'wanker' and their cognates. However, it is fair to infer that Ryanair has resisted the blandishments of brand image consultants, marketing makeover artists, service quality advisers and similar purveyors of business 'bolloxology', as the high priest of low fares delicately puts it (Done 2004).

Yet, for all his foul-mouthed fulmination at Mephistophelean marketers and their satanic ilk, O'Leary is the demi-pontiff of ambi-branding. Sure, he owes much to his holiness Herb Kelleher, but the gospel according to Michael is heretical to the point of schismatic. It is ole-time, fire-and-brimstone marketing predicated on a plethora of Ps.

Pummel costs Ryanair's business model, like that of its Texan forebear, rests firmly on the ruthless pursuit of cost reductions (Felsted 2003). Every frill or fancy or frippery or finery or frivolity that airline passengers formerly enjoyed on national flag-carriers has either been excised completely or treated as a revenue-generating optional extra. In-flight catering, first-class cabins, frequent-flyer programmes, free on-board magazines, generous baggage allowances, lavish departure lounges, plentiful cabin crew and adequate leg room have all been abolished or unbundled, as have paper tickets, assigned seating, covered jetways and compensation payments for delayed or cancelled flights. Reclinable seats, window blinds, liveried headrests, backseat pockets, hold-stowed baggage and, believe it or not, courtesy sick bags are also on their way out. So single-minded is Ryanair's pursuit of low costs that wheelchairs are regarded as optional extras that must be paid for by their users.

Costs are also kept down by flying a single aircraft, the 737 (which can be bought in bulk and maintained more easily), making maximum use of the fleet (through fast turn-around times and squeezing in more flights per day), eschewing elaborate hub-and-spoke route networks (which facilitate passenger connections but are beset by delays), avoiding busy international airports in favour of sleepy secondary facilities on the peripheries of major conurbations (the grateful operators of which are 'encouraged' to provide incentives, rebates, promotional support, etc.), selling tickets via the Internet (which is not only more cost-effective than the alternatives but enables the company to maximize revenue through 'yield management' procedures) and, not least, by keeping a very tight reign on employee-related expenses. Wages are low, hours are long, holidays are short, demands are many, perks are few, or paid for. Ryanair's employees pay for their uniforms, refreshments, health checks, airport passes, vetting procedures, car parking spaces and, incredibly, Christmas parties. They are even encouraged to 'acquire' their ballpoint pens, Post-it notes, paper clips and analogous paraphernalia.[3]

COMMENCING DESCENT

Price promotions It is little wonder, given Ryanair's congenital cost-consciousness, that it is sometimes known as Eire O'Flot. If not quite the Trabant of commercial aviation, it is definitely the Daewoo. Indeed, 'doing a Ryanair' is an increasingly popular Irish expression, one that means more than merely travelling by the eponymous airline; it also carries connotations of the cheap 'n' nasty, with the emphasis on nasty (Creaton 2004). The upside of the downside, however, is exceptionally low fares. Ticket prices haven't simply been savaged by the attack dog of commercial aviation, they have been slaughtered, disembowelled and their innards eaten raw. London for £29, Glasgow for £59, Paris for £79, Hamburg for £99, Stockholm for £39.99. And those are the expensive seats.

On top of its everyday low prices, Ryanair is renowned for its periodic price promotions, which are unfailingly, if tenuously, linked to some spurious special occasion, celebration or anniversary (*The Business* 2003). Christmas specials, Easter specials, summertime specials, St Patrick's Day specials and specials that announce the opening of new routes or milestones on the company's march to global domination are regular occurrences. Specials that spoil the specials of its low-cost rivals are no less regular, as are knock-em-dead, never-to-be-repeated (until the next time) price spectaculars. The one hundredth anniversary of the Wright Brothers' flight, for example, prompted Ryanair to offer 100,000 seats at 50p. When its monthly passenger numbers first exceeded those of BA – by 240,000 – it offered 240,000 fares at give-away prices. Ryanair responded to 9/11, not with retrenchment or risk-avoidance, but its biggest-ever sale (one million seats at £9.99) and a keep-flying, keep-the-flag-flying, keep-on-keeping-on rallying cry ('Let's Fight Back!'). Indeed, it doesn't take too much imagination to guess what's going to happen in 2005, the twentieth anniversary of Ryanair's glorious inception-cum-immaculate conception.

Publicity stunts Arresting as they are, Ryanair's believe-it-or-not price promotions are fairly small fry compared to some of the company's publicity stunts. On one occasion, it took advantage of an attempted hijacking at Stansted airport and announced, 'It's amazing what lengths people will go to, to fly cheaper than Ryanair'. The Airline Pilot's Association was not amused and said so, to massive press coverage. On another occasion, O'Leary led an assault on a rival airline's headquarters, complete with Second World War tank and a small army of steel-helmeted, fatigues-wearing volunteers. When Ryanair's grunts were turned back at the security gate, they burst into a platoon marching song specially composed for the occasion, 'I've been told and it's no lie/easyJet's fares are way too high' (Bowley 2003). On yet another infamous occasion, O'Leary took advantage of the Vatican's revelation of the Third Fatima prophecy by proclaiming that the Pope also revealed the Fourth Secret of Fatima: Ryanair's fares are lowest. This claim was accompanied by press ads featuring the Holy Father imparting the good news to an awestruck nun. Catholics were outraged, the press had a field day and O'Leary laughed all the way to the publicity bank.

O'Leary's credo, clearly, is that there's no such thing as enough publicity, good, bad or otherwise. The last of these is well illustrated by the case of Jane O'Keeffe, who benefited from one of Ryanair's earliest publicity stunts (Creaton 2004). Way back in 1988, she was the company's one-millionth passenger and was awarded free flights for life. Nine years later, when she tried to book some seats, Jane was brusquely informed that the deal was off. Her understandable complaints to the chief executive were met with a tirade of personal abuse, where no expletive was left undeleted. Ms O'Keeffe sued for her rights and, when the case eventually came to court, Ryanair refused to settle. The judge ruled against the defendant, awarded costs to the plaintiff and, to cap it all, described O'Leary as a belligerent bully. Far from being a complete PR disaster, however, the CEO's parsimonious attitude reflected well on Michael O'Scrooge. As the *Financial Times* observed, 'O'Leary's investors must have loved the fact that their money was entrusted to such a miser' (Bowley 2003: 20).

TOUCH DOWN

Passenger persecution O'Keeffe, of course, is just one among many disgruntled passengers. Trying though they were, her experiences are no more traumatic than many of those who fly with Eire O'Flot. The low-cost carrier makes no bones about the fact that its customers are on their own when flights are cancelled or delayed. Put out passengers are not compensated with cups of coffee or meal vouchers, much less hotel rooms or taxis at the airline's expense. The tickets, after all, don't cost much more than a meal in a fast food restaurant, so why should Ryanair feed and water and ferry and accommodate those it has inconvenienced? If buses and trains don't do it, there's no reason why O'Leary should. He's not the patron saint of passengers, you know!

Ryanair's couldn't-care-less approach to customer care also applies to refunds and baggage. Not only are refunds never paid out, even if a passenger's travel plans are disrupted by the death of a grandparent, but the bereaved customer is told to 'fuck off' for having the temerity to ask. What's more, if they want their pre-paid airport tax returned, as is their legal right, Ryanair imposes an administrative charge that exactly matches the amount in question. Granted, as corporate mantras go, 'fuck off granny' and 'no fucking refunds, you fuckers' are somewhat unusual in a world of 'customer is king' mission statements. However, unlike the purported customer-huggers, Ryanair really means what it says, especially with regard to baggage. If baggage is lost, too bad, it'll turn up eventually. If it is damaged, the customer is at fault for not packing it properly. 'The company', opines O'Leary, 'is not the compensator of last resort for inappropriate or badly packed luggage' (Creaton 2004: 188). The basic problem, he goes on, is that passengers take far too much stuff with them. And it's got to stop.

Ryanair's modus operandi is 'when in doubt, blame the customer' and the company, presumably, is often racked by doubts. Not content with berating customers who burden themselves with unnecessary baggage, or commit the unforgivable sin of wanting their money back, O'Leary hurls insults at them for good measure. He regularly describes them as 'the great unwashed', calls them 'morons' if they fail to find cheap fares on the company website, and takes perverse pride in the accusation that his is the lager louts' and stag parties' airline of choice. Indeed, when his Internet ticketing facility made the not inconsequential mistake of charging customers several times over for the service, he claimed that consumers' websurfing shortcomings were the cause of their problems. Hardly surprising, then, that Barbara Cassani, CEO of a rival low-cost carrier, was moved to comment, 'They glorify making the experience as uncomfortable as possible. If a customer has a problem, they enjoy telling you to piss off. They believe that if customers aren't hurting, their costs aren't low enough' (Calder 2003: 113).

Persistent prevarication In addition to maligning customers, Ryanair is never reluctant to mislead them. The rock-bottom prices quoted in its ads are often difficult to find in practice. Only a limited number of seats is available at the promotional price – which also conveniently excludes taxes and airport charges – and once the cheap seats are filled the rest pay more (although Ryanair's fares are still lower than most flag-carriers). The specials, likewise, are less special than they appear, not least the Easter specials, which don't apply to flights over the holiday weekend itself. Destinations, too, are described with the kind of poetic licence that'd put Seamus Heaney to shame. Flights to 'Frankfurt' actually go to Hahn, a former airforce base 128km from the city. 'Stockholm' is served from Vasterås, 100km due south. 'Hamburg' is reached via Lubeck, an hour's train journey from the dubious delights of the Reeperbann. Passengers to 'Brussels' are deplaned in Charleroi, a comparatively modest 46km distant from the alleged destination, those to 'Olso' are deposited in Torp, a mere 100km away, and visitors to 'Paris' find themselves in Beauvais, 60km north of the City of Light. At one time, moreover, travellers to 'Barcelona' and 'Copenhagen' were being flown to Perpignan (in France) and Malmö (in Sweden) respectively. It seems that bait-and-switch is alive and well and living in Dublin.[4]

In fairness, and unlike its full-service rivals, Ryanair doesn't rip customers off with well-padded ticket prices, expensive add-ons and fancy folderol. 'We give the people what they fucking want', says Ryanair's unrepentant chief executive. The company, he also points out, receives less than one complaint per 1,000 passengers, which compares well with other low-cost airlines. However, as it only responds to written complaints and, as most people know that complaining is pointless in any event, Ryanair's record flatters to deceive. The reality is better captured in one of O'Leary's priceless outbursts, 'Do you know how many people British Airways has got working in customer service? Two hundred of the fuckers. Do you know how many I've got? Three, and two of them are part-time' (Adams 2004: 31).

BAGGAGE RECLAIM

Pugilistic pugnacity Ryanair's contrarian take on customer orientation, and resolute refusal to respond to dissatisfied customers' demands, is deeply ironic, not to say profoundly paradoxical. When the company itself is the customer – as it is with suppliers, airport administrators, advertising agencies, aircraft manufacturers and so forth – Ryanair is the most demanding customer imaginable and constantly dissatisfied to boot. It drives extremely hard bargains, negotiates ever-tougher deals and thinks nothing of brutally abandoning suppliers in order to bring them into line. When the caterer that delivered ice to Ryanair's aircraft tried to raise its prices, the carrier simply did without ice cubes until the uppity supplier saw sense (or, rather, passengers did without ice in their expensive soft drinks and overpriced alcoholic beverages). When the owners of Rimini airport attempted to increase Ryanair's landing fees, the service to 'Bologna' promptly transferred to an adjacent facility at Farli (whose operators were much more forthcoming on the incentives front). When the world aviation industry was in its apocalyptic post-September 11 slump, Ryanair seized the day and screwed Boeing into the ground on a new aircraft order (so massive was the company's discount on a hundred 737s, that O'Leary was moved to boast, 'we raped them').

Ryanair's rapacity is not confined to suppliers. Competitors too come in for rough-and-tumble treatment. British Airways was blasted in a notorious 'EXPENSIVE BA****DS' press advertisement which so incensed the world's favourite airline that it took the Irish upstart to court (Calder 2003). Unfortunately for BA, the judge ruled that the flag-carrier was indeed ripping its customers off as Ryanair intimated. O'Leary was delirious. Air France and Alitalia have also been lambasted by O'Leary the Lip – to the point of painting 'Arrivederci Alitalia' on the side of its aircraft – as has almost every other European carrier. Sabena was summarily dismissed as 'a bunch of swindlers', Buzz flew 'shitty aircraft on shitty routes', Go and its fragrant figurehead, Barbara Cassani, was duly declared 'a dog', easyJet, bizarrely, is 'not the brightest sandwich at the picnic', and, when the CEO of Lufthansa suggested that Germans aren't really interested in low fares, the Mouth from Mullingar riposted, 'How the fuck does he know? He's never offered them any. The Germans will crawl bollock-naked over broken glass to get them' (Bowley 2003: 21).[5]

Personality cultivation It is one of the quirks of the airline business that as travel has become ever more sanitized, ever more nondescript, near enough noisome, its chief executive officers have become ever less anodyne, ever less corporate, near enough countercultural. Stuffed shirts, shrinking violets and self-effacing shoe-gazers have no place in the upper echelons of the aviation industry. Attention-grabbers, headline-huggers and alpha male chest-beaters (of both genders) dominate its boardrooms, terrorize its executive suites and go mano-a-mano with fellow capo-di-capos. This is especially so in the no-frills sector, where the high jinx and low blows of its CEOs can generate copious high-impact, low-cost press coverage, which keeps the organization in the public eye and serves as a walking, talking, gunslinging billboard for its wares. Freddie Laker, Richard Branson and the peerless Herb Kelleher are the archetypes of this brash, ballsy, buccaneering mode of brand building and its latter-day avatars include Stelios Haji-Ioannou (of easyJet), Barbara Cassani (of Go) and, as the foregoing discussion indicates, Mr larger-than-lifeness himself, Michael O'Leary.

According to Lloyd (2003: 5), O'Leary has a 'Barnum-like genius for attracting attention' and, while he's not a patch on the imperishable P.T., there's no doubt that he fits the aviator-showman stereotype (hyperbole, hoopla, lots of hot air, etc.). Be that as it may, the really interesting thing about O'Leary's personality cultivation practices is the massive disjunction between the persona and the person (Jowit and Byrne 2003). He is presented as an ill-educated hick from the sticks, who plays football with the baggage handlers, eats beans 'n' chips in the staff canteen and swears like a drunken sailor who's mislaid his wooden leg. He dresses in a farm labourer ensemble, aspires to owning a couple of country pubs, disdains the chardonnay-quaffing chattering classes, and makes much of his down-to-earth upbringing in the market town of Mullingar. However, the O'Leary reality is that 'he is in fact a highly educated, gently reared scion of Irish country aristocrats' (Bowley 2003: 23). He was schooled at Ireland's Eton, Clongowes Wood College (James Joyce's Alma Mater), read business studies at Ireland's Oxbridge, Trinity College Dublin, and worked for a blue-chip accountancy practice, Stokes Kennedy Crowley, before becoming Tony Ryan's financial enforcer. He lives in a palatial stately home, Gigginstown House, where he breeds Black Angus cattle and runs a stable of thoroughbred racehorses, including Economy Drive and War of Attrition. He has an acclaimed art collection, owns a villa or two in Italy, is a regular patron of exclusive Dublin eateries and, far from being a Celtic Che Guevara, is a bit of a mummy's boy, who takes his dirty laundry home at weekends, once answered to the nickname 'Duckie' and occasionally loudly announces, apropos of nothing, 'I'm not gay'. Mind you, he has a £500-million fortune to soften any blows to his far from fragile ego.

ARRIVALS HALL

Michael O'Leary, clearly, is an inscrutable individual, as is the ambi-brand he bestrides and personifies. He is a working-class hero with a silver spoon in his mouth. He loathes the media circus, allegedly, but is a PR ringmaster of rare ability. He has no time for fishy marketers, yet leaps like a salmon up the estuary of marketing mediocrity. He treats his customers diabolically – although not nearly as diabolically as he treats his suppliers – and they keep coming back for more. He opens routes to ostensible backwaters, which can't logically sustain the service, only to prove the pessimists wrong. He comes across as a flamboyant, finagling, flim-flam man, to put it politely, however his company's accounting practices are extremely conservative and each competitive move is carefully planned (Creaton 2004). He complains bitterly about government support for failing national carriers, such as Aer Lingus and Alitalia, but heads the hand-out queue when it comes to regional incentives, to say nothing of the route-subsidizing practices of local airport authorities. He perpetually plays the part of small start-up that's being persecuted by the big bully-boys of the industry, though the reality is that Ryanair is the most profitable airline in the world and, if not quite the biggest, certainly the meanest bully on the block (*The Economist* 2004).

Ryanair's brilliance, in sum, is not simply due to its pile-it-high-sell-it-cheap approach to commercial aviation, important though that is. It is not attributable to its like-it-or-lump-it philosophy of customer service, although the company's consumers seem to like lumping it. It is not a consequence of Ryanair's concept-centric rather than customer-centric organizational ethos (the concept, of course, being Southwest's phenomenal no-frills format). It is not even down to the redoubtable Michael O'Leary, who is the embodiment of the brand, the Cúchulainn of commercial aviation. Ryanair's success cannot be separated from the marketing-savvy culture that surrounds it. In a world where consumers are branded from birth and can deconstruct campaigns in double-quick time, brands that rebuff branding and the associated 'bolloxology' are, ironically, the best branded of all. Marketers might not like the fact that an accountant is showing them how to do it. O'Leary may be a retro throwback to the bad old days of Barnumesque ballyhoo. But when every other organization is expressing its undying love for the consumer – love that promises more than it provides – being told to piss off is, perversely, much more honest and much more authentic (or at least less hypocritical), than the 'manipulative pseudo intimacy' that obtains elsewhere (Zuboff and Maxmin 2003: 11).

CONCLUSION

If the branding textbooks are to be believed, we live in a monovalent world, a world of one-word-one-brand, a world where brand managers are urged to acquire a piece of terminological real estate and make it their own. Virgin is fun. Coca-Cola is it. McDonald's is family. Budweiser is true. Danone is health. BMW is performance. Calvin Klein is sex. Absolut is art. Evian is purity. Avis is effort. Guinness is fortitude. Marlboro is freedom. Nordstrom is service. Polo is discernment. Volvo is safety. Oxfam is relief. Starbucks is respite. Intel is inside. Microsoft is megalomania.

This branding monoglot came to the fore in the late 1950s, when Rosser Reeves developed the idea of the Unique Selling Proposition and relentlessly hammered it home, a bit like his legendary Anacin adverts. It was reinforced in the 1970s, when Al Ries and Jack Trout positioned themselves as the gurus of positioning, a kind of perceptual pallisading process whereby brands occupy a clearly identified position in consumer cognition. The monosphere is still going strong, though it now trades under terms like brand identity, essence, DNA, spirit, promise, personality, mission, vision, value, soul, mindshare and many more.

The fundamental problem, however, is that the very idea of one-word-one-brand is untenable in today's incurably ambiguous world. Assumptions of stable linguistic meaning have foundered on the razor-sharp shoals of post-structuralism. Chaos theory, the tipping point and those infuriating fluttering butterflies in the Amazonian rain forest that cause hurricanes in Hong Kong, constantly remind us of the hair-trigger character of our incorrigibly unstable times. The old idea of the unified self, or personality, has been superseded by a mutable postmodern sense of self, where people possess a multiplicity of personae, or roles, that they adopt as occasions demand – 'wife and mother', 'career woman', 'sports fanatic', 'fashion victim', 'culture vulture' and so on. In such vacillating circumstances, new approaches to branding are needed. Ambi-brands represent one such possibility.

KEY POINT

- 'Ambi-brands' – those flexible brands that draw upon culture, advertising, and play different roles – pose problems for traditional branding theory.

QUESTIONS FOR DISCUSSION

1 Is ambi-branding appropriate for our paradoxical times or will it add to the confusion and clutter?
2 McDonald's recent difficulties exemplify the problems of a monovalent brand in a plurivalent world. Discuss.
3 Can brand managers really learn from creative artists, like novelists and poets, or do creatives simply tell us what we already know?

NOTES

1 In addition to his overview in *Keywords*, Raymond Williams wrote a short book on culture in 1981.
2 Word-of-mouth marketing is hard to beat, but word-of-God marketing is out of this world.
3 Keep a close watch on your watch next time you check in.
4 Needless to say, Ryanair's anti-customer orientation has come in for more than a modicum of criticism. Its disingenuous price promotions are regularly condemned by the ASA, Britain's official advertising watchdog. It is the butt of whatever-next jokes, exaggerated tales of travellers' travails and water cooler exchanges of the 'my Ryanair experience was worse than yours' variety. Every so often the newspapers are filled with horror stories featuring stranded passengers left to fend for themselves in some foreign hellhole (invariably with young children or aged parents in tow). The company's callous treatment of disabled customers, who are required to stump up £18 for wheelchair assistance, is a particular bone of contention (see Creaton 2004).
5 Above and beyond 'sticking it to Lufty', Ryanair's pugnacity extends to almost every conceivable stakeholder. These include the European Union, which runs 'an evil empire', merchant bankers, who 'piss away money', Britain's air traffic control system, which is 'a fucking shambles', industry pressure groups like the Air Traffic Users Committee, who are 'a bunch of halfwits', assorted trade unions, which are typically told to 'take the fucking deal on the table or fuck off', and do-nothing travel agents who are 'wankers' to a man and 'should be taken out and shot' (Osborn 2003). O'Leary's special ire, however, is reserved for the Irish government, the Irish airports authority and, inevitably, the Irish state airline. As you can imagine what this ire involves, I'll spare your blushes any further.

REFERENCES

Adams, R. (2004) 'Flying costs', *London Review of Books* 2 September: 30–31.
Barwise, P. (2003) 'Preface', in R. Clifton and J. Simmons (eds) *Brands and Branding*, Princeton, NJ: Bloomberg: xii–xv.
Benjamin, W. (1973) 'The work of Art in the age of mechanical reproduction', in *Illuminations,* trans. H. Zohn, London: Fontana: 211–244.

Benjamin, W. (1999) *The Arcades Project*, trans. H. Eiland and K. McLaughlin, Cambridge, MA: Belknap.

Bowley, G. (2003) 'How low can you go?', *Financial Times Magazine* 21 June: 16–23.

Brown, S. (1995) *Postmodern Marketing*, London: Routledge.

Brown, S. (2003) *Free Gift Inside!!* Oxford: Capstone.

Calder, S. (2003) *No Frills: The Truth Behind the Low-Cost Revolution in the Skies*, London: Virgin Books.

Collins, J. (2002) *Making Culture into Popular Entertainment*, Oxford: Blackwell.

Creaton, Siobhan (2004) *Ryanair: How a Small Irish Airline Conquered Europe*, London: Aurum.

de Chernatony, L. (2001) *From Brand Vision to Brand Evaluation*, Oxford: Butterworth-Heinemann.

Done, K. (2004) 'Ryanair talks of disaster, but the low-cost revolution flies on', *Financial Times* 7 February: 9.

Featherstone, M. (1991) *Consumer Culture and Postmodernism*, London: Sage.

Felsted, A. (2003) 'Everyone is looking for the secret under the bed. Can Michael O'Leary sustain Ryanair's low-cost strategy?', *Financial Times* 4 November: 17.

Fournier, S. (1998) 'Consumers and their brands: developing relationship theory in consumer research', *Journal of Consumer Research* 24, 3: 343–373.

Freiberg, K. and Frieberg, J. (1996) *Nuts! Southwest Airlines' Crazy Recipe for Business and Personal Success*, New York: Texere.

Holt, D. B. (2003) 'What becomes an icon most?', *Harvard Business Review* 81, 3: 43–49.

Jenks, C. (1993) *Culture*, London: Routledge.

Jowit, J. and Byrne, N. (2003) 'Q. Would you buy a low-cost flight from this man? A. Millions do every year', *Observer* 15 June: 16.

Kotler, P. (2003) 'Brands', in *Marketing Insights From A to Z*, New York: John Wiley: 8–14.

Lloyd, J. (2003) 'Editor's letter', *Financial Times Magazine* 21 June: 5.

Osborn, A. (2003) 'Ryanair chief strafes Eurocrats and rivals', *The Guardian* 24 October: 22.

Seabrook, J. (2000) *Nobrow: The Culture of Marketing – The Marketing of Culture*, New York: Knopf.

Shakar, A. (2001) *The Savage Girl*, New York: Scribner.

Simmons, J. (2004) *My Sister's A Barista: How They Made Starbucks a Home From Home*, London: Cyan.

The Business (2003) 'Peter Pan has the last laugh', *The Business* 9 June: 17.

The Economist (2004) 'Turbulent skies', *The Economist* 10 July: 67–69.

Vincent, L. (2002) *Legendary Brands: Unleashing the Power of Storytelling to Create a Winning Marketing Strategy*, Chicago, IL: Dearborn.

Wallace, D. F. (1996) *Infinite Jest: A Novel*, Boston, MA: Little, Brown.

Wallace, D. F. (2004) 'Mister Squishy', in *Oblivion: Stories*, London: Abacus: 3–66.

White, C. (2004) *The Middle Mind: Why Americans Don't Think for Themselves*, New York: Allen Lane.

Williams, R. (1981) *Culture*, London: Fontana.

Williams, R. (1983) 'Culture', in *Keywords: A Vocabulary of Culture and Society*, London: Fontana, 87–93.

Zuboff, S. and Maxmin, J. (2003) *The Support Economy: Why Corporations are Failing Individuals and the Next Episode of Capitalism*, London: Allen Lane.

Chapter 4

The two business cultures of luxury brands

Jean-Noël Kapferer

Luxury brands have always sustained the attention of analysts and observers as well as investors. Representing what is ultimate in quality of products and services, they are endowed with a considerable goodwill attached to their mostly immaterial added values. As such they are extreme illustrations of the power of intangibles in our modern world. Luxury brands are not new: some like Fabergé are more than two centuries old; Lacoste was created in 1933. However, new luxury brands are still created. One is struck by the emergence and worldwide success of luxury brands which did not exist thirty years ago or so: Armani, Dolce & Gabbana, Versace, Boss, Calvin Klein, Ralph Lauren, Donna Karan. Beyond being new, these brands seem to operate differently than former ones, meeting new demands of global markets for luxury. Their success reveals that a new vision of luxury is now spreading, matched by a new business model for luxury brand creation and rapid development. In fact, two major brand and business models cohabit in the luxury market. Behind these two models of luxury branding one finds very opposite underlying cultural assumptions about luxury, its legitimacy and its sources of desirability.

WHAT IS A LUXURY?

Before we address the issue of understanding how two very different business models are now in competition in the worldwide luxury market, we must first understand what is a luxury. Luxury is indeed an elusive concept. Typically, everyone can readily identify which brands deserve to be called luxury brands and which cannot. However, most people find it hard to formulate a precise definition of luxury. As a rule, most scholars start by proposing their own definition. Instead of adding another definition, ours, to the mass of already existing definitions of what is a luxury item, it is more fruitful to start from a premise: luxury is a concept with fuzzy frontiers. No definition will strictly delineate it. Where does luxury stop and where does upper range start for instance? Is what has been called mass-stage products (a contraction of mass prestige) or new luxury still luxury?

Our analysis of most proposed definitions will show that they are implicitly based on a specific business model, a specific view shaped by the current luxury brands of the country, for instance. This is why we prefer to look at luxury from different angles: economic, semiotic, sociology and psychology.

For economists, luxury goods are an oddity. In economic terms, luxury objects are those whose price/quality relationship is the highest of the market. However, for an economist quality means tangible functions. Thus McKinsey defines luxury brands as those brands that have constantly been able to justify a significantly higher price than the price of products with comparable tangible functions (Kapferer 1997: 252). Such a definition helps in so far as it suggests that this big price gap measures something intangible – reputation and image. Whereas upper-range products deliver the most options and quality attributes as the basis of their price, but with less immaterial source for their price premium. The limit of McKinsey's definition however is that it is a relative definition. Is mere price gap enough? Isn't there a minimum absolute price? Can all products become luxury goods? Nike trainers are much more expensive than the copies which come from the same Korean manufacturing companies that also produce Nike shoes. However, Nike is not a luxury brand. Certainly Nike's premium prices are based on image, but still very few people would consider it as a luxury brand.

What does etymology tell us? Where does the luxury word come from? In fact, although semantically it has a lot of the connotations of *lux* (the Latin word for light), the roots of the word luxury are elsewhere. Why then do so many people associate luxury with *lux* (lightness, brightness)? Because it is flattering the ego, the self-concept of the local luxury brands. In fact this semantic halo is self-justifying: it gives an apparently trustworthy endorsement to a specific practice, a specific business model to speak in modern terms. Some would say it is a useful lie (Sicard 2003). If one believes that luxury comes from *lux* one is ready to accept that like light, luxury is enlightening, glitters, is brilliant: each and every item is like a jewel and shines like gold. The fact that luxury is visible is also essential: luxury must be seen, must be visible by oneself but most of all by others. This is why it is so important that branding be made extremely visible to all others. At a symbolic level, light means life, fertility. This is why, linking luxury to light (*lux*) one associates luxury with extreme creation. Now this concept of luxury may fit with Versace or Givenchy or Dior, but it does not fit with Donna Karan, Calvin Klein or Armani. Nothing is more discreet than a Calvin Klein dress. Obviously the association with *lux* does not fit. It is a self-justifying semantic manoeuvre.

The real etymology comes from agriculture: *luxus* means growing apart, or in a non-straight manner. An extension of this root can be found in the word *luxatio*: you catch an ankle *luxatio* if you step aside too briskly. Therefore *luxus* is a difference, a step aside from usual conventions. Luxuriance means something characterized by richness and extravagance, often tending to excess (*Webster's Dictionary*). When this step concerns ethics and mores it leads to extreme and criticized behaviours: interestingly the French word *luxure* refers to one of the ten deadly sins, the one related to sex.

Sociology and history also have a lot to teach us about the concept. For decades luxury was the appendage of the aristocracy. To be invited and live at the court of the king and queen one had to stand up to his/her rank: this was done by spending an enormous amount of money in goods of the highest quality. Since aristocracy was a non-working ruling class, the goods were not judged by their functionality but by the amount of pleasure they delivered and by their rarity. Clothes designers were appointed to the royal court to design tailor-made clothes with the most sophisticated fabrics and the rarest material. Being appointed by the king/queen was the extreme sign of honour for such craftsmen. Luxury was in the product itself. The key word was 'rare'.

It is only later that the designers, the obscure tailors, opened shops and became known by their name. An inversion took place: now the aristocracy, but most of all the rising bourgeoisie, visited these stores, which had become fashionable places to patronize, where one had to be seen. The name of the creator and his shop started to be visible and important since they indicated if one was trendy and how much one had paid. The constant quest of the bourgeoisie, devoid of aristocratic lineage, was to create its own hierarchy: that of work and money. Luxury more than any other product is visible: therefore it positions the owner.

What does psychology tell us about luxury, its meaning? If a word has only one root, then meaning is shaped by culture. Luxury brands are global, as is the word luxury. However, one knows that global brand management is fraught with dangers because under apparently simple terms everyone uses, there are hidden differences of under-standing. There is an illusion of shared understanding (Kapferer 2004), especially if, as is the case in all global companies, most local managers have to speak English, another language for them. Among a common age group, research has shown that the same term (luxury) was not associated to the same attributes (Kapferer 1998): thus a fully inter-national sample of young MBAs at HEC Paris revealed four types of luxury, weighing differently how some attributes were typical of the concept. As a consequence, the proto-typical brand of each type was very different. Each of the following set of brands did in fact exemplify a very specific vision of what is a luxury, they cohabit in a single country and even in a single age segment: Hermès/Cartier, Gucci/Boss, Vuitton/Porsche, Chivas/Mercedes. The first set illustrates a luxury concept defined by such key attributes as 'beauty of the object', 'excellence of products'. The second refers to a luxury concept made of 'creativity', and 'beauty of the object'. In the third, understanding of luxury, 'magic' and 'never out of fashion' are typical sine qua non attributes. The last type refers to luxury characterized by a feeling of 'belonging to a minority', a 'small club of owners' (Kapferer 1998: 47).

International surveys cast an even more dramatic light on deep differences of understanding as far as luxury is concerned. In a recent study, Risc asked European, American and Japanese persons who had bought luxury products and brands to associate attributes to the concept of luxury. Interestingly, the profiles are quite close between continents: the first three items are expensive, high quality and prestige. There is, however, a striking difference between Japan on one side and Europe/USA on the other as far as the fourth and fifth defining attributes are concerned: Japanese consumers do not associate luxury to 'exceptional' and 'rare', whereas they are two key defining items elsewhere in the West (Kapferer 2004). Instead the Japanese expect luxury to be artful, almost a piece of art.

PHYSICAL OR VIRTUAL RARITY?

There seems to be two visions of luxury separating the East and the West: one, which associates luxury to rarity, while the other does not. This is why, for instance, Vuitton makes 40 per cent of its sales in Japan. Most 'office ladies' carry or will carry a Vuitton handbag. Now the commercial success of Vuitton is such that exactly the same luxury item is bought by thousands of people. Such diffusion would rapidly dilute brand equity anywhere in the Western world (Kapferer 2004: 264). It does not at all in Japan: here the national and cultural norm of 'saving the face' means that each one should be eager to wear the item held as the symbol of good taste. In addition, unlike the Western consumer, the Japanese consumer is not driven by individualistic motives. Instead he/she wants to be as little noticed as possible, by blending in with the crowd.

This Japanese trait does indeed facilitate the management of luxury brands in Japan. The task is more complex in the West. Brands are not made to be worshipped but used to make a profit and contribute to growth. This is why people invest in the stock of LVMH group, the leading luxury group in the world. This expectation from the stock exchange leads companies to ask their managers to produce continuous growth.

One first answer to this demand is to globalize the brands: this is why luxury brands are targeting Asia. But how should they grow in Europe or the USA? The more they build sales the less rare they are. In doing so they may ruin brand equity because the luxury concept is much associated with rarity among Western consumers.

What is the solution to this paradox: how to grow while remaining rare? The answer can be found in making an important distinction between actual rarity and virtual rarity. Actual rarity is based on ingredients, processes or craftsmanship. If an ingredient is available in very scarce quantities it is de facto rare: thus an 18-year-old Chivas will by definition be very expensive (the financial costs of maintaining barrels of whisky during 18 years are high). As a result of this process, it will also be rare. If a handbag is made of ostrich or sharkskin it will also be quite rare. Although everyone dreams about such rare items, they are not satisfying from a corporate standpoint: there are built-in limitations to sales growth attached to this product-based rarity (Catry 2005).

One should instead create impressions of rarity, virtual rarity: what are the classic strategies to do so?

■ the choice of a restricted selective and exclusive distribution such as Louis Vuitton fully owned stores or Hermès stores;
■ creating a permanent but non-lasting out-of-stock situation on specific items;

- communicating by word of mouth that there will not be enough supply for all people;
- manufacturing the product after it has been ordered, to emphasize the impression of exclusivity created by this one-to-one apparent customization;
- creating a halo of exclusivity by the sponsorship of top stars, super models, fashion designers, and creators: this is how Absolut Vodka maintained its exclusive image while becoming the third worldwide spirit in sales;
- creating special and very rare products whose goal is only to stimulate the buzz and press fallouts: for instance Glenlivet created a special product called the Millennium. This famous single malt brand announced it would produce malt and sell it in full barrels, kept 15 years, and sold at the eve of the year 2000. The barrel was priced at 15,000 euros. This created a large echo in the media, thus increasing the feeling of an exclusive brand. Most of the sales of this brand, however, concern the regular Glenlivet available in all regular liquor stores;
- another typical strategy is to create a feeling of exclusivity by the special advantages gained by belonging to a restricted club. Here the brand emphasizes service to foster its image while expanding its product sales;
- finally, one major strategy is to divide the business in two parts: one will be made of actually very rare products, exceptional, promoted by event which themselves are unique and by creators or designers who master both art and the media (John Galliano, Tom Ford, Mark Jacobs). The second part is made of products far less expensive and mass-produced, which will benefit from the halo effect created by the exclusive part. This is *mass-stige*: are Yves Saint Laurent cosmetics still luxury? No, of course not. However, they are endowed with the image of this world-reknowned designer and capitalize on it to sell a higher dream at a higher price.

TWO DIFFERENT APPROACHES TO LUXURY BRAND BUILDING

The only real success is commercial, yet there are many roads to this destination. An examination of the success of US brands such as Ralph Lauren, Calvin Klein and DKNY proves that it is possible to become an overnight success in the luxury market without the long pedigree of a Christian Dior, Chanel or Givenchy. True, these newer brands have not yet demonstrated their ability to endure and survive beyond the death of their founders, but their commercial success is evidence of their attractiveness to customers the world over. We need to distinguish between two different business models for brands. The first includes brands with a 'history' behind them, while the second covers brands that, lacking such a history of their own, have invented a 'story' for themselves. It comes as no surprise that these companies are US-based: this young, modern country is a past master in the art of weaving dreams from stories. After all, both Hollywood and Disneyland are American inventions.

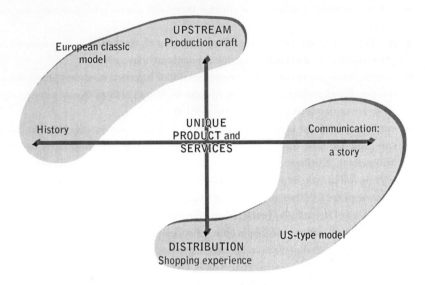

UPSTREAM
Production craft

European classic
model

History

UNIQUE
PRODUCT and
SERVICES

Communication:

a story

DISTRIBUTION
Shopping experience

US-type model

Figure 4.1 *The two business cultures of luxury brands.*

Furthermore, the European luxury brands – rooted as they are in a craftsperson-based tradition predicated upon rare, unique pieces of work – place considerable emphasis on the actual product as a factor in their success, while the US brands concentrate much more on merchandizing, and the atmosphere and image created by the outlets dedicated to their brand, in the realm of customer contact and distribution. What we see is the creation of a dichotomy between 'history' and the product on the one hand, and 'stories' and distribution on the other. Let us examine and compare these two brand and business models in more detail.

The first brand and business model may be represented by the luxury pyramid (Kapferer 2004: 69). At the top of the pyramid, there is the *griffe* – the creator's signature engraved on a unique work. A *griffe* (French word for claw) refers to instinct, unpredictability, pure creation of a single person. This highlights what threatens it most: copies. Brands, on the other hand, are threatened by fakes or counterfeits. The second level of this pyramid is that of luxury brands produced in small series within a workshop: a 'manufacture' in its etymological sense, which is seen as the sole warrant of a 'good-facture'. Examples include Hermès, Rolls-Royce and Cartier. The third level of the pyramid is that of streamlined mass-production: here we find Dior and Yves Saint Laurent cosmetics, and YSL Diffusion clothes or DKNY. At this level of industrialization, the brand's fame generates an aura of intangible added-values for expensive and prime quality products, which nonetheless gradually tend to look more and more like the rest of the market.

In this model, luxury management is based on the interactions between the three levels. The perpetuation of *griffes* depends on their integration in financial groups that are able to provide the necessary resources for the first level, and on their licensing to industrial groups able to create, launch and distribute worldwide products at the third level (such as P&G, Unilever and l'Oréal). Profit accrues at this level, and is the only means to make the huge investments on the *griffe* pay off. These investments are necessary to recreate the dream around the brand. Reality consumes dreams: the more we buy a luxury brand, the less we dream of it.

Hence, somewhat paradoxically, the more a luxury brand gets purchased, the more its aura needs to be permanently recreated.

This is exactly how the LVMH group operates. The business model is best explained in the actual words of Bernard Arnault, the CEO of LVMH, the world's leading luxury group, which owns 41 luxury brands such Louis Vuitton, Moët & Chandon, Dom Pérignon, Hennessy cognac as well as Dior, Tag Heuer watches, etc. What are the key factors in the success of its brands? Arnault (2000: 65) lists them in the following order: First, product quality; then creativity; image; company spirit; a drive to reinvent oneself and to be the best. Writing earlier in his book with reference to Dior, the ultimate luxury brand, he notes, 'Behind Dior, there is a legitimacy . . . roots . . . an exceptional evocative power . . . a genuine magic, to say nothing of its potential for economic growth' (p. 26).

As we can see, in this pyramid model, with its base that expands to feed the brand's overall cashflow (through licensing, extensions and a less selective distribution system), there must be a constant regeneration of value at the tip. This is where creativity, signature and creator come in, supplying the brand with its artistic inventiveness. Here we are in the realm of art, not mere styling. Each show is a pure artistic event. Unlike the second brand and business model (as we shall see), it is not a question of presenting clothing, which will be worn in a year's time. As Arnault puts it, 'One does not invite a thousand guests to watch a procession of dresses which could be seen on a coat hanger or in a show room' (p. 70), 'most competitors prefer to show off mass-produced clothing on their catwalks, or indulge in American-style marketing. We are not interested in working this way' (p. 73), and 'Marc Jacobs, John Galliano and Alexander McQueen are innovators; fashion inventors; artists who create' (p. 75). This quote is very insightful: luxury brands belong to art and should be managed as the Medici aristocrats did when they invited the greatest artists to live and paint in Firenze. Each defilé is an art exhibition: it demonstrates artistic supremacy. The creativity of the signature label, at the tip of the pyramid, is at the heart of the business model: within a few years of the arrival of John Galliano at Dior, sales had increased fourfold. Never before had Dior been talked about so much worldwide. Dior was back at the centre of world artistic creation for women.

The disadvantage of this model – and after all, every model has a disadvantage – is that the more accessible secondary lines are entrusted to other designers, and the further away you move from the tip of the pyramid, the less creativity there is. In this model, there is a strong danger that brand extensions will show little of the creativity of the brand itself: they will merely exploit its name. Their goal is to sell to the masses and make a profit from the aura of the prestigious name sold on widely distributed products.

The second brand and business model may have originated in the United States, but we should also include the likes of Armani and Boss in this category. It can be described as a flat, circular, constellation-like model (Kapferer 2004: 71). At the centre of this constellation is the brand core, while all manifestations of the brand (its extensions, licences and so on) are around the edge, at a more or less equal distance from the centre. Consequently these extensions are all treated with equal care, since each of them brings its own individual expression of this core value to its target market. Each portrays the brand in an equally important way, and plays its own part in shaping it. For example, Ralph Lauren's home textile extension (bed sheets, blankets, tablecloths, bath towels and so on) is a complete expression of the patrician East Coast ideal and its values: indeed, the tactic of merchandizing the range in the corners of department stores aims to create an idealized reconstruction of a room in a house. There are price differences between all these extensions: however, the variance is far less stretched than in the former model.

This second model can include brand 'places' such as The House of Ralph Lauren – superstores which not only stock the entire brand range and its various collections and extensions, but are also specifically designed to give flesh, structure and meaning to the brand ideal. Ralph Lifshitz, Ralph Lauren's founder, built his brand on an ideal: that of American aristocracy, symbolized by Boston high society. Ralph Lauren's flagship stores are three-dimensional recreations of this fanciful illusion.

The same model is also used by brands such as Lacoste (Kapferer and Gaston-Breton 2002), created in 1933 in the days of tennis champion René Lacoste, a Davis Cup winner together with his friends 'Les Mousquetaires', and nicknamed 'The Crocodile' for his tenacity. Ever since then, the brand's values, which are encapsulated in his famous *chemise* (meaning 'shirt': the word itself is important), have been upheld by the Lacoste family and a collection of partners, their licensed producers and distributors. Lacoste thus has a certain authenticity and a genuine history, yet at the same time follows this second business model.

Indeed, the creation of this model has nothing to do with chance: it is an economic necessity for any brand which continues to be sold at an accessible price point. There is no way of sustaining an exclusive distribution network with an average retail price of around 65 dollars or euros – that is, the price of a Lacoste shirt – or 50 dollars, the price of a Ralph Lauren polo shirt. The economics only become feasible with multiple extensions. Following our model, this can be done in two ways. The first is horizontal product extension to increase brand recognition, providing that elusive access to large-scale advertising budgets, and breaking into different distribution channels or different locations inside the same department store. Lacoste perfumes, shoes and bags increase the perceived presence and status of the brand.

The second is vertical product extension to increase average till prices. Today, for example, Lacoste has segmented its product range into three groups – sport, sportswear and Club – yet has steered clear of formal wear, which is outside the brand's sphere of legitimacy. This segmentation makes it possible for customers to wear Lacoste in a variety of situations: sport, leisure and 'dress-down Friday wear'. At the same time, the average product price is increasing according to the particular segment: the high-quality materials used in a Club jacket explain why. Of course, the product ranges of all Lacoste's extensions are arranged around this same segmentation. Ralph Lauren uses a similar model: its Purple Label Collection features Italian-made outfits produced from quality materials, and a price tag to match: 6,000 euros per outfit.

This brand extension policy makes matters easier for distributors, who have come to understand that the rate of return increases as the physical sales area expands. Each store can now offer a rich assortment of products, which are no longer mere accessories, but extensions in their own right – and in so doing, can increase the value of the average shopping trip. It should be noted that 'pyramid-based' brands face a rather perverse problem. If they create too many accessible extensions, they reduce the profitability of the sales outlets. In a Chanel boutique, it makes more sense to spend 10 minutes selling a customer a Chanel bag – given the margin it offers – rather than a perfume or cosmetics from the Chanel Precision range. Clearly, the extension policy is inseparable from the distribution policy.

DIVERSITY IN LUXURY

To conclude, it is noticeable that newcomers in the luxury market have been able to turn around the issue of lack of authenticity. Unlike brands such as Lacoste, Chanel, Dior and Yves Saint Laurent which grew after the fame of a historic designer or of a famous tennis player, Boss, Calvin Klein and Ralph Lauren are pure creations of marketing built around persons who symbolize the brand but were not designers themselves. That did not prevent them from succeeding for they invented their own story to compensate the lack of true history. They enacted their story not so much in products but in stores and for one of them by taking the name of the brand itself. In doing so they revealed that history may no longer be a driver of luxury, at least for a number of new customers, such as the youth who is strongly ahistorical. Modern youth likes enhanced experiences: it has been formed by Hollywood, videogames, virtual reality. Should one then rally to this new model? Of course not, since choice is based on diversity of alternatives. There is a need for diversity in the market. Also, every brand should capitalize on its strengths.

Finally, it remains to be proven that these new breed of brands will survive as long as the former ones. Only experience will answer this question. At some point in time, illusion may not work anymore and authenticity could become the very exclusive benefit of luxury brands.

KEY POINT

■ Two models of luxury brands coexist, based upon opposing cultural assumptions about luxury: one rooted in history, rarity and craftsmanship, often associated with European luxury brands, and another based upon stories, image and marketing finesse, often linked to American success.

QUESTIONS FOR DISCUSSION

1 Choose several luxury brands and discuss them within the two models discussed here. Do the two models seem to apply?
2 What are some of the key cultural assumptions about luxury that inform luxury branding?
3 Are some brands more authentic than others, as this chapter suggests? In what way?
4 Does this approach to brand culture apply only to luxury brands?
5 How does the *griffe* concept enhance our understanding of brands?

REFERENCES

Arnault, B. (2000) *La passion creative*, Paris: Plon.
Catry, B. (2005) 'Le luxe peut être cher, mais doit-il être rare?', *Revue Française de Gestion* 156 (July/August).
Kapferer, J.-N. (1997) 'Managing luxury brands', *Journal of Brand Management* 4, 4: 251–260.
Kapferer, J.-N. (1998) 'Why are we seduced by luxury brands?', *Journal of Brand Management* 6, 1: 44–49.
Kapferer, J.-N. (2004) *The New Strategic Brand Management*, London: Kogan Page.
Kapferer, P. and Gaston-Breton, T. (2002) *Lacoste: The legend*, Paris: Cherche Midi.
Sicard, M. C. (2003) *Luxe, Mensonge et Marketing*, Paris: Village Mondial.

Chapter 5

Managing leader and partner brands

The brand association base

Henrik Uggla

This chapter provides a theoretical overview of brand leveraging and identifies some problems related to brand boundaries and the popular notion of fit. A brand association base model is introduced that connects brands in the surrounding environment to a leader brand. Moreover, it is suggested that marketers can benefit from a closer look at the areas between brands and between brands and the end-consumer. Implications for brand leveraging research and semiotic research are outlined.

BACKGROUND

During the last two decades, marketing in general, and the field of strategic brand management in particular, has been inherently biased toward the idea of building immaterial marketing resources from the bottom line (e.g. Aaker 1997; Doyle 2002; Kapferer 2004). In a ground-breaking article (Farquhar *et al*. 1992) underscored that in building a brand, marketers should endeavour to link the brand to an association that has enough flexibility to provide a platform for both current positioning and subsequent leveraging. Although this kind of argument provides a first important step towards a deeper focus on brand leveraging, it provides a quite restricted vision of the opportunity space for brand collaboration, based on the idea of a non-collaborative situation with a single brand that should be leveraged.

Contemporary marketing and brand management practices cannot justify a theoretical paradigm entirely devoted to the issue of building brand resources. Instead, brand management might be better described as a balance between building and borrowing brand value through associations between brands in collaborative settings. For example, the owners of the Post brand of breakfast cereals might build and self-brand an association with a certain ingredient taste (cranberries) or borrow that taste from an already established and appreciated brand in the market through licensing (Ocean Spray Cranberries). But ingredient branding is just one of many brand leveraging strategies, beside co-branding, brand alliances and all sorts of licensing and franchising. From this larger inclusive perspective, brand leveraging might be viewed as the art of balancing between making or buying brand equity from the marketplace or even borrowing it from valuable sources of reputation in culture (Uggla 2001; Schroeder 2000, 2002).

BRAND LEVERAGE THEORY

Brand leverage theory integrates brand extension and brand alliance research. Aaker and Keller (1990) distinguished three bases of fit – complement, substitute and transfer of skill – between the original brand and the extension product category. They also found interactive effects, predicting brand extension success, between different variables. For example, host brand quality is not enough to create a successful brand extension, it must interact with *fit* in order to become successfully evaluated by consumers (Aaker and Keller 1990; Keller and Aaker 1992). Tauber (1988) developed two criteria for brand extensions: fit and *leverage* between the host brand and new product categories.

In comparison, he views fit as natural link that is established between the brand and the new product and leverage as the differentiating attribute or benefit in the new category. Park and colleagues (1996) introduced the idea of viewing composite brand alliances as an indirect form of brand extension; they show that a *co-branded version* of a product can help to overcome potentially incongruent or negatively correlated attributes between. Their model is based on two levels of fit: brand and product fit. Jevons and de Chernatony (2002) viewed the degree of brand collaboration as a function of type of business relationships (close or distant) and brand connection (strong or weak).

According to them, a close relationship between brands combined with a close business relationship will enable category extensions, with a supervisory interaction. On the contrary, a close relationship between brands combined with a distant business relationship will shape advisory interaction between brands and awareness shaping co-branding. A less academic but more pragmatic model was developed by Blackett and Boad (1999). They argued that co-branding should be viewed as a lasting collaboration between two independent brands with an increasing degree of shared value creation, ranging from reach awareness co-branding aimed at reaching out to new customer bases and sharing or leveraging established brand awareness, values endorsement co-branding, based on a reinforcement of each other's values, ingredient co-branding through branded ingredients, complementary competence co-branding through new product development. Another approach is presented by Cegarra and Michel (2000). They distinguish between functional versus conceptual co-branding. In the conceptual co-branding situation, customers evaluate attributes then category typicality. In contrast, functional co-branding is based on category evaluation in the first instance and then product attributes.

In summary, co-branding or other types of alliances between brands can be viewed as a strategy for reaching out beyond the brands' outer core and using the brands' more latent potential for leverage through the core competence of a partner brand (Bucklin and Sengupta 1993). In this chapter I will develop a strategic model focused on the transfer of meaning between brands as viewed from the perspective of a leader brand.

THE BRAND ASSOCIATION BASE

The brand association base is a strategic brand alliance model for all types of links between brands and their connection to other brands and categories (see Figure 5.1). The brand association base is founded on research within the realm of strategic brand management with relevant underlying research streams in cognitive psychology and semiotics. The brand association base can be defined in the following way:

> The brand associations managed by a leader brand (category), extended through iden-
> tity transfer or leveraged through image transfer through partner brands (categories)
> or institutional associations, that contributes in a positive/negative way to customer
> derived meaning for the brand (image) and value (equity).

In the next section, the four cornerstones of the brand association base model – the leader brand, the partner brand, institutional associations and brand image – will be further developed.

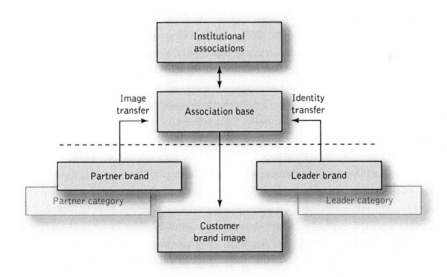

Figure 5.1 *The brand association base.*

The leader brand

The leader brand is the most downstream brand in a brand alliance context (Malaval 2001). It is the primary brand, associated to a secondary brand (Hillyer and Tikoo 1995). The co-brand Ecco shoes with Gore-Tex fabrics, consists of a leader brand (Ecco) and a partner brand (Gore-Tex).

Four important criteria delimit and define the leader brand in a brand alliance or co-branding context: category driver, control over the marketing and distribution system, status as a modified brand and owner of a customer base. For example, Ecco sells quality shoes (category) in their own stores (marketing and distribution), the Gore-Tex ingredient brand modifies the Ecco line of shoes for the segment of waterproof shoes (modifier brand) and Ecco owns a customer base of potential shoe buyers. In the co-branding architecture of Ford Explorer Eddie Bauer Edition, Ford Explorer is the leader brand that is modified up-market through the Eddie Bauer partner brand. In this case, the leader brand reaches up to a higher market segment through the premium associations transferred through the partner brand. In England, Seiko is a leader brand in relation to Oxford University Press. Seiko and Oxford University Press have developed a digital crossword solver that is marketed by Seiko through its consumer product website, and the content provided by Oxford University Press is the ingredient co-brand. In the service sector, the leader brands often appear as organizers of meaning from partner brands. A sign of this strategic direction is that most theme parks now have their own partner brand managers that develop platforms and conditions for brand alliances.

Universal Studios has established relations with a number of important partners. A strategic consideration for the leader brand relates to how it should be positioned in relation to its partners. The roles and positions of partner brands will depend upon the more specific product market context where these partners appear. In the case of Universal Studios, a basic distinction has been created between partners, sponsors and supplier brands. Partner, sponsor and supplier brands differ as to their positions in the graphic portfolio, in marketing communication and amount of space in the theme parks. The leader brand connects to the larger association base through *identity transfer*. An important strategic consideration for the leader brand relates to how much of this brand should be transparent in relation to partners and how they should be co-positioned in a brand alliance effort. In a distribution-led brand alliance, the leader brand might be used as an umbrella and a portal. For example, Togo's great sandwiches serve as an umbrella leader brand in the multi-unit franchising alliance with Dunkin' Donuts and Baskin-Robbins ice cream. In product co-branding the positioning of the leader brand might be more balanced. The co-brand Bianchi-Ducati mountain bike represents a visible balance between the leader brand (Bianchi) and the partner brand (Ducati).

The partner brand

Partner brand associations are defined here as associations secondary to the identity and more immediate territory of the leader brand. A partner brand can reinforce the value proposition of a leader brand in functional and or symbolic ways. It can bring functional brand associations to a leader brand. Gore-Tex reinforces the functional brand promise of Ecco shoes through its 'Guaranteed To Keep You Dry' promise. Partner brands can reinforce symbolic and self-expressive associations for a leader brand (Uggla 2004). Designer and architect Michael Graves has reinforced symbolic associations for the US retailer Target through the Michael Graves product line. In this case, the partner brand has reinforced world-class design associations for the leader brand (Aaker 2004; Nunes *et al.* 2002).

Partner brand associations contribute in the strategic context with brand equity to the overarching leader brand and its association base in either of two ways, *asymmetrical* or *symmetrical* forms of collaboration (i.e. ingredient or co-branding). Asymmetrical collaboration refers to positioning based on a *visible asymmetry* in the graphic representation and expression of collaborating brands, in many cases, such as Intel Inside in computers, Gore-Tex in apparel and Reuteri in mineral water and food, the branded ingredient can contribute with a deepened functional dimension to the value proposition of the host brand, create synergy effects and facilitate positioning of the leader brand. If the partner brand is positioned as an ingredient, this ingredient branding strategy can also affect the leader brand's possibility of entering into new categories in the future (Desai and Keller 2002). To sum up, a partner brand can create differentiation for the leader brand and for itself, downstream in a value chain. It can transfer both functional, emotional and symbolic associations to the leader brand. From the leader brand and the partner brand, I shall now explore the concept of institutional associations.

Cultural and institutional associations

Institutional associations are the outcome of culturally entrenched meaning that can be transformed into value for a brand. The specific cultural content of these associations can be based on connections to science, history, knowledge and even art. Illy is a global premium brand of espresso coffee with institutional and content-rich associations. It has relationships to higher education through its 'Universitá del Caffe' based on theory and application classes on the subject of coffee. In addition, links to art are established through the illy collection of mugs designed by Jeff Koons and other contemporary artists.

These associations have meaning and recognition in a given cultural context. Their categorization base depends on socio-culturally shared meaning structures and/or scientific authority (Rosa and Porac 2002) and can be compared with a non-product related association (Keller 2003). A key feature of this kind of association is that since it is already embedded in a larger surrounding context and culture, it also contains a certain amount of value. For example, the American Dental Association is a trusted institution that transfers reputation and trust to Crest toothpaste (Nunes *et al.* 2002).

81

An important distinction should be made between institutional associations and institutional brand associations. Illy is a commercial brand, a university is an institution. However, 'Universitá del Caffe' by illy represents an institutional brand association. The same accounts for associations to science or art. A hospital is an institution, and under very specific and reciprocal circumstances it can contribute with culturally embedded associations to a brand. Consequently, the Ronald McDonald house can be said to contain institutionalized brand associations. Art, and in particular artists such as Andy Warhol, has transformed and upgraded brand identity associations into institutionalized brand associations. For example, Warhol's serial paintings of Coca-Cola, Marilyn Monroe and Campbell's Soup can be viewed in this way (Schroeder 2002).

Strategic incentives for leader versus partner brands

The strategic incentives and motives to collaborate differ with respect to the brands position within the association base system. A basic distinction can be made between functional, emotional and symbolic incentives from the perspective of each part. A basic functional motive for the leader brand will be the extension of the brand territory beyond the brand's outer core, to reinforce an attribute from a partner, or leverage the quality associations of a partner brand. The partner brand can also use the leader brand for classic category extension. In this case the partner brand is moved through a process of image-transfer, through source to target (Riezebos 2003).

For example, when the ingredient brand Dupont Supplex with Lycra only by Dupont® collaborates with the Stay-In-Place Sport Bra, it also represents a category

Table 5.1 *Incentives for leader and partner brands*

	Leader brand	Partner brand
Functional benefits	Extend brand territory through indirect extensions Reinforce and endorse an isolated attribute and benefit Reduce competitive advantage of the market leader Create stronger association with quality Capitalize on a core competence	Extend to new categories Leverage channel equity Expand the customer base Create more usage Capitalize on brand awareness
Emotional benefits	Reinforce emotional benefits through image transfer of functional or symbolic benefits	Extend the value proposition Create a deeper brand personality
Symbolic benefits	Image-transfer of design and self expression Use partner as a silver bullet brand	Image-transfer of end-user and usage imagery from the leader brand customer base

extension for the partner brand into the 'sport bra' category. Other important functional motives for the partner brand include possible expansion of the customer base, leverage of channel equity and end-consumer awareness established by the leader brand and the opportunity to create more usage and end-consumer demand. Emotional benefits for the leader brand include the reinforcement of functional or symbolic benefits from the partner brand. In comparison, the partner brand can *enrich* and *deepen* its own brand personality and extend the value proposition through the leader brand. Finally, both parts can create and leverage symbolic benefits through partner brand arrangements. A leader brand such as Siemens can use Porsche design in order to strengthen self-expressive benefits and the partner brand can capitalize on spillover effects of a symbolic nature from the leader brand's customer base.

Customer brand image

The customer will derive her or his perceived equity from one or more elements related to the association base as outlined above. The customer brand image will ultimately depend on the brand knowledge and attitude towards the brands inherent to the system and the underlying categories, but it will also be dependent upon the more particular ways that these brands appear and interact together through a co-branding effect and a spillover effect (Baumgarth 2000; Simonin and Ruth 1998). For example, the brand image derived from a co-promotion campaign between the leader brand Motorola (cellular phones) and the partner brand Victorinox (Swiss Army knife) will be more or less than the sum of the brand equity structures given by these as individual brands. In a general sense, the customer will attribute more importance to the brand with a product class prerogative, the brand that sets and decide the category toward the end customer. For example, in the co-branding effort between Häagen-Dazs and Baileys, around a liqueur-flavoured ice cream, more importance will generally be given to the ice-cream leader brand than the modifying partner brand (Riezebos 2003).

Psychologically, the evaluation will also be dependent upon the salience and awareness level of the partner brand in consumer memory and its perceived contribution to the leader brand (Hillyer and Tikoo 1995). For example, if the consumer feels that the Gore-Tex membrane ingredient partner brand with its brand promise 'Guaranteed To Keep You Dry' contributes strongly to the desired benefits of the leader brand, this will strongly affect the value and substitutability among leader brands in a consideration set. Moreover, the consumer perception of the brand alliance affects the associations of the partner brands. Less familiar partner brands experience stronger spillover effects than stronger and more recognized brands (Simonin and Ruth 1998).

From a fit perspective, the evaluation of leader and partner brand goes beyond conventional fit dimensions (cf. Aaker and Keller 1990) and is based both on product category and brand fit. Research on complex category conjunction indicates that low or even incongruent fit dimensions can lead to a more elaborate psychological processing and emerging attributes in the evaluation process of two brands (Bristol 2002). When the consumer evaluates the brand alliance, more elaborate processing and attention will be given to a non-complementary alliance between a leader brand and a partner brand with respect to the underlying product categories involved. The reason for this is that the consumer will engage in a cognitive elaboration of what these products have in common. In the next section, an attempt will be made to link the psychological observations made above to the semiotic dynamics in this brand identity system.

SEMIOTIC BRAND ALLIANCE STRUCTURE

From a semiotic perspective, a brand is a sign with a relationship to an underlying object and to someone who interprets this sign (i.e. the interpretant, Peirce 1931–58; see also Chapters 7 and 11 in this volume). In semiotic theory, a distinction is made between a symbol, an icon and an index (Eco 1979; Peirce 1931–58; Nöth 1995). A symbol is an arbitrary sign whose meaning is established by convention. We have been led to think that the Nike swoosh stands for sports fashion, but it is not a natural connection. In comparison, an icon represents its underlying object. The man/woman pictograms indicating the men's room and the ladies' room in a restaurant are icons. Whereas an index is connected to its underlying object through existential connections. Smoke is an index of fire and in the realm of strategic brand management we might say that a qualified endorser is an index for the endorsed brand. In other words, Michael Jordan is an index for Nike.

If the leader brand wants to dominate its brand association base, it should strive to create asymmetrical brand alliances and only use its partner brand as an icon or an index; however, complete control over partner brands can hardly be achieved (Blackett 1999). In some cases, partner brand associations can be transformed into leader brand associations over time. For example, Michael Jordan started in an asymmetrical brand-to-brand relationship as an endorser for Nike, transformed into status of a sub brand (i.e. Nike Air Jordan) and eventually became a leader brand in his own right (e.g. Michael Jordan Steakhouses). In semiotic terms, Jordan transformed his brand from an index to a symbol. In some cases, partner brand associations become so strong and important as drivers for end-consumer decision that they become a natural part of the overarching brand structure of the *leader brand*. For example, Gore-Tex started out as an ingredient brand.

TOWARDS AN INTEGRATED SEMIOTIC MODEL OF BRAND LEVERAGING

If it is taken into account the two mega paradigms in semiotic theory developed by Saussure and Pierce and the full complexity of psycho semiotic meaning transformation

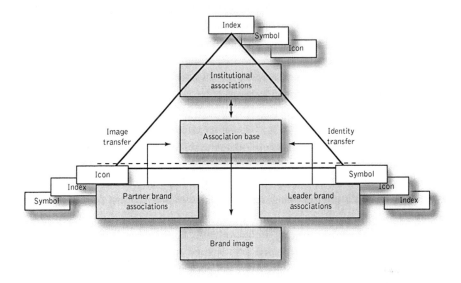

Figure 5.2 *The semiotic brand association base.*

with respect to the order and structure between partner and leader brands in a sign system, it is possible to present a more integrated semiotic brand leveraging model that more fully combines the pragmatic sign taxonomies offered by Pierce and the sign-to-sign sensitivity in a linguistic model. From such a point of view, the emergence of a brand image might be seen as an interplay of brand signs in a system that can affect end-consumer perception of the most important brand and the order and power relationship with brand meaning (e.g. my Gore-Tex jacket from Peak Performance rather than my Peak Performance jacket with Gore-Tex). Ideally, such a sign-to-sign system should provide a potential stance from either of several brands in a system (i.e. leader or partner brands) from a culturally embedded perspective outside the more immediate commercial marketing context (institutional level) or from any potential interpretant or mind, concerned with sense-making of the sign(s).

IMPLICATIONS FOR BRAND THEORY AND SEMIOTIC RESEARCH

The present chapter has offered a theoretical and pragmatic response to concerns raised in the theoretical discussion of brand management on the necessity of obtaining a greater understanding of how meaning can be leveraged in a cultural brand system. The brand association base can potentially reconcile some of the inherent contradictions with brand boundaries. The ideas developed in the present chapter also partially contribute to the issue of developing more refined models of specific application areas in branding, particularly alignment between a brand and its surrounding culture, co-branding, ingredient co-branding, ingredient branding and complex brand architecture in relation to a strategic design of brand identity and brand equity systems.

Moreover, the chapter has expanded the use of semiotics in brand management from more traditional approaches such as content analysis of ads into a new application area within strategic brand management in terms of brand leveraging. The semiotic model can be a nice complement to more cognitive models (cf. Farquhar *et al*. 1992; Aaker and Joachimsthaler 2000; Keller 2003). The model encourages a more reflective brand strategy and research approach that emphasizes the ability for change rather than stability in brand systems and brand constellations. Finally, the model can contribute to our understanding of brand knowledge, and the relative instability of that construct as the status of the stimuli input can change in consumer mind and memory (e.g. from icon to index).

The semiotic brand-leveraging model extends the Peircean distinctions of icon–index–symbol into a new application area beyond more traditional applications in advertising, design, product development and packaging (Mick *et al*. 2004). In comparison, many of the more traditional approaches have been concerned with the elements of brand building, rather than brand leveraging. Put into a holistic semiotic marketing context, traditional research streams focused on potentializing and actualizing meanings in and around the objects. In contrast, the semiotic brand-leveraging model puts a main focus on potentializing and actualizing meanings between signs (brands) and their underlying objects (products). The semiotic brand-leveraging model can be applied in order to further refine semiotic marketing research devoted to hypermarkets and retail environments involving sign-complexity. It can be used in order to plan and position objects or designs with dual-sign structures – such as a Sony Ericsson mobile phone. Or it can be further developed in a more theoretical direction through subdivision into different forms. For example, by combining Kawama's (1985) Peirician framework with the brand association base model, a more subtle taxonomy might emerge, allowing for distinctions such as an icosyndex partner brand. In sum, the semiotic brand-leveraging model expands the horizon of semiotic marketing research by describing the image transfer processes in a new way beyond the traditional cognitive models.

KEY POINT

■ The brand that orchestrates a brand alliance with other brands can be called a leader brand. Within this alliance, institutional associations – based on deep-rooted cultural values – add legitimacy to a brand.

QUESTIONS FOR DISCUSSION

1 How can a partner brand be changed from icon to symbol in a partner brand strategy?

2 It has been suggested that Michael Jordan has transformed from a partner brand for Nike into a leader brand. Can you find other celebrity endorsers with the same power? Consider the movies, sport and fashion industry.

3 Which type of leader brand (weak or strong) has most to gain from collaboration with a highly recognized partner (ingredient brand) such as SHIMANO, Gore-Tex, Intel Inside or Lycra?

4 What are the major strengths, versus risks and drawbacks in partner branding based on the brand association base model?

5 In the United States SUN-MAID® Californian raisins has extended its brand into Instant muffins, using a line extension from their core product (SUN-MAID® Extra Moist Californian Raisins) as an ingredient brand, visible on the packaging. Is it smart to become both leader and partner brand in the same offering?

REFERENCES

Aaker, D. A. (1997) 'Should you take your brand to where the action is?', *Harvard Business Review* (September–October): 25–35.

Aaker, D. A. (2004) *Brand Portfolio Strategy: Creating Relevance, Differentiation, Energy, Leverage and Clarity*, New York: The Free Press.

Aaker, D. A. and Keller, K. L. (1990) 'Consumer evaluations of brand extensions', *Journal of Marketing* 54 (Winter): 27–41.

Aaker, D. A. and Joachimsthaler, E. (2000) *Brand Leadership*, New York: The Free Press.

Baumgarth, C. (2000) 'Fit-reasons of co-branding: a qualitative study', working paper, Department of Business Administration, School of Economics, University of Siegen, Germany.

Blackett, T. (1999) 'Co-branding comes of age', *Intellectual Property* (November): 5–9.

Blackett, T. and Boad, B. (1999) *Co-branding – The Science of Alliance*, Basingstoke: Macmillan.

Bristol, T. (2002) 'Potential points of brand leverage: consumers emergent attributes', *Journal of Product and Brand Management* 11, 4: 1–13.

Bucklin, L. P. and Sengupta, S. (1993) 'Organizing successful co-marketing alliances', *Journal of Marketing* 57: 32-46.

Cegarra, J. and Michel, G. (2000) 'Co-branding: clarification du concept et proposition d'un modele devaluation', http://panoramix.univ-paris1.fr/GREGOR/Site

Desai, K. K. and Keller, K. L. (2002) 'The effects of ingredient branding strategies on host brand extendibility', *Journal of Marketing* 66 (January): 73–93.

Doyle, P. (2002) 'Shareholder-value based brand strategies', *Journal of Brand Management* 9, 1: 20–30.

Eco, U. (1979) *A Theory of Semiotics*, Bloomington: Indiana University Press.

Farquhar, P. H., Han, J., Herr, P. and Ijiri, Y. (1992) 'Strategies for leveraging master brands', *Marketing Research* (September): 32–39.

Hillyer, C. and Tikoo, S. (1995) 'Effect of cobranding on consumer product evaluations', *Advances in Consumer Research* 22: 123–127.

Jevons, C. and de Chernatony, L. (2002) 'Interrelationships and interactions between brands: a conceptual taxonomy'. Proceedings of the Thirty-first EMAC Conference, University of Minho, School of Management and Economics, Portugal.

Kapferer, J. N. (2004) *The New Strategic Brand Management*, London: Kogan Page.

Kawama, T. (1985) 'A semiotic approach to product forms', in T. A. Seboek and J. Umiker Seboek (eds) *The Semiotic Web*, Berlin: Mouton de Gruyter: 625–638.

Keller, K. L. (2003) *Strategic Brand Management*, London: Prentice Hall.

Keller, K. L. and Aaker, D. A. (1992) 'The effects of sequential introductions of brand extensions', *Journal of Marketing Research* 29, 1: 35–50.

Malaval, P. (2001) *Strategy and Management of Industrial Brands*, Boston, MA: Kluwer.

Mick, D. G., Burroughs, J., Hetzel, P. and Brannen, M. Y. (2004) 'Pursuing the meaning of meaning in the commercial world: an international view of marketing and consumer research founded on semiotics', *Semiotica* 152, 1/4: 1–74.

Nöth, W. (1995) *Handbook of Semiotics*, Bloomington: Indiana University Press.

Nunes, P. F., Dull, S. F. and Lynch, P. D. (2002) 'When two brands are better than one', *Outlook* 1: 16–23.

Park, W. C., Jun, S. Y. and Shocker, A. D. (1996) 'Composite branding alliances: an investigation of extension and feedback effects', *Journal of Marketing Research* 33 (November): 454–465.

Peirce, C. S. (1931–58) *Collected Papers*, C. Hartshorne, P. Weiss and H. Burks (eds) Cambridge, MA: Harvard University Press.

Rosa, J. A. and Porac, J. F. (2002) 'Categorization bases and their influence on product category knowledge structures', *Psychology and Marketing* 19, 6: 503–532.

Riezebos, R. (2003) *Brand Management: A Theoretical and Practical Approach*, Harlow: Prentice Hall.

Schroeder, J. E. (2000) 'Édouard Manet, Calvin Klein and the strategic use of scandal', in S. Brown and A. Patterson (eds) *Imagining Marketing: Art, Aesthetics, and the Avant-Garde*, London: Routledge: 36–51.

Schroeder, J. E. (2002) *Visual Consumption*, London: Routledge.

Simonin, B. L. and Ruth, J. A. (1998) 'Is a company known by the company it keeps? Assessing spillover effects of brand alliances on consumer brand attitudes', *Journal of Marketing Research* 35, 1: 30–42.

Tauber, E. M. (1988) 'Brand leverage – strategy for growth in a cost-control world', *Journal of Advertising Research* (August/September).

Uggla, H. (2001) *Organisation av Varumärken*, Malmö: Liber Ekonomi.

Uggla, H. (2004) 'The brand association base: a conceptual model for strategically leveraging partner brand equity', *Journal of Brand Management* 12, 2: 105–123.

Part II
Clarifying brand concepts

Chapter 6

Brands as a global ideoscape

Søren Askegaard

INTRODUCTION

Consumer research in brands has a long history, starting with Gardner and Levy's (1955) classic paper 'The product and the brand'. Initially, branding was seen as one particular kind of marketing communication strategy where values were added to the product through a specific meaning universe (often in the shape of a consumer slice-of-life narrative) presented in an advertisement. Nowadays, with a much wider range of 'branding types', we have to consider the term in a larger sense. Without proposing a definition, here I will take the notion of branding to be a strategically produced and disseminated commercial sign (or a set of signs) that is referring to the value universe of a commodity.

However, in spite of Gardner and Levy's clear emphasis that a brand primarily is 'a public image', this aspect of the brand has until recently been neglected by the research in brands. Nor has there traditionally been a lot of research in the role of brands on a global scale from a consumer research perspective. Either the literature has been managerially oriented in the search for global branding opportunities in the tradition following Levitt (1983). Or, as witnessed by the growing bulk of research in globalizing consumer culture, it has largely focused on consumption and consumer culture generally (e.g. Ger and Belk 1996) without a specific focus on brands in general or specific brands in particular.

In recent years there have been indications of a growing interest for understanding how brands function, both at a macro and a micro level (e.g. Fournier 1998). What characterizes this research is that the brand is not placed in a global cultural context. The brand remains a neutral element without specific importance to the macro-social level. The brand and the consumption of it, however, are not culturally neutral. When transnational companies implement brands in a cultural context this potentially has profound consequences for the cultural development. Ritzer (1993) has argued how the fast food industry, notably the diffusion of McDonald's burger chain, has had funda-mental consequences for American society as the connected rationalization processes of rationalizations fundamentally has changed the Americans' food culture. In a follow-up volume (Ritzer 1998), he tries to expand the argument by giving examples of the way this development also encompasses a number of other cultural institutions (the women's role, the dinner table as rallying ground, the understanding of work). The debate following Ritzer's (and others') work has generally tended to lead to a less pessimistic take on the bulldozing homogenization effects of globalization, by demonstrating consumer agency in producing brand meanings and usages independently of the global corporations' strategic intentions and also to processes of resistance against the cultural changes caused by 'McDonaldizations' and global branding universes. This little introductory example is an illustration of the potential importance and impact of that 'public image' of the brand, of which Gardner and Levy spoke half a century ago, and it shows how a single brand can influence and change basic cultural institutions and spark off a whole discourse on cultural change patterns.

This chapter argues that brands and branding can be seen as a central historical and institutional force that has profound impacts on the perception of the marketplace and the consumer as social categories. The term 'ideoscape' is borrowed from Appadurai (1990) who uses it to describe a set of central ideas coming out of the Enlightenment tradition (democracy, welfare, freedom, etc.) and pertaining to the construction of the modern global political environment. With the growing impact of market institutions on almost all aspects of our lives, it does not take much imagination to see 'brands' and 'branding' as part of an increasingly dominant market economic and commercial ideoscape, carried by organizations such as WTO, by marketing and management practices and by the contemporary sovereign status of the liberal market economy. As (part of) such an ideoscape, branding is becoming central to the structuring of commercial and economic activities in still larger parts of the world. It is not the purpose to 'prove' the thesis but to situate it in relation to prior research in branding and globalization and to illustrate it by drawing on other reflections on the macro-construction of market realities, notably the work of Wilk (1995), Garsten and Hasselström (2004) and Wenger (2000).

BRAND RESEARCH

It should hardly be a surprise, then, that there has been a growing managerial and academic interest in brands and the process of branding. For the past fifteen years or so, marketers and financial stakeholders have been increasingly focused on the value of brands. Mergers and acquisitions have demonstrated investors' willingness to pay large sums of money for well-established brand names and the expected portfolio of customer goodwill. Brands have become increasingly important assets, as illustrated by the focus on the concept of brand equity dating from this period. However, there has not been unequivocal support for the idea that the value of brands is increasing. Voices have been raised concerning various threats to the value and future marketing role of brands, pointing to the growing importance of private labels or weakening consumer loyalty. In addition, generalized consumer resistance and a veritable anti-branding movement has, paradoxically, become a central part in the contemporary brand universe (Klein 1999; Holt 2002). But the death of the brand has been announced prematurely before. And in the face of growing competition in global markets and rising costs and clutter in mass-media advertising, leading to demands for efficiency, integrated communication and a search for alternative communication vehicles, the presence and importance of brands has arguably never been greater globally.

Consequently, the scholarly and managerial literature on brands has flourished in the past years. A number of brand management 'gurus', local as well as global, have set the agenda for the thinking and management of brands throughout the 1990s and into the twenty-first century. Interestingly, only very sporadically has the brand management literature taken a seriously based consumer perspective on brands. The consumer is treated as the background on which the great variety of tactical and strategic brand management tools can be tried and tested, but rarely is the consumers' response to or relation to the brand in focus per se. Possibly, this is due to the fact that the same group of researchers that inspired more culturally and social constructivist-oriented approaches in consumer research also had a tendency to maintain that the discipline of consumer research should be freed from its bonds to managerial practices and become a scientific discipline in its own right (e.g. Belk 1986). Brand research might have been judged to be too closely associated with the primacy of managerial purposes.

This, however, is definitely changing. More and more alternative voices have appeared during the latter half of the 1990s, drawing attention to consumers' symbolic use of brands in their construction of group identities, meanings of everyday practices and meanings attached to personal self-images. Hence, the social constitution of brand meaning and the importance of brand narratives for the sociological and social psychological role of brands are no longer taboo for interpretivist consumer researchers (for an overview of some of these contributions, see Arnould and Thompson 2005).

Even some representatives of the more classical brand management approach are demonstrating increasing awareness of the social role of brands, at least in a micro-perspective. As argued by Keller (2003), consumer knowledge about brands is multidimensional and encompasses a wide range of references to symbolic entities that are attached to the brand, fleshing out its value: endorsers, places-of-origin, events, ingredients, company alliances, and so forth. Basically, he argues that the meaning of a brand is fundamentally linked – in the consumers' mind – to the brand's relationship to people, places, things and other brands. The counter-argument presented here is that this logic can be turned around; that increasingly, the meaning of things, places and people is created through their linkage to brands. Keller indicates this through his double arrows in the models he presents but, given his cognitive psychological focus, he fails to fully recognize the institutional power embedded in contemporary 'brandscapes' (see Chapter 12 in this volume).

GLOBALIZATION AND THE POWER OF BRANDS

> Few expressions of globalization are so visible, widespread and pervasive as the world-wide proliferation of internationally traded consumer brands, the global ascendancy of popular cultural icons and artefacts and the simultaneous communication of events by satellite broadcasts to hundreds of millions of people at a time on all continents. The most public symbols of globalization consist of Coca-Cola, Madonna and the news on CNN.
>
> (Held *et al.* 1999: 327)

Everybody seems to agree on statements such as this one; but fewer actually follow the belief up with closer investigations of the role of brands in the globalizing process as they are lived and experienced in markets all over the world. Still, as Waters (2001) points out, one of the major globalizing factors is the spreading of a canon of management discourse all over the world, which is having a profound everywhere on organizational and business practices and ideas. Brands and branding is as much part of this process as many other central strategic business concepts and practices.

Contrary to the classical Levitt-inspired approach that sees globalization as an annihilation of spatial references, the globalization of consumer culture can be seen as a plethora of spatial references. It is a process of challenge to traditional consumer cultures of predominantly local discourse from a global fragmentation (Firat 1997) of national cultural references (e.g. the presence of similar ethnic restaurants in the world's metropolitan areas) and global brands with added one or more drops of 'Americana' (McDonald's, Coca-Cola, etc.) or 'Europeana' (the Paris–Milan–London axis when it comes to a number of luxury brands). Even developing countries may today enjoy benefits from such spatial references (Anholt 2003). Thus, there is in each brand a built-in cultural reference that refers to an origin, even for 'global' brands. But this place of origin will coexist in each consumer's life with a large number of other potential spatial references. Hence, it is reasonable to recognize that modern consumer culture has multiple layers of references.

Brands, likewise, are equally complex in their meaning formation. Nevertheless, one may argue that brands are among the most significant ideoscapes in the globalization processes. They are a central metaphor for understanding marketplace actor practices in the positioning game of modern (corporate and consumer) identity formation. Consequently, a long range of collective social practices and reflections concerning identity formation are based on brands as vehicles in 'authenticating acts and authoritative performances' (Arnould and Price 2000) individually as well as in community formation (Muñiz and O'Guinn 2001).

It is not that the globalization theme has been ignored in the managerial literature; quite the contrary, since Levitt (1983) was one of the first to introduce a wider use of the notion. But the debate has focused on the presence or absence of strategic opportunities for standardizing marketing efforts, leading to an ongoing debate of standardization versus adaptation. Or the debate has concentrated more on organizational issues such as coordination problems and centralization versus decentralization. Aaker and Joachimsthaler (2000) refer to both of these traditions without actually discussing the implications of globalization processes for complexifying notions such as brand equity or brand identity. If we turn to the already-cited interpretivist and consumer-oriented brand literature, which supposedly should be more open towards the cultural complex-ities and implications of the nexus of globalization and branding, the international – not to speak of the global – dimension has been almost completely ignored, at least until work by Holt (2002) and Thompson and Arsel (2004).

Hence, most of the debate must be found outside the specifically marketing or management-oriented literature. One of the most influential critics, whose discussion of the global influence of branding and the managerial control processes attached to it took as its point of departure one particular brand and its metaphorical use as a general reference to a wide set of social change processes, is Ritzer (1993, 1998) with his McDonaldization thesis. The symbolic universe constructed by branding, and the control mechanisms installed within corporations to secure and master this symbolic universe, owes a lot to the processes of efficiency, calculability, predictability and control, which Ritzer summarizes under the term McDonaldization.

Ritzer mainly sees globalization in terms of Americanization, and links this process to the perceived economic and cultural advantages of McDonaldization. In a central passage, he argues with Appadurai's (1990: 301) contention that 'deterritorialization, in general, is one of the central forces in the modern world' since money, commodities and, one could add, symbolic expressions such as brands, incessantly flow around the world. Yes, Ritzer says, but 'while this view well describes fast food restaurants and credit cards, the "territory" from which they emanate, largely the United States, as well as the territories to which they are exported, remains of central importance' (Ritzer 1998: 12). As contemporary research in product images has demonstrated, the Westernness, Americanness or exoticness attached to consumer brands is crucial for understanding their worldwide proliferation (e.g. Ger and Belk 1996).

In a similar vein, but stressing the exploitative rather than the merely cultural effect of global brands, Canadian journalist Naomi Klein has created a(nother) global movement through her book *No Logo* (Klein 1999). Here, she argues for a growing awareness of and resistance to the power of global brands, by debunking the sometimes harsh reality of production relations and business strategies behind the alluring symbolic universes presented by diverse brands. This has led to new types of consumer resistance more specifically oriented towards brands (Holt 2002).

Obviously, many voices criticize what is seen as the exaggerated power and homog-enization effect of the global brands and argue extensively for the power of localization of global phenomena in a variety of contexts. Miller (1995) argues that even the glob-ality of Coca-Cola may be highly overestimated since, in Trinidad, the local usage and inscription of Coca-Cola in cultural patterns and practices largely overshadows the symbolic universe of the global brand. But, on the other hand, as Ritzer (1998) contends,

95

it is important to distinguish between levels and scope in terms of the power potential of local agency, and he is 'hard pressed to see McHuevos, McLaks or elegant dates at fast food restaurants as significant local variations on the homogenizing processes of McDonaldization' (p. 86).

Maybe the most fruitful take on the situation is Wilk's (1995) notion of 'global systems of common difference', indicating the existence of powerful structuring ideas and practices that are global and globalizing in themselves, but that allow for a certain degree of local variation, much like the example of the global McDonald's format with a local touch. As suggested by Askegaard and Csaba (2000) in an analysis of symbolic relations between Coca-Cola and Pepsi Cola and a local brand Jolly Cola in the Danish market, local brands may manage to hold off global brands, but they still reproduce, reinforce and promote the general system and discourse of branding and may, thereby, eventually pave the way for the 'real thing'.

The brand as a phenomenon may thus be seen as part of which Ritzer (1998) called the new means of consumption. Phenomena like chain stores, shopping malls, credit cards, Internet shopping, etc. are characterized as 'new means of consumption' – 'things owned by capitalists and rendered by them as necessary to customers in order for them to consume' (Ritzer 1998: 91). The new means of consumption take on an enchanting, sometimes religious character. The brand, although not specifically mentioned by Ritzer, has certainly taken on such a position, with many customers worshipping and devoting considerable time and energy to brand care. Brands are used to create communities (Muñiz and O'Guinn 2001), to create festivals and concerts (by sponsorship), and to add a spiritual dimension to what used to be 'merely a product'. Brands, just as the other new means of consumption do, take on religious dimensions, something which today is a deliberate part of corporate communication, motivation and identity-building strategies (Kunde 2000).

BRANDS AS A GLOBAL IDEOSCAPE

The process of globalization has been described as a compression of time and space where geographical space or landscape loses its meaning relatively compared to other structured and structuring 'scapes'. In other words, a number of social processes become more and more independent of geographical distance. Some of the most essential new structurations are the symbolic universes that consist of the global 'mediascapes' and the global 'ideoscapes' as Appadurai (1990) has labelled them. The global brands and their meaning universes constitute central elements in these mediated messages through their representations of central ideas about 'the good life', initiating new value systems and measures. The question is to what extent these global brands also initiate new 'transnational' communities (Beck 2000), and what kind of bonding the common reference to global brands provides. Global brands are not absorbed in local consumer cultural contexts through processes of direct copying and imitation of their cultures of origin, neither in transitional societies (e.g. Wilk 1998), nor in other developed consumer societies (Miller 1995). Thus globalization is not synonymous with homogenization, but rather with a plurality of consumption forms that exist more or less parallel in the different contexts.

Brands' – global as well as local – symbolic universes are definitely among the world's most powerful image-generating mediascapes, 'image-centred, narrative-based accounts of strips of reality, and what they offer to those who experience and transform them is a series of elements (such as characters, plots and textual forms) out of which scripts can be formed of imagined lives, their own as well as those of others living in other places' (Appadurai 1990: 299). But this is mainly oriented towards the content of the brands' symbolic universes. When it comes to the brand format, it is more fruitful to consider it as part of what Appadurai calls ideoscapes. As earlier stated, he explicitly refers to the political imagery of modernity, a legacy of the Enlightenment, as the central globalizing ideoscape. But, as we have seen, today the liberating forces of modernization may be perceived to reside just as much in the development of a modern business culture as in Enlightenment-based political culture. This is possibly most evident in the developmental path adopted by the newly industrialized and industrializing countries of Asia. Consequently, it can be argued that alongside the political ideoscape is an equally important business ideoscape, which profoundly transforms the economic and social activities in the world. Brands as a phenomenon and branding as a strategic practice constitute central elements in this globalizing business ideoscape.

This is where we shall return to Wilk's (1995) idea of global structures of common difference, since it very well illustrates what is meant by branding as a global ideoscape. Wilk underlines that he sees the global cultural system as one that promotes diversity in content but hegemony of form: 'Global structures organize diversity, rather than replicating uniformity [. . .] we are portraying, dramatising and communicating our differences to each other in ways that are more widely intelligible' (p. 118). A brand is such a hegemonic vehicle of diversity, a widely intelligible way of communicating a potentially infinite number of corporate, product and consumer identities.

It should be noted here, that it is not the process of signification that is new. Material culture has carried symbolic meanings in all human societies. What is changing is the introduction of the strategically and commercially produced signifier, which leads to the commoditization of not only material culture but also of the symbolic forms encapsulating it. No longer merely a cultural sign, the branding once and for all establishes the consumer good as a commodity sign, and thereby opens up for the reflexive process about the commodity–signs communicative potential that leads to the increasing focus not only on branding but on lifestyles, consumer identity projects, consumer tastes and statuses, designs and aesthetization of everyday life – in short, creating a consumer culture.

This leads to a new type of person dominating larger and larger aspects of social life: market man or *homo mercans*:

an individual oriented towards market transactions. He or she is embedded in a discourse that places prime value on the marketability of goods and services as well as sills, competencies, manners and attitudes. [. . .] Market man is forged out of the interplay between different technologies: technologies of production, which allow us to transform and manipulate things; of sign systems, which allow us to use meanings, symbols or significations; of power, which directs the conduct of individuals; and of the self, which allows us to affect our way of being so as to reach a certain state of being.

(Garsten and Hasselström 2004: 213)

Branding as a communicative form is thus instituting a new personality type and, along with that, a new community of practice (Wenger 2000), an essentialization of a (brand) language, where the cultural forms of brands and branding are made sense of retrospectively as narratives, provided of course that one actually is a member of the community, i.e. is able to master its practices (or, in other words, has brand literacy). Branding as a community of practice is simultaneously a cognitive domain that defines distinctions, objects, actors, contracts and roles that, in turn, lead to the emergence of identities (of brands, companies, consumers, etc.).

Branding as a (global) ideoscape thus provides the ideological basis for the estab-lishment of new meaning systems, new practices and new identity forms for the members of the consumer culture. It provides the logical basis for the whole idea of 'experience economy', of new distinctions between social groups, of new types of (brand) commu-nities, new central stories in people's lives and new identification patterns of both oneself and others.

These reflections can be illustrated by drawing some insights from an ongoing research project in Nepal, where the focus is on the changes in market relationships following the new practice of local producers to brand their goods. Branding, in the Nepalese context, is increasingly experienced as an imperative, both for reasons of competitiveness with export markets but also because of the changing nature of local consumers. Nepalese people in larger numbers have had glimpses into the lifestyles of the surrounding world, seen and heard presentations of new ideas and fashions and witnessed the newest technical achievements through satellite TV, 24-hour radio broadcasting and a proliferation of different newspapers and magazines. Televisions and VCRs have become standard features of urban middle-class homes all over the world. These consumers want to quench their desire for the popular foreign-branded products held in esteem as part of the canon of a modern consumer lifestyle and a little sinful transgression, both characteristics of modern consumer desire. Just as Garsten and Hasselström (2004) point out the double character of the market as both a model of and for the society, so branding in many ways is becoming both a model of and a model for symbolic relationships between human beings – witnessed by consumers' increased focus on their own lifestyles and self-projects: 'the marketed self' both as a body and as a biographical narrative.

Even though local branding in Nepal today is in its infancy, it is already spreading beyond the consumer goods sector and its imperative is felt wherever market competition is instituted. The privatization of media services attracted many producers to establish various commercial FM radio stations, making this field a highly competitive one and hence forcing the stations to engage in a brand-profiling of themselves by focusing on the various attributes of their broadcasting methods and policies in order to attract listeners. Even ancient cultural practices such as yoga centres are increasingly repositioned and branded in the market as, for example, health clubs.

Consumers' frames of reference also expand beyond the boundaries of their own lived experience through such avenues as more widespread and higher education and new travel and tourism possibilities, which, together with the mass media, increasingly demonstrate to all new members of the global consumer society the plethora of 'possible lives', that for many are, to use Appadurai's (1990) description, at the same time desirable and abhorrent, attainable and out of reach.

All these changes are bringing new awareness to both producers and consumers of the meanings attached to products and brands in a consumer society context and consequently are leading to changes of behaviour regarding the production and marketing as well as the consumption of local products. Branding has thus become a new and pervasive marketing tool for product and service industries in both the public and the private sectors. And new status systems and distinctions between the 'haves' and the 'have-nots' are instituted through never-ending spirals of consumer desire for yet another commodity sign, paradoxically leading to the realization that even in the world's poorest countries, like Nepal, Baudrillard's (1998) point that consumer society is antithetical to an affluent society in a certain way holds true.

CONCLUSION

Just as is the case with Appadurai's (1990) political ideoscape consisting of phenomena such as democracy, human rights, etc., the global ideoscape of branding is coloured with local variations depending on the market context in question. The seeming uniformity of the business vernacular covers a great variety of local dialects. Hence, the message of this chapter is not the homogenization of the world's consumer markets in terms of similar 'brandscapes', but rather the homogenization of this world's markets in terms of the consciousness of the necessity of special symbolic attributions to consumer goods in contemporary market-based economies.

The case of Nepal, even in the short rendition that can be given here, clearly demonstrates how the branding logic transforms the local competition and consumption universes and thereby constitutes an important step towards the creation of what is often called a modern consumer society. The branding process is the result of intensified competition, and it in turn brings this competition into a vast new dimension of product and brand symbolism with even more intensification as the consequence, that is unless the power is so unequally distributed in the market that a (quasi-)monopoly arises. Branding also causes a new consumer to form, a consumer who is brand conscious in the largest sense: a consumer for whom these new symbolic universes gradually become some of the most central parts of his or her identity formation, both individually and in groups.

Holt (2002) has already pointed out the 'institutional isomorphism' at stake in the impact of marketing managerial decisions on the evolution of consumer culture. Branding as a managerial institution and consumer culture are co-constitutive of each other and changes in one will generate changes in the other, not in a linear way but sometimes working in the same cultural direction, sometimes forming counter-attacks to each other. This raises the issue of the morality of the consumer good and the brand. If we are to believe the preceding arguments, there is no doubt that consumer–brand relationships in the broadest sense have a profound impact also on consumers' (as citizens) relationship to each other and, ultimately, to the society they live in and its cultural forms. This is far from a simple discussion with easily adoptable moral judgements. And though it might be the most urgent question rising from these reflections, it will unfortunately go far beyond the scope of this chapter to open it here

As indicated in the introduction, the discourse on branding has become even more dominant in recent business literature. This power of brands is also illustrated by the insight that, whereas in Gardner and Levy's (1955) days, brands were symbolic extensions of products, today products are in an increasing number of cases becoming the material extension of a brand. Brand architects and branding specialists are flooding the market with suggestions for mastering the difficult process of taming the symbolic tiger, and for making it obey in a variety of settings from single-branded products to the general corporate identity. One may suggest that this process is a reflection of a growing awareness of the world as a social and symbolic construction. Not that it is admitted by (all of) the brand experts, but the failure of branding and corporate image specialists to persuasively convey a no-nonsense message – since no-nonsense is also a symbolic position (Holt 2002) – indicates that the demon of symbolic construction of the product universe has escaped the bottle. We may not be caught in a branding frenzy ten years from now, since the branding specialists also live from renewing their symbolic catalogue, but the song remains the same.

KEY POINT

■ Brands and branding are a powerful social and cultural institution and an important vehicle of globalization – a process most visible in marketizing economies with embryonic consumer cultures.

QUESTIONS FOR DISCUSSION

1 When is the (consumer's) freedom of choice in a material way supportive of the (citizen's) freedom of choice in a political way, and when is it not?

2 On a positive note, what roles can branding play in global development?

3 What other approaches to the symbolic economy of commodities other than branding might we think of?

4 Select several brands and discuss them within the ideoscape perspective. Does it apply to these brands?

5 How does this approach complement or contradict other approaches to branding?

REFERENCES

Aaker, D. A. and Joachimsthaler, E. (2000) *Brand Leadership*, New York: The Free Press.

Anholt, S. (2003) *Brand New Justice: The Upside of Global Branding*, London: Butterworth-Heinemann.

Appadurai, A. (1990) 'Disjuncture and difference in the global cultural economy', in M. Featherstone (ed.) *Global Culture*, London: Sage: 295–310.

Arnould, E. and Price, L. (2000) 'Authenticating acts and authoritative performances: questing for self and community', in C. Huffman, S. Ratneshwar and D. Mick (eds) *The Why of Consumption: Contemporary Perspectives on Consumer Motives, Goals and Desires*, London: Routledge: 140–163.

Arnould, E. J. and Thompson, C. (2005) 'Consumer culture theory (CCT): twenty years of research', *Journal of Consumer Research* 31 (March): 868–883.

Askegaard, S. and Csaba, F. F. (2000) 'The good, the bad, and the jolly: taste, image and the symbolic resistance to the Coca-Colonization of Denmark', in S. Brown and A. Patterson (eds) *Imagining Marketing*, London: Routledge: 124–140.

Baudrillard, J. (1998 [1969]) *Consumer Society*, London: Sage.

Beck, U. (2000) 'The cosmopolitan perspective: sociology for the second age of modernity', *British Journal of Sociology* 51, 1: 79–105.

Belk, R. W. (1986) 'What should ACR want to be when it grows up?', in R. J. Lutz (ed.) *Advances in Consumer Research*, vol. 13, Provo, UT: Association for Consumer Research: 423–424.

Firat, A. F. (1997) 'Globalization of fragmentation – a framework for understanding contemporary global markets', *Journal of International Marketing* 5, 2: 77–86.

Fournier, S. (1998) 'Consumers and their brands: developing relationship theory in consumer research', *Journal of Consumer Research* 24 (March): 343–373.

Gardner, B. B. and Levy, S. J. (1955) 'The product and the brand', *Harvard Business Review* (March–April): 33–99

Garsten, C. and Hasselström, A. (2004) 'Homo mercans and the fashioning of markets', in C. Garsten and M. Lindh de Montoya (eds) *Market Matters. Exploring Cultural Processes in the Global Marketplace*, London: Palgrave: 209–232.

101

Ger, G. and Belk, R. W. (1996) 'I'd like to buy the world a Coke: consumptionscapes in the less affluent world', *Journal of Consumer Policy* 19: 271–304.

Held, D., McGrew, A., Goldblatt, D. and Perraton, J. (1999) *Global Transformations*, Cambridge: Polity Press.

Holt, D. B. (2002) 'Why do brands cause trouble? A dialectical theory of consumer culture and branding', *Journal of Consumer Research* 29 (June): 70–90.

Keller, K. L. (2003) 'Brand synthesis: the multidimensionality of brand meaning', *Journal of Consumer Research* 29 (March): 595–600.

Klein, N. (1999) *No Logo: Taking Aim at the Brand Bullies*, New York: Picador.

Kunde, J. (2000) *Corporate Religion*, London: Pearson.

Levitt, T. (1983) 'The globalization of markets', *Harvard Business Review* 61 (May–June): 92–102.

Miller, D. (1995) 'Consumption as the vanguard of history', in D. Miller (ed.) *Acknowledging Consumption*, London: Routledge: 1–57.

Miller, D. (1998) 'Coca-Cola, a black, sweet drink from Trinidad', in D. Miller (ed.) *Why Some Things Matter*, Chicago, IL: Chicago University Press: 169–187.

Muñiz, A. M. Jr and O'Guinn, T. C. (2001) 'Brand community', *Journal of Consumer Research* 27 (March): 412–432.

Ritzer, G. (1993) *The McDonaldization of Society: An Investigation into the Chancing Character of Contemporary Social Life*, Thousand Oaks, CA: Pine Forge Press.

Ritzer, G. (1998) *The McDonaldization Thesis: Explorations and Extensions*, London: Sage.

Thompson, C. and Arsel, Z. (2004) 'The Starbucks brandscape and consumers' (anticorporate) experiences of glocalization', *Journal of Consumer Research* 31 (December): 631–642.

Waters, M. (2001) *Globalization*, London: Routledge.

Wenger, E. (2000) *Communities of Practice: Learning, Meaning and Identity*, Cambridge: Cambridge University Press.

Wilk, R. (1995) 'Learning to be local in Belize: global systems of common difference', in D. Miller (ed.) *Worlds Apart: Modernity Through the Prism of the Local*, London: Routledge: 110–133.

Wilk, R. (1998) 'Emulation, imitation, and global consumerism', *Organization and Environment* 11, 3: 314–333.

Chapter 7

Brave new brands

Cultural branding between Utopia and A-topia

Benoît Heilbrunn

Imagination is good and evil, for in the midst of it man can master the vortex of possibilities and realize the human figure proposed in creation, as he could not do a prior to the knowledge of good and evil . . . Greatest danger and greatest opportunity at once . . . To unite the two urges of the imagination implies to equip the absolute potency of passion with the one direction that renders it capable of great love and great service. Thus and not otherwise can man become whole.

(Martin Buber, 'The good and evil imagination', in *Good and Evil*, 1952: 93–7)

INTRODUCTION

Brands have become an essential dimension of the so-called marketing democracy. They now represent economic entities but also sources of power and legitimacy which impose modes of thinking and behaving. A brand may be viewed not solely as a sign added to products to differentiate them from competing goods, but as a semiotic engine whose function is to constantly produce meaning and values. A brand is therefore a narrative entity that imposes itself as a natural source of ideological and biological power in the Foucaldian sense of power, which is a set of 'actions on others' actions'. Power does not act directly; it presupposes rather than annuls the capacity of individuals as agents; it acts upon, and through, an open set of practical and ethical possibilities (Foucault 1977; Gordon 1991). Thus brands now embrace most of the figurative/transfigurative activities (Kearney 1998) of human existence (from perceiving and acting to thinking and speaking). Furthermore, the ideology promoted both explicitly and implicitly by brands is also closely related to the main paradigm of consumption that equals consumption with happiness. Based on these assumptions, the chapter will now attempt to show how strong brands promote ideological and imaginative systems that are constantly based on utopian models. This means that branding ideologies borrow from theologico-political models developed since the book *Utopia* (1516) by Thomas More.

UTOPIA, YOU'VE SAID U-TOPIA . . .

Utopia is a word originating from both the Greek and the Latin, first used by Thomas More in his now classic *Utopia*. Utopia literally means 'no-where', that is a place that stands in no place, a sort of absent presence, an unreal reality, a kind of nostalgic elsewhere, an alterity with no identification. This name is therefore linked to a series of paradoxes: Amaurotus, the Capital of the Island, is a ghost city; its river Anhydris is a river with no water; its chief, Ademus, a prince with no people to govern; its inhabitants, the Aplaopolites, are citizens without a city; and their neighbours, the Achoreans, are inhabitants with no country. Utopia is thus based on a philological transformation (a sort of prestidigitation) which aims mainly at announcing the plausibility of a world upside down and at the same time to cast shadow over the legitimacy of an upright world. What are the main features of this Utopia?

- Reproducibility: the Island which is separated from the rest of the world comprises 54 cities which are all based on the same architectural model; there is a big similarity among houses in each city; the streets and houses of the city are built according to a geometrical pattern, with peasant houses and gardens which are exchanged between the citizens every ten years.
- The importance of work which is the basis of society and which creates prosperity. Stores are always full of merchandise thanks to the economy's efficiency and the rationally planned distribution system. The working system is organized in such a way that members of the commonwealth learn the craft for which they are most suited. Working hours alternate with leisure activities: six hours of the day are devoted to work, while the rest of the time is spent in healthy recreation and learning.
- The absence of possession, property and savings. There are no tailors or designers so that everyone focuses his/her attention on important things. All citizens wear the same clothes of undyed wool with distinctions only for sex or marital status. The Utopians do not value gold or silver, but use them to manufacture fetters and chamber pots.
- The two fundamental dogmas on which all Utopians agree are first the immortality of the soul and second the presence in the universe of a Providence. Utopian citizens believe in the existence of rewards and punishments after death.

UTOPIA AS REPRESENTATION AND FICTION

These patterns fill a specific function regarding reality, history and social relationships. This function is essentially a critical one whose aim is to show through the picture drawn by the utopian writer or designer, the *differences* between social reality and a projected model of social existence. The utopian representation possesses this critical power without being aware of it; the critical impact of Utopia is not the model itself, but the difference between the model and reality. But this critical discourse, which is a latent characteristic of all Utopias, is not separated from dominant systems of values and ideas: it expresses itself through the structures, the notions of those systems by which individuals represent their real conditions of existence. Utopia functions as a possible intervention of reason in the social field and is nothing else than the real, iconic or textual picture of this 'possibility'. Utopia thus has a two-sided nature; on the one hand it expresses what is absolutely new, the 'possible as such', that is what is unthinkable in the common categories of thought used by the people at a given time; it must thus employ fiction or fable to express what it has to say. On the other hand, it appears impossible for Utopia to transcend the ordinary language of a period and of a place, that is it cannot totally transgress the codes by which people make reality significant to them.

So the utopian language is a representation of an ideal mode of collective existence that at the same time must innovate to improve the existing state of affairs, and at the same time must represent this innovation through the vocabulary used by people to interpret reality. The fictional and representative power of a utopian world must be based on the ordinary system of representation. Utopia serves as a rhetorical device. It may be conceived as a metaphor whose aim is to convey across time some guiding principles of ideal societies though a criticism of existing political systems.

UTOPIA AND IDEOLOGY

Beyond this representational and fictional power lies a propensity of the utopian system to promote a strong ideology. We may then follow Marin's statements about the relationship between ideology and Utopia (Marin 1973, 1977):

1 An ideology is a system of representations of the imaginary relationships that individuals have with their real living conditions.
2 Utopia is an ideological locus: it belongs to the ideological discourse.
3 Utopia is an ideological locus where ideology is put into play and called into question. Utopia is the stage where an ideology is performed and represented.
4 A myth is a narration that fantastically 'resolves' a fundamental contradiction in a given society.

The utopian system is also based on an inner contradiction, which is structured by the category of the neutral.

TOWARDS AN IDEOLOGY OF NEUTRALITY

Utopia is a place out of place; it essentially refers to the category of the neutral (Marin 1973). What is neutral is neither true nor false, neither masculine nor feminine, neither active nor passive, neither this, neither that. Neutrality exists as a contradiction, and more essentially as a differentiation of contrary terms, which are maintained in a polemic movement. Neuter allows an impossible synthesis, a productive differentiation, and the reconciliation of an acting contradiction. Neutral is the name given to limits, to contradiction itself (Marin 1977: 51).

Neutrality could define itself in a relationship to a dynamic totality whose parts are in opposition, in position of a marked difference. Neuter functions as a conjunction of contraries. It is placed in the centre of the structure, it constitutes its organizational principle and it allows the substitution of elements in the total shape of the system. Power is what exerts itself through the potential reference of the neuter. The state for instance presents itself as neutral, and plays as an arbitrator between different parties. Utopia recuperates the unbearable neutral with a logic joining together the contradictory terms. Utopia makes it possible to think of and to formulate the contradiction signified by that notion of neutral. As a fiction, Utopia transforms contradiction into a representation. Utopia, as defined by Thomas More and as developed in many further fictional, political or philosophical texts, assumes a certain number of paradoxes.

THE ZIGZAG OF BRANDS

The representational and fictional function of Utopia may in fact very well be applied to brands. A brand always more or less promotes a critical discourse on existing products and brands, that is on a given market situation. A brand always more or less implies that what it has to offer is better or different from what already exists and what competitors offer. A brand is a kind of value offer, which can only be legitimized through the claim of a significant difference, be it material (a 'better' or 'new' product, new colours or materials, new functions, etc.) or discursive (the way the brand speaks about its products). A brand acts as a narrative programme, which must promote a system of material and discursive differences so as to justify and legitimize its existence among other brands and so as to create consumers' preference.

A brand cannot create a total innovation to avoid the risk of being rejected by the market because of an unacceptable degree of newness and strangeness; a brand must therefore communicate and build its rhetorical power on existing market codes using a psychological framework which is familiar to market actors (consumers, retailers, etc.). It means the brand should position its products using (even if it deforms them) existing market categories, existing terminology, etc. Brand innovation should thus always zigzag between the two extremes, which are pure originality and banality. A brand discourse is thus always more or less utopian by nature.

106

BIG, BING, BRAND: FROM MANAGEMENT TO GOVERNMENT

Furthermore, it can be said that the symbolic power of brands has evolved tremendously in occidental societies. In an era of 'world disenchantment' (Gauchet 1985), new ideological sources of power emerge. There seems to be a sort of displacement of current ideology sources from the theological and the political towards the economic. In a 'desecularized' context, economic entities (and mostly brands) have taken the symbolic place left empty by the retreat of the divine. Brands now pre-empt symbolic spheres that used to be the privilege of either religion or the political spheres. Among the numerous examples which could be quoted are:

- the borrowing of Judeo-Christian myths by brands: Santa Claus and its use by Coca-Cola provides a good example of this cultural and ideological borrowing;
- highly symbolic activities are now managed by economic entities: retailers like Carrefour organize social events like weddings (they take in charge wedding lists for instance), they also sell coffins (the French retailer Leclerc has created a sub-brand which provides funerary services) and attempt to exert their power as soon as a baby is born; young mothers in hospital are provided with sponsored baskets containing branded diapers, baby bottles and other baby products so as to create a strong emotional attachment towards these brands in a moment which is both symbolically and emotionally of a high significance for parents;
- the management of urban quarters or even cities might be delegated to economic entities. Disney manages attraction parks but also a whole city in the United States with its own banks and supermarkets; Disney provides its own currencies to be used in the American parks where it is possible to buy products with 'Disney dollars', etc.

There thus seems to be a radical evolution of the role of brands from management to government. Some brands have become governing brands; we understand governmentality in the Foucaldian sense as 'the conduct of conduct', that is to say, a form of activity aiming to shape, guide or affect the conduct of some person or persons. In this sense, governmentality concerns brand–consumers relationships but also more globally relations within societies. Through the power of their ubiquity, their visibility and their ability to promote endless discourse, brands shape the way we see ourselves, others and the world in general. They govern part of the way we consider our daily universe and most of our daily actions through very prescriptive discourses. We now would like to show that in order to participate in any kind of societal governmentality, brands act as utopian entities that promote a strong ideology through a series of paradoxes. This means that the dialectic category of totality is unknown to Utopia. Utopia is dominated by a postulate of anti-dialectic homogeneity: it is essentially a schizophrenic universe.

107

'HAPPINESS IS A WARM GUN'

Brands promote one of contemporary society's key values: happiness. They promote an ideology based on the infusion of happiness: the better versus the best in a context of competition, differentiation creates a type of discourse not solely based on 'think different' or 'this is better than that', but on 'this is "The" Best', as if there were no possible alternative. Differentiation, a key branding concept, only exists through the possibility to propose joy, satisfaction and pleasure which are the key values structuring the imaginary universe of consumer society. A discourse on happiness is always more or less linked to a kind of theologico-political paradigm. Utopia as a narrative on the ideal society is a good illustration of this necessary conjunction of economic, theological and political principles. Utopia is opposed to 'dystopia' which means negation and unhappiness.

Let us go back to the More's Utopia. Two kinds of philosophies are expressed here. In the book two sects with opposite values coexist. On the one hand, there are those who only believe in life after death and who renounce earthly pleasures to get immortality. They are single and do not eat meat. On the other hand, there are those who have no objection to pleasure (as long as it does not impede work) and approve of marriage because they think that procreation is a necessary duty. There is in Utopia a sort of neutral religious philosophy which is neither humanist nor Christian and which is in fact based as Marin showed on both a criticism of false pleasures (which represents in fact a criticism of nobility) and a criticism of honest pleasures (which represents a critical ethics of asceticism). There thus seems to be two kinds of values expressed in the utopian universe: first, a narrative programme based on practical and critical values, and second, a narrative programme based on life or existential values.

This dichotomy relates to the two main registers of values potentially conveyed by branding discourses. First, values linked to a narrative programme of usage, and second, values linked to a narrative programme of life. As Floch (1988) illustrated, these values may be distributed on a semiotic square that gives the potential values ascribed to brands. They are shown in Figure 7.1.

It is now time to show that brands carry inner contradictions in the sense they always more or less articulate both sides of the semiotic square. We may even say that the power of a brand lies in its ability to articulate both practical and utopian values. Brands are paradoxical entities with a doublethink approach (see this notion of doublethink in George Orwell's *Nineteen Eighty-Four*). Brands have a propensity to create solliptical universes governed by their own rules. They function as small utopian models that articulate two kinds of values, which seem at first glance contradictory. This is what we previously called the dilemma of brands (Heilbrunn 1998a). We will now have a look at four examples taken from different consumption universes.

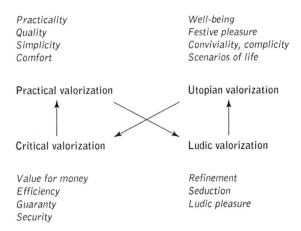

Practicality
Quality
Simplicity
Comfort

Practical valorization

Value for money
Efficiency
Guaranty
Security

Well-being
Festive pleasure
Conviviality, complicity
Scenarios of life

Utopian valorization

Critical valorization

Ludic valorization

Refinement
Seduction
Ludic pleasure

Figure 7.1 *The semiotic square of valorizations.*

Source: adapted from Floch (1988).

Club Med and the rationalization of leisure activities

Club Med illustrates the contemporary rationalization of recreational activities. Recreation can be thought of as a way to escape the rationalization of daily routines; but however, over the years these escapes have themselves become rationalized, embodying the same principles as bureaucracies and fast-food restaurants (Ritzer 1996: 21). Today's vacations are a good illustration of the rationalization of recreation. People might act 'efficiently', in a rigidly controlled manner, visiting many sights while travelling in conveyances, staying in hotels equipped with TV, VCR, Nintendo, CD players, or in rationalized campgrounds offering little or no contact with the unpredictability of nature and eating in fast-food restaurants just like those at home (Ritzer 1996: 21). These examples of which Club Med is very representative show that the escape routes from rationality have, to a larger degree, become rationalized (Ritzer 1996: 21). This is absolutely consistent with Weber's anticipation of a society of people locked into a series of rational structures, who could move only from one rational system to another.

McDonald's, food and fun

Ritzer has also very well illustrated the fact that the main principles driving McDonald's philosophy of action are contradictory by nature. They are:

- efficiency: streamlining the process, simplifying the product, putting customers to work, etc.
- calculability: emphasizing quantity rather than quality, giving the illusion of quantity, reducing processes of production and service to numbers

109

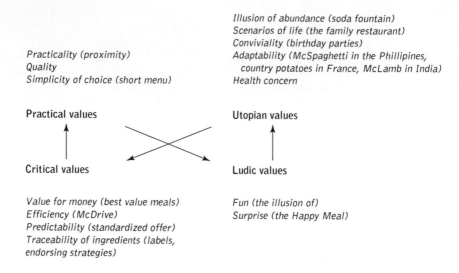

Practicality (proximity)
Quality
Simplicity of choice (short menu)

Illusion of abundance (soda fountain)
Scenarios of life (the family restaurant)
Conviviality (birthday parties)
Adaptability (McSpaghetti in the Phillipines,
    country potatoes in France, McLamb in India)
Health concern

Practical values

Utopian values

Critical values

Ludic values

Value for money (best value meals)
Efficiency (McDrive)
Predictability (standardized offer)
Traceability of ingredients (labels,
endorsing strategies)

Fun (the illusion of)
Surprise (the Happy Meal)

Figure 7.2 *Types of values defended by McDonald's.*

- predictability: replicating the setting, scripting interaction with customers, delivering predictable products and predicting employee's behaviour
- control exerted on customers, products and processes
- the appearance of leisure: along with the illusion of efficiency, McDonald's illustrates the propensity of restaurants to become theatrical and to become amusement parks for food. McDonald's uses for this purpose a ubiquitous clown, but also an array of cartoon characters to remind people that fun awaits them on their next visit (Ritzer 1996: 125).

The reconciliation of apparently contradictory values may be seen on the semiotic square on which we have tried to position all the possible material and discursive value manifestations of the McDonald's brand (Figure 7.2).

Carrefour at the crossroads of life and consumption

Carrefour is a leading French retailer, the first to launch private labels in France in 1976. The advertising campaign focused on critical values and represented a very severe criticism addressed to national brands that were said to inject useless marketing devices such as packaging brand names and other marketing devices in order to justify a price premium. The campaign established the 'produits libres' (free products) as the alternative to traditional national brands. The 'produits libres' were said to be a return to the mere substance of products, a return to the product's essence at a decent price after an era of brand over-exaggeration. Since then, the retailer's discourse has evolved towards more

- 'I am not sun-tanning, I am increasing my productivity'
- 'With Carrefour one builds up one's mental fibre day after day'
- 'Carrefour simplifies the choice of computers by selecting the best products'

- 'We are not eating, we are taking care of ourselves'
- 'Health is something one builds up every day'
- 'We are not in front of a computer, we are travelling'
- 'We are not eating, we are training our taste buds'
- 'We do not drive, we free ourselves'

Practical values

Utopian values

Critical values

Ludic values

- 'We don't fish, we recycle our savings'
- 'Everyone should have access to everything one needs to live well'
- 'Our aim is to develop healthy and tasty products at a reasonable price'

- 'I am not drinking milk, I am doing some physics'
- 'One's first car always opens up new horizons'

Figure 7.3 *Values defended by Carrefour in its institutional campaign.*

existential values. This is demonstrated quite clearly in the organization of hypermarkets which are conceived more and more as life-universes rather than sheer trade-universes. This emphasis on life-values is shown for example by the insertion of hypermarkets into shopping malls and the gradual introduction into stores of newspaper stands, cafeterias, art exhibitions and greenhouses, so that the shopping trip is conceived by customers as more of an experience than as a burden consisting of filling up a trolley. This ideological move towards utopian values may also be seen in a massive advertising campaign that is very interesting because it illustrates in fact the articulation of two value registers. On the one hand, the emphasis on practical and critical values through such claims as 'quality products', 'reliable products', 'good value for money products', etc.; on the other hand, the emphasis is laid on utopian and ludic values through such claims as 'consumption helps to construct one's life', 'one does not eat, one trains one's taste buds'. The power of the brand lies in the ability to promote both a-priori non-compatible value registers. This is exactly the kind of inner contradiction principle which makes Carrefour a utopian brand (see Figure 7.3).

Disneyland and the de-structuring of time

Disneyland is a good example of the materialization of a utopian brand's discourse through spatialization. The organization of space is a constitutive dimension of any Utopia; Utopia represents a crisis of the historical historic temporalization. Historic time as concrete and reversible is a stranger to Utopia. The realization of any Utopia means the stop of historical time. Utopian time is essentially de-structured, degraded. Time is suspended. In *Brave New World* (1932), Aldous Huxley makes a remarkable suggestion: to assure the stability of human institutions and to subtract them from time ascendancy, he suggests there be no interval between desire and satisfaction. This distortion of time as well as the materialization of utopian values is highly visible in Disneyland. Disney alienates the spectator of the park by a distorted and fantasy representation of daily life, through a fascinating picture of the past and the future, of what is strange and what is familiar: comfort, luxury, consumption, scientific progress, technological innovation, superpower, morality.

Marin has shown for instance how the material organization of Disney shows the inner contradictions of the utopian model (see Figure 7.4). The park is organized around Main Street USA, which acts as a universal operator and helps develop the narrative chosen by the park. It has three main functions: (1) a *phatic* function which allows all the possible stories to be narrated; (2) a *referential* function: through it, reality becomes a fantasy and an image, a reality; (3) an *integrative* function: this space divides Disneyland into two parts, left and right, and which relates these two parts to each other. Main Street USA also has a semantic content. It is the place where the visitor may buy, in a nineteenth-century American decor, real commodities with either real money or Disney money. Main Street USA is a locus of exchange of meanings and symbols in the imaginary land of Disney, but also the real place of exchange of money and commodity. This place is also an evocation of the past and this is an attempt to reconcile and exchange, in this very place, the past

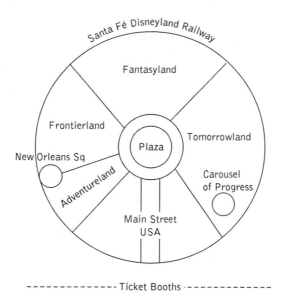

Figure 7.4 *Disneyland: a degenerate Utopia*
Source: Marin (1977).

and the present, that is an ideal past and a real present. It is the symbolic centre through which all the contrary poles are exchanged, in both the economic and semantic meanings of the term. This place assures the fictional reconciliation of several opposite worlds and by this narrative the visitor performs, enacts, reconciliation (Marin 1977: 58).

BRANDS AS TRANSFORMATIVE DEVICES

Brands are paradoxical because they promote contradictory principles, but also because they make different and often opposite levels coexist. They essentially act as transformative agents that allow contradictory principles to coincide (see Figure 7.5). These dimensions, which necessarily coexist in any brand's discourse, are the following:

- Conjunction of nature and culture: brands are technological as well as semantic devices, which transform natural ingredients into products. What is a product but a cultural and marketed object which results from an industrialization process of transformation to something which is culturally consumable, that is which fits in existing cultural categories. Be it the transformation of milk into Danone's yoghurt, the transformation of water into Evian, the transformation of leather into Hermès luggage, of cotton into a Levi's pair of jeans, or the transformation of a cow into a series of McDonald's hamburgers, branding is a magical device of transformation based on the serialization of objects, the consumability of objects. Brands make objects appear as cultural entities (culture is seen here according to Mary Douglas's perspective as an entity which provides a categorization of goods and makes categories visible). This transformation occurs through the

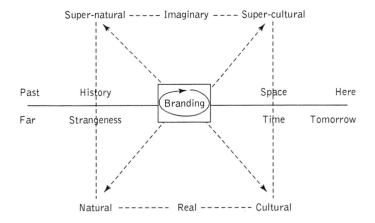

Figure 7.5 Utopian brands as transformative devices.

Source: adapted from Marin (1977).

conjunction of material processes (industrialization, technological know-how, etc.) and through discursive devices, which help to position the object in a cultural dimension through packaging, advertising discourses, etc. Furthermore, re-transforming this cultural object into a so-called natural object might reverse the process. A brand like Body Shop is a good example of this tendency to position a cultural object as a 'natural' one, legitimizing it through the use of so-called natural ingredients, or the ethical choice not to test any products on animals. A brand might therefore transform a natural object into a cultural product and this cultural product into a naturalized object again. This naturalization of culture is a widely used strategy to fit to environmental expectations (biological food products, hygiene products, etc.) but also because of a kind of nostalgia expressed by urban citizens to live closer to 'nature' and their will to consume so called 'natural products'.

- Conjunction of super-natural and super-cultural: following the culturalization of nature and the symmetrical effect, which is the naturalization of culture, exists the possibility to 'super-culturalize' products. This is especially true for technological products; the main rhetorical device of innovation is, for instance, to show a technological mastering and control of the brand which carries the ability to find new materials, new processes, new uses of the product (the Walkman is a good illustration) or even to redefine psychological categories by which consumers view the various consumption fields. The Dockers brand is a good example of such a strategy. This sub-brand of Levi's established itself by mixing-up two existing perceptual categories in the clothing industry and by proposing the 'casual-business-wear' category. In this case a brand is an super-culturalized device, which establishes new cultural categories. A symmetrical device is the super-naturalization process, by which the brand transforms through a kind of magic.

- Conjunction of the imaginary and the real as illustrated by Disneyland, where characters from imaginary universes permanently coexist with visitors or salespersons who definitely belong to the real world. Disneyland functions as a permanent exchange between spheres of the imaginary and spheres of reality.

- Conjunction of past and present dimensions: a brand exists in a temporal dimen-sion and its history gives it a legitimacy and is the main variable through which its equity is built up. Brands need continually to reassess the customers they have acquired for a long time because this time length implies the development of a know-how, the possibility to build long-term relationships with trade partners (intermediaries) and customers. To really get instilled in consumers' life, brands need to root their existence in a historical time. There is an implicit postulate by which a time period (at least one generation) is what gives brands competence, that is the ability to perform; the time dimension implicitly roots a sort of perfor-mance excellence. If one goes back to the narrative scheme which articulates the four stages of any brand–consumer relationship, it is quite obvious that the temporal dimension (in a long historical perspective) is what allows the brand to show the acquisition of competence and thus the ability to perform, thus being able, implicitly or not, to accomplish its original mission and therefore to be credited with a positive sanction, that is to be recognized as a hero (Heilbrunn 1998a, 1999).

■ Conjunction of the very distant and the here and now: a brand often shows its power to make the distant close (that is to abolish distance) and to make the close distant (through a sort of re-enchantment power over our dull daily lives). Distance is an important paradigm, be it geographical distance (the brand brings back exotic products and ingredients into our occidental sphere) or a cultural distance (the brand borrows sources of discourses from various cultural influences). At the same time, distance needs to be abolished in order to get a kind of proximity with consumers. Brands act as rhetorical devices whose function is jointly to create and to abolish distance.

CONCLUSION

Strong brands are often said to impose strong ideological discourses characterized by definite positions and by strongly established differences with competitors. Paradoxically, the opposite could also be said, that is the power of a brand lies in its ability to infuse a contradictory system of values based on the category of the neutral.

Following Louis Marin's pioneering semiotic decoding of Disneyland, the decoding of a brand's discourses and ideologies outline the strong propensity of brands to elaborate so-called utopian models that represent in fact a-topian models. By a sort of magical transformation, brands help opposite values to be reconciled. By a kind of paradox, the so-called strongly established position of a brand is transformed into an out-of-time and out-of-space position, a sort of un-position, as if it were an a-position.

KEY POINT

■ A brand function as a utopian model whose aim is to propose to consumers a sort of road to paradise. Strong brands promote ideological systems that are constantly based on utopian models, which contain a series of inherent contradictions and paradoxes which brands are able to reconcile through a narrative programme.

QUESTIONS FOR DISCUSSION

1 How are brands like Utopias? Choose several examples and analyse.
2 What are some of the symbolic powers of brands?
3 What role does happiness play in contemporary brand strategy?
4 This chapter argues that brands are transformative devices. Discuss this, using an example.
5 What are some ideological aspects of popular brands?

BIBLIOGRAPHY

Ackroyd, P. (1999) *The Life of Thomas More*, London: Vintage.

Baudrillard, J. (1992) *L'Illusion de la fin*, Paris: Galilée.

Buber, M. (1952) *Good and Evil*, New York: Scribner's.

De Certeau, M. (1985) 'Practices of space', in M. Blonsky (ed.) *On Signs*, Baltimore, MA: Johns Hopkins University Press.

Deleuze, G. and Guattari, F. (1972) *L'anti-Oedipe. Capitalisme et schizophrénie*, Paris: Éditions de Minuit.

Deleuze, G. and Guattari, F. (1980) *Mille-Plateaux. Capitalisme et schizophrénie 2*, Paris: Éditions de Minuit.

Floch, J.-M. (1988) 'The contribution of structural semiotics to the design of a hypermarket', *International Journal of Research in Marketing* 4: 233–252.

Foucault, M. (1977) *Discipline and Punish. The Birth of the Prison*, London: Penguin.

Fox, A. (1993) *Utopia. An Elusive Vision*, New York: Twayne Publishers.

Fox, S. (1984) *The Mirror Makers. A History of American Advertising and Its Creators*, New York: Vintage.

Gauchet, M. (1985) *Le désenchantement du monde. Une histoire politique de la religion*, Paris: Gallimard. Translated as *The Disenchantement of the World. A Political History of Religion*, Princeton, NJ: Princeton University Press, 1997.

Godin, C. (1997) *La Totalité 4. La pensée réalisée*, Seyssel: Champ Vallon.

Godin, C. (1998) *La Totalité 2. Les pensées totalisantes*, Seyssel: Champ Vallon.

Gordon, C. (1991) 'Governmental rationality: an introduction', in G. Burchell, C. Gordon and P. Miller (eds) *The Foucault Effect. Studies in Governmentality*, Chicago, IL: University of Chicago Press.

Gottdiener, M. (1995) *Postmodern Semiotics. Material Culture and the Forms of Postmodern Life*, Oxford: Blackwell.

Heilbrunn, B. (1998a) 'In search of the lost aura: the object in the age of marketing re-illumination', in S. Brown, A. M. Doherty and B. Clarke (eds) *Romancing the Market*, London: Routledge: 187–201.

Heilbrunn, B. (1998b) 'My brand the hero: a semiotic analysis of the consumer–brand relationship', in M. Lambkin, G. R. Foxall, F. Van Raaij and B. Heilbrunn (eds) *European Perspectives in Consumer Behaviour*, London: Prentice Hall.

Heilbrunn, B. (1999) 'When Snow White dates Mister Clean . . . !!! A narrative approach to advertising discourse'. Paper presented at the Association for Consumer Research European Conference, Jouy en Josas, June.

Kearney, R. (1998) *Poetics of Imagining. Modern to Post-modern*, Edinburgh: Edinburgh University Press.

Latouche, S. (1992) *L'occidentalisation du monde. Essai sur la signification, la portée et les limites de l'uniformisation planétaire*, Paris: La Découverte.

Levitas, R. (1990) *The Concept of Utopia*, New York: Philip Allan.

Maclaran, P. and Stevens, L. (1998) 'Romancing the Utopian marketplace: dallying with Bakhtin in the Powerscourt Townhouse centre', in S. Brown, A. M. Doherty and B. Clarke (eds) *Romancing the Market*, London: Routledge: 172–186.

Manguel, A. and Guadalupi, G. (1980) *The Dictionary of Imaginary Places*, New York: Macmillan.

Marin, L. (1973) *Utopiques: jeux d'espaces*, Paris: Éditions de Minuit. Translated as *Utopics: The Semiological Play of Textual Spaces*, Atlantic Highlands, NJ: Humanities Press, 1984.

Marin, L. (1977) 'Disneyland: a degenerate utopia', *Glyph* 1, 1: 50–66.

Paquot, T. (1994) *L'utopie ou l'idéal piégé*, Paris: Hatier.

The Project on Disney (1995) *Inside the Mouse: Work and Play at Disneyworld*, Durham, NC: Duke University Press.

Ricoeur, P. (1986) *Lectures on Ideology and Utopia*, New York: Columbia University Press. Translated in French as *L'idéologie et l'utopie*, Paris: Seuil, 1997.

Ritzer, G. (1996) *The McDonaldization of Society. An Investigation into the Changing Character of Contemporary Social Life*, revised edition, Thousand Oaks, CA: Pine Forge Press.

Ritzer, G. (1999) *Enchanting a Disenchanted World. Revolutionizing the Means of Consumption*, Thousand Oaks, CA: Pine Forge Press.

Servier, J. (1967) *Histoire de l'utopie*, Paris: Gallimard.

Tafuri, M. (1976) *Architecture and Utopia. Design and Capitalist Development*, Cambridge, MA: The MIT Press.

Thompson, J. B. (1990) *Ideology and Modern Culture*, Stanford, CA: Stanford University Press.

Virilio, P. (1975) *Bunker Archéologie*, Paris: Centre Georges Pompidou.

Chapter 8

Rethinking identity in brand management

Fabian Faurholt Csaba and Anders Bengtsson

The companies which produce all this identity work, mostly design consultancies with a bias towards graphics, but some PR companies, advertising agencies, marketing consultancies and other specialists too, have not made the job of explaining the identity activity any easier. In fact many of them have compounded the confusion.

(Olins 2003: xiii)

Branding has moved from identifying products to managing the meaning of brands through elaborate brand identity systems. Previously, the fundamental function of branding was to identify a product and an assurance of standard and quality, thereby suggesting difference from alternative offerings. Differentiation is essential in that it prevents a good or service from being reduced to a commodity, with fierce price competition as a result (Levitt 1980). Over time, new approaches to the differentiation of products and brands have appeared and had their day. Rosser Reeves's (1961) Unique Selling Proposition (USP) and Ries and Trout's (1986) positioning approach, image management (Park *et al.* 1986), and brand personality (Aaker 1997; Batra *et al.* 1993; Gardner and Levy 1955) have become part of the staple of differentiation techniques within marketing. Since the late 1980s, differentiation has mainly been discussed in terms of branding, and for about a decade, brand identity has been a key concept in dominant branding models. This shift can be seen as advancement towards a more sophisticated version of branding which suggests that, to stand out and be successful, brands must be imbued with human characteristics and traits (Aaker 1996; Kapferer 2004).

In the vast branding literature, there are many different views of brand identity. Much of the work, however, lacks theoretical depth and applies complex concepts (such as identity) in a taken-for-granted manner. Authors offer little or no acknowledgement of each other's contributions to the understanding of brand identity, which has resulted in inconsistent definitions of the concept. Even the academically informed brand management literature fails to consider the theoretical roots of identity and debates on identity in related fields, such as cultural studies, sociology and organizational studies. As a consequence, the brand management literature does not address the limitations of identity as a guiding metaphor or the assumptions behind it. If brand management theory is to account for the cultural processes in which brands are given meaning and value, then we need to rethink its concept of identity.

In this chapter, we first offer a short review of the application of the term identity in literature on brand management. We then analyse brand identity in terms of the common metaphors employed to understand brands in the management literature. The review and analysis uncovers main four assumptions about identity in work on brand management, which we hold up against conceptualizations of identity in contemporary social theory and cultural studies. Illustrating how companies increasingly find their brands involved or entangled in negotiations or politics of identity, we assert the importance of building theory of social and cultural identity into brand management. Finally, we outline four alternative ways of approaching and understanding identity in brand management.

BRAND MANAGEMENT AND THE CONCEPT OF IDENTITY

The application of the term 'identity' to branding appears to have started in the field of corporate communication. In Wally Olins's (1989) classic text on corporate identity, he discusses the meaning of identity and defines a system of three brand identity structures. In one of these structures – branded identity – brands are not presented to the public under a corporate umbrella and thus have their own identity, independent of any corporate identity. His approach to identity emerged from enquiry into the visual representations of organizations. Identity vehicles such as brand names, logos, symbols, characters, spokespeople, slogans, packages and buildings should be managed to organize and strengthen the corporation's expressions. Corporate identity had been discussed since at least the early 1970s and the term 'identity' came to the fore in organization studies in the early 1980s together with a growing interest in symbolic and ideational dimensions of organizational life (Cornelissen 2002: 259).

In marketing, Jean-Noël Kapferer was the first to launch a comprehensive framework in which he characterizes identity as the brand's innermost substance. In this version of brand identity, it is the brand strategist's task to strategically make use of the identity in order to control the meaning, aim and self-image of the brand (Kapferer 2004). In Kapferer's view, 'identity' thus resides on the sender's side and 'image', which is seen as a result and interpretation of identity, is generated in the marketplace through the decoding of messages that are sent out by the brand strategist. In this way, brand identity reflects the organization and should be found internally rather than being dictated by the public. The reason for this is that if the brand strategist allows consumers to define the brand, it is likely to lose its identity. According to Kapferer, a strong brand is created by focusing on its essence, where communication managers 'look beyond the surface for the brand's innermost substance' (Kapferer 1997: 99). Kapferer develops a 'brand identity prism', in which he subdivides brand identity into six categories, each con-

119

tributing to 'a well-structured entity' (ibid.: 105). In his later writings, Kapferer (2001) seems to change his idea about identity and argues that consumers often define brand identity and they do so in terms of concrete and tangible attributes. He continues to argue that in order to figure out whether or not an attribute is part of brand identity, it is necessary to ask the *consumers* if the brand remains intact without the particular attribute (Kapferer 2001).

Another authoritative voice in the brand identity discussion is David Aaker (1996) who offers a brand identity system that has much in common with the ideas outlined by Kapferer. According to Aaker, identity is constituted by a set of unique associations that should be defined by the brand strategist. The associations chosen by the brand strategist hence 'represent what the brand stands for' (Aaker 1996: 68). In his conceptualization of brand identity, Aaker points to four overarching perspectives: brand as product, brand as organization, brand as person and brand as symbol. Each of these contains sub-components that should be considered in articulating what the brand should stand for in the customers' minds (Aaker 1996: 78). In addition, Aaker makes the distinction between core identity and an extended identity. The core identity represents the central timeless essence of the brand, which should address issues such as the soul of the brand, the brand's fundamental beliefs and the competencies as well as the values of the organization behind the brand. The extended identity includes the core identity but is more elaborate and provides texture and completeness to the brand's identity. In an updated version of the brand identity system, Aaker and Joachimsthaler (2000) make a further distinction by introducing brand essence. The essence is part of the core identity and is the single thought that captures the soul of the brand and it should function as glue in order to hold various core identity elements together. Although Aaker and Joachimsthaler argue that a single identity across markets and products should be the starting point, they do acknowledge that a company might need to work with multiple identities. They contend that a product line or a country is not enough to justify a different identity. Rather, what should be adjusted is the execution or the interpretation of the identity. In some cases, however, it can be necessary to have different identities for the brand. When this is necessary, the brand strategists should strive to have at least a few key associations in common at the core of the identity.

In his discussion of various managerial interpretations of 'brand', Leslie de Chernatony (2001) designates identity as one of the perspectives that define what a brand is. In defining what brand identity is, he draws on corporate identity theory, and suggests, 'identity is about the ethos, aims and values that present a sense of individuality differentiating a brand' (de Chernatony 2001: 36). He further identifies five interrelated elements that generate the notion of a brand identity: brand vision and culture, positioning, personality, relationship and presentation. These identity elements are established in a process that starts with the definition of the company's vision and culture. Having defined the core ideas of the people behind the brand, it is then possible to create a positioning strategy that communicates functional attributes and a personality that communicates emotional attributes. To create a successful identity, de Chernatony

120

asserts, it is necessary for a company to have an understanding of internal relationships as well as external relationships with consumers and other stakeholders. The challenge with brand identity, according to de Chernatony, is for the brand strategist 'to find ways of blending these components [of identity] to gain maximum internal reinforcement' (ibid.: 38). Having created a strong internal brand identity through the mixing of various identity elements, it then becomes possible to communicate this essence to consumers and stakeholders.

As suggested, accounts of brand identity have been influenced by work on corporate identity and organizational identity. In some writings, the application of the metaphor of identity in the study of organizational culture has served to legitimize the concept of brand identity (Kapferer 1997). It is worth noting that use of the metaphor of identity has been explored extensively in both organizational theory and corporate identity theory and has been criticized for making questionable parallels to human identity (Balmer 2001; Cornelissen 2002; Gioia *et al.* 2000). Czarniawska (2000) has distinguished between an inherited and an emergent view of identity in organizational theory. The inherited view assumes a 'true self' that is authentic, coherent and deep, while the emergent view – influenced by postmodern thought – links identity to a selfhood that is constructed, contingent and performed. Such critical reflections on the use of the concept or metaphor of identity are scarce in the general branding literature. And surely drawing parallels between humans and the branded objects is more questionable than drawing analogies between individual and organizational self-reflective questioning (Gioia 1998). In the following section, we will look at two contributions that have reflected on epistemology in brand management, and challenged its taken-for-granted and inherited concepts.

IDENTITY AS METAPHOR IN BRAND THEORY

Recent studies have examined the root metaphors employed in discourse on branding, and reflected on their impact on the way brands are conceived of in academic and management practice (Davies and Chun 2003; Hanby 1999). Hanby distinguishes between two main streams of thought on brands, a 'classical view' of brands as a 'lifeless manipulable artefact', and a more recent view, conceiving brand as 'a living entity' (1999: 12). The classical view, which he associates with the American Marketing Association's 1960 definition of brands,[1] reflects a mechanistic metaphor and treats brands from the perspective of the brand owner. Brands are conceptualized as extended products, which can be understood in terms of their constituent elements (name, package, service, guarantees and quality features). The brand is not larger than the sum of its parts, so elements can be replaced without loss of meaning. The classical view is, in Hanby's words, 'owner-oriented, reductionist and grounded in economics' (1999: 9) and brands could be manipulated by the brand strategist to differentiate them from alternative offerings and ensure a price premium.

121

According to Hanby, the notion of 'brands as living entity' emerged in the 1980s, as positivism and objectivism relaxed their grip on the marketing discipline. This view is based on an organic metaphor and emphasizes the role brands play in consumers' lives. It describes brands as holistic entities, which have personalities, inner essences, and grow and evolve over time. Hanby suggests that Kapferer's brand identity construct represents the most complete exposition of this view (1999: 9). Hanby notes that current academic texts on brands mix the seemingly incongruent mechanistic and organic views, but he does not elaborate much on the merits or aptness of the metaphors in advancing knowledge of brands and the brand construct. He does note, however, that the organic metaphor seems more suited for differentiating brands on non-functional dimensions. His conclusive discussion is concerned with the need for companies to understand and manage their brands in accordance with the prevailing organizational root metaphors.

While not addressing brand identity, Davies and Chun offer a more detailed examination of metaphors in brand theory than Hanby. They advance three root metaphors that are each accompanied by a set of associated sub-metaphors. The three root metaphors are: brand as differentiating mark, brand as person and brand as asset. This scheme does not correspond perfectly with Hanby's, but it is clear that 'brand as living entity' and 'brand as person' are roughly similar and the mechanistic 'lifeless manipulable artefact'-view can be linked to the notion of 'brand as differentiating mark'. Under the 'brand as person'-label they trace five sub-metaphors: brand personality, brand relationship, brand loyalty, brand reputation and brand values. All suggest that human capacities and characteristics can be attributed to brands. We imbue brands with personalities, reputations and values, or we form relationships with brands and sometimes even feel loyalty towards them.

Considering Hanby's pronouncement of brand identity as the fullest expression of the brand as living entity metaphor and its significance in the work of some of the most influential brands theorists (e.g. Kapferer 2004 and Aaker 1996), we would have expected it in Davies and Chun's otherwise comprehensive analysis. But when we apply brand identity to their typology, it is clear that it complicates matters. Brand identity is a composite construct in both Kapferer's and Aaker's approaches, and their models of brand identity draw on both the 'brand as differentiating mark' and 'brand as person'-metaphors. Aaker's identity dimensions, for instance, include both 'brand-as-symbol', which is one of the sub-metaphors in Davies and Chun's 'differentiating mark' category, and 'brand-as-person'. Apparently neither Aaker nor Kapferer are concerned about mixing metaphors and perhaps the flexibility and ambiguity of their brand identity constructs are what makes their models such open and versatile tools for interpreting and managing the complex symbols we know as brands. We might argue that this equivocation obscures rather than clarifies our thinking, but as a term 'identity' can be applied to both inanimate objects and simply mean 'a set of characteristics by which a thing is recognized or known', or to individuals, referring to the 'behavioural or personal traits by which an individual is recognizable as a member of a group' or simply 'distinct personality' (*American Heritage Dictionary* 1993: 674). It is only when identity is applied to brands in the latter sense that we are dealing with metaphor per se.

On the basis of our review of the branding literature and the considerations of the metaphors behind the brand concept, we might outline four central assumptions about identity in brand management:

1 Definable by brand strategist
2 Enduring and stable
3 Essential
4 Distinction between internal–external.

Definable by brand strategist

A common theme in the reviewed literature is the idea that the brand strategist should define brand identity. In this way, it is the marketer's task to define the brand essence, the core and extended identity and communicate this to consumers in order to evoke a brand image that corresponds to the brand's identity. The underlying notion in current branding theory is that identity can be defined, observed, moulded and managed. This corresponds to a functionalistic perspective on identity as suggested by Balmer (2001) and reflects the mechanistic approach noted by Hanby (1999). It reveals that contemporary theories of brand identity are based on the idea that brand managers and conspirators act as cultural engineers (cf. Holt 2002). In this way, brand identity portrays marketers as alchemists who can mix a variety of elements in order to dictate how consumers should live their lives. Holt, of course, declares this paradigm of branding passé which has been replaced by a more subtle postmodern style of branding, which now itself is under pressure.

In the brand management literature, potential gaps between brand image and brand identity can be attributed to a variety of sources: poor market knowledge of the brand, poor brand communication, or poor understanding in the organization of the brand's essence or core identity. Failing to take charge of brand identity can cause the company to fall into an image trap, that is, following the market's interpretation of the brand (Aaker 1996). Kapferer states for instance that the brand strategist should not let the public dictate brand language. But the question is to what extent the brand strategist can dictate brand language and how much it is actually up to consumers to perform this articulation. By focusing too much on brand identity (understood as projection of management), brand strategists risk getting caught up in reversal of the brand image trap, in which the management of the brand becomes a self-absorbed and self-seductive identity game (Christensen and Cheney 2000). Recent post-positivistic enquiries have developed theoretical models which illustrate the dialectical relationship with consumers and brands (Fournier 1998; Holt 2002). This line of research shows that the meaning development of brands sometimes is out of the marketer's control. It could be argued that it is impossible for consumers to negotiate a brand's identity.

However, in a world where consumers are becoming increasingly reflexive, they do not just uncritically buy into the symbolic universe provided by brand strategists. Rather, as companies pursue their branding strategies, consumers gradually develop brand literacy and can second-guess brand managers' intentions of their brand-building efforts.

The idea that consumers think of brands in terms of personalities (Aaker 1997) or initiate relationships with brands (Fournier 1998) assumes that brands can take on human qualities and thus be seen as a case of anthropomorphism. The very idea that a brand itself – not the company behind it – is regarded by consumers as an actual relationship partner (Fournier 1998) is a highly contentious claim. This claim would seem to overturn our conventional notions of subjects and objects of consumption, of selfhood and possessions (Belk 1988). The question is whether consumers really have relationships with brands just because they describe them as *if* they were human characters. But regardless of whether we accept that brands are subject-like entities and thus can have an identity or merely are used by consumers in the process of identity formation and negotiation, it becomes apparent that we need conceptualizations that take into account the consumers' role in linking identity and brands. Whether interpreting brand personalities or being engaged in brand relationships, consumers not only respond to brand identities but also more or less actively negotiate the brand in relation to their own cultural and social identity (Fournier 1998). Therefore, it is clear that the process of defining brand identity is not the prerogative of the brand strategist. Rather, brand identity is co-produced with consumers and other stakeholders. This element of co-production of brands is particularly evident in brand communities, in which well-organized consumer groups become active carriers of brand meanings, not mere followers of the company's idea of the brand (McAlexander *et al.* 2002; Muñiz and O'Guinn 2001).

Enduring and stable

Another concern we have with existing conceptualizations is that identity is seen as an enduring and stable entity. In the brand identity literature, brand image is portrayed as volatile and shifting and consequently can provide little guidance for the marketer. Instead, brand identity is assumed to be stable, and something that the marketer must be true to. In the literature review, we have identified a variety of metaphors assuming identity to be enduring. Brand identity is increasingly discussed as the brand's DNA or as a genetic structure, which is inherent in the brand. While the academic literature is consistent regarding identity and its durable properties, it is interesting that some accounts from practitioners' branding texts critique the idea that a brand should have a fixed identity. Instead, it is suggested that brands need to have fluid identities in order to reflect the speed of innovation and the dynamic nature of the market (Grant 1999). Similarly, in organizational theory, the association of identity with stability and endurance has been challenged. The issue has become how to balance stability and fluidity in organizational identity. In seeking flexibility and negotiating rapid change, organizations cope through 'adaptive instability' in identity to maintain an appearance of stability and order (Gioia 1998).

Essential

In the literature reviewed, there are assumptions that brand identity represents the essence of a brand and constitutes a true substance. The DNA metaphor (e.g. Ryder 2003) that is commonly used furthermore emphasizes that brand identity is considered as an essential component that is embedded in the brand. As Ellwood (2000: 146) suggests, '[t]he brand DNA is the core essence of what the brand means and should be present in all formats of the brand's expression'. This way of thinking echoes the dominant idea that marketing inherited from economics (see Vargo and Lusch 2004), that value (in this context identity) is embedded within the product. However, we argue with Holt (2002) that brand identity is constructed in a dialectical process between the marketer and the consumer. In conjunction with the idea about the essential qualities, brand identity is discussed in terms of false and true identities, where it is the marketer's task to define the 'true identity' (Perry and Wisnom 2003). By arguing that identity is about the truth of the brand, the brand identity literature implicitly designates the image of a brand as a false or at least a non-true representation of the brand. However, as Christensen and Askegaard (2001) philosophically remind us, there are no true or false representations of a brand.

'Essentialism' also limits flexibility and expressivity in branding. Again, we might take a glance at organizational identity. Gioia suggests that organizations, just like individuals, maintain some ambiguity in their identity: 'If the organizational identity is not precisely pinned down, it can accommodate many different presentations and actions; it can accommodate many pursuits; and it can engage in unplanned change without appearing to violate its basic (and ostensibly enduring) values' (Gioia 1998: 23–24).

Distinction between internal–external

Another problem in existing accounts of brand identity is the assumption of a clear distinction between internal and external audiences (cf. Christensen and Askegaard 2001). In the brand management literature, identity is generally construed as a concept internal to the organization and image as the way consumers or other external stakeholders interpret brand identity. This distinction is unfortunate because the boundaries between internal and external audiences often are blurred. Furthermore, this distinction neglects the fact that not only brand strategists and internal organizational stakeholders but also consumers and other actors in the marketplace negotiate brand identity.

In summary, many of the prescriptions that emerge from the dominant discourse on brand identity seem inadequate and need reconsideration. This partly reflects the functionalistic approach and an oversimplification of the process of imbuing brands with

125

meaning. Our analysis suggests the underlying concepts of and assumptions about identity in the literature are not grounded theoretically. It might be argued that the concepts of identity in brand management are used metaphorically, and that it makes little sense to hold these assumptions about identity up against contemporary theory of human and social identity. However, in the processes of constructing and negotiating brand identity, all actors draw on collective symbols and social conventions. If companies are to create and manage brands that are relevant to the market and in tune with the changing and increasingly complex social and cultural environment, they need to understand societal processes of identity formation. In the following section, we will highlight some of the main themes in contemporary theory and debates on cultural and social identity.

SOCIAL AND CULTURAL IDENTITY THEORY

In recent years, identity has emerged as a key theme in human and social sciences. A variety of explanations for the exploding attention to identity can be stated. Giddens (1991) associates the problematic of self-identity with modernity and its defining trait of reflexivity. In traditional societies attributes relevant to identity such as lineage, gender, class and social status are relatively fixed. As these sureties are challenged, erode and turn more fluid, the self becomes a reflexive process and identity a more fundamental existential issue. As the forces of modernity impose themselves, the result is – according to Sennett – an endless and obsessive preoccupation with social identity (in Giddens 1991). The mobility, displacement and uprooting of people and mixture of cultures associated with globalization and the ensuing challenge to nation-states pose more questions concerning cultural, national, racial and ethnic identities. In the past decades, new social movements and subcultures defining themselves in opposition to dominant societal values – feminist, anti-racist, gay rights movements – have further destabilized taken-for-granted notions of subjectivity and identity. It is these critical engagements that have brought identity into focus in social and cultural theory, for as Mercer (quoted in Woodward 1997: 15) points out: 'identity only becomes an issue when it is in crisis, when something assumed to be fixed, coherent and stable is displaced by the experience of doubt and uncertainty.'

Efforts to explore and understand the nature, sources and formation of social and cultural identity do not represent a coherent body of work. The multifarious contributions draw on a wide array of research traditions and do not provide a common conceptual framework or generally agreed-upon agenda. It has even been suggested that attempts to conceptualize identity are, if not futile, then problematical since most enquiries are critical of the notion of integral, originary and unified identity (Hall 1996). For this reason, it is not useful to engage in an extended effort to define precisely what social identity is. However, this point is itself a key insight and themes that may inform analysis of identity in branding do emerge from the literature. In the following section, we will briefly review some of these themes and relate them to the theory and practice of branding.

Castells (1997) sees identity as people's source of meaning and experience, and offers a useful working definition of identity. Identity (as it refers to social actors), he argues, is the 'process of construction of meaning on the basis of a cultural attribute, or related set of cultural attributes, that is/are given priority over other sources of meaning' (Castells 1997: 6). Some of the primary cultural (or culturally constructed) attributes related to identity formation are gender, race, ethnicity, sexual orientation, nationality, generation and age. Identity building is often related to the legitimization or resistance of social domination. In the process, identity negotiation may involve struggles to redefine the position of social actors in society and transforming social structures (Castells 1997).

From this description, we can outline five assertions on the nature of social and cultural identity:

1   Identities are reflexive and dynamic, not fixed and essential (Hall 1996). To underline this dynamic and active character of identity, Hall suggests that identity is better understood as 'identification'.
2   In acts of identification, identity is discursively constituted through narratives of the self or collective 'selfhood' (Giddens 1991).
3   Given the many cultural attributes at work in identity formation and the struggles over social positions these processes entail, identity should be approached as multiple, conflicting and contested (Miller et al. 1998).
4   Identity is contingent in the sense that it is constructed in relation to others or something outside (du Gay 1996).
5   Identity is articulated through relations with particular people, places and material goods (Miller et al. 1998).

How might we bring these assertions on social and cultural identity to bear upon the theory and practice of brand management? First, as Figure 8.1 shows, the notions about identity in brand management are inconsistent with conceptions in current social theory. Assumptions about identity in the brand management field resemble those of the 'inherited view' in organizational theory as described by Czarniawska (2000). This indicates that the dominant discourse on brand management is based on outdated conceptual premises. But are the assertions on social identity really relevant to brand management? In the following section we will address this issue.

RETHINKING BRANDS AND IDENTITY

First of all, we should point out that issues of cultural and social identity are – although often under other labels – already central elements in marketing theory and practice. In the recognition of patterns of social difference affecting consumption, segmentation and

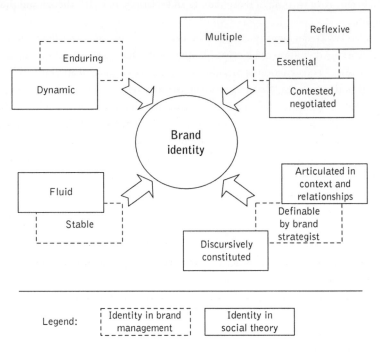

Figure 8.1 *Concepts of identity in brand management and social theory.*

targeting have always – perhaps without saying it directly – dealt with the factors that shape social and cultural identity. And so has consumer behaviour. But, as we have suggested, very few studies have directly interrogated brand identity in the light of recent theory of social and cultural identity. Fournier (1998) applies postmodern consumer theory in analysing the articulation of class, gender and generation identity in accounts of brand relationships, but identity is not a central concern. Elliott and Wattanasuwan (1998) address how brands act as symbolic resources in the construction of identity, in other words, how identity is articulated through relations with brands. Brands can help consumers establish and communicate some of the fundamental cultural categories such as social status, gender and age. Their study is primarily concerned with consumers' uses of brands and they do not confront the concept of brand identity. They suggest, however, that brands can be used to counter some of the threats to the self posed by postmodern fragmentation, loss of meaning and loss of individuality, by virtue of the consistency of meaning and significance they offer. Brand identities, they imply, must be more stable than the (post)modern consumers' identity. But the connection between questions of consumer identity formation and brand identity clearly demands further consideration.

In the practice of brand management, companies are constantly engaged with issues of social and cultural identity. Companies lacking sensitivity towards and understanding of the processes, dimensions and negotiations of identity, are getting caught up in increasingly tricky identity politics in which they risk the wrath or indifference of consumers, lost marketing opportunities and costly market failures. In recent work on brands there are numerous examples. We will briefly review examples of how companies have been drawn into confronting various aspects of the identity negation.

Goldman and Papson (1998) describe Nike's efforts in the 1980s and 1990s to alter its representation of gender identity in acknowledgement of feminist criticism of gender roles and stereotypes and the growing importance of female sports. The subject of Nike and its efforts to understand and attract women has almost become a cliché. In the movie *What Women Want* (2000), Mel Gibson stars as a chauvinistic ad executive who, after an accident, is gifted with powers to hear exactly what women think and desire. These powers are put to use in a new Nike campaign to women. The film illustrates Nike's ongoing real-life efforts to appeal to women, for instance their Nike Goddess concept, and as such illustrates challenges of handling gender issues in branding very well.

To extend its dominant position in the men's market for sports clothing in the USA to the fast-growing market for women's sports goods, Nike was forced to transform itself from a 'men's club' into an organization capable of dealing with complex and highly sensitive issues of gender representation. After experimenting with ways of avoiding representing women in terms of the 'male gaze', Nike's advertisements adopted rhetoric of self-determination and personal choice to identify with women's increasing resistance against ideologies of biological necessity (Goldman and Papson 1998: 127). Nike's embracing of images of female equality and empowerment illustrates how market demands and politics of identity directly effect decisions concerning brand identity.

American food and beverage giant Quaker Oats Company provides another example of the complexities of brand identity negotiation. Quaker Oats' challenge in salvaging its classic and iconic Aunt Jemima brand from accusations from the black community of reproducing racial stereotypes in what was seen as anachronistic, racist brand imagery (Kern-Foxworth 1994) offers an illustration of how ethnic and racial identity issues become central in branding. While the controversies surrounding Aunt Jemima depict how racial identity can cause trouble for brands, Naomi Klein's (1999) and Paul Smith's (1997) discussions of how Adidas and Tommy Hilfiger realized how to vitalize their brands with racially coded 'ghetto cool' suggest that successful brand building increasingly depends on the ability to work with cultural identity. Outside the USA, growing ethnic and racial minorities and resulting tensions mean that companies in Europe and elsewhere increasingly are forced to deal with issues of racial and ethnic identity.

Identity politics also enter branding theory and practice. Kates (2002) provides detailed insights into the role brands play in the formation and struggles over sexually defined identity in his study of gay men's brand relationships. Interest in marketing to gays and lesbians has increased greatly in recent years and gay communities have more and more openly voiced their opinions about representations of gays in advertising and branding activities. Increasingly gays have attacked companies for negative typecasting or ignoring gays. On the other hand, brands of companies who have recognized gay rights, values or life in their advertising, human resources management or other areas of management have gained great currency in the gay community. Examples include Abercrombie & Fitch, IKEA, Ford Motor Co. and Calvin Klein (see www.homoeconomics.de and www.commercialcloset.org). Of course, many companies have been reluctant to openly identify their brands with gay and lesbian imagery or causes. The balancing act of appealing to gay and liberal tastes without alienating homophobic or confusing conservative stakeholders is a tricky business. In flirting with gay segments or imagery, many companies have communicated covertly to gays or implied gayness with a wink. Michael Wilke (1997) used the term 'gay-vague' about commercials hinting at same-sex relationships through portrayals of ambiguous relationships, blurred gender distinctions, wayward same-sex glances or touching, camp/kitsch, or coded references to gay culture. Companies often deny intensions to portray gays, but undermine such statements by placing the ads in gay media.

If these examples are the sign of things to come and processes of globalization and detraditionalization further destabilize identity, it seems brand managers in the future will be forced to deal with the intricacies of identity politics and the resistance and legitimizing of identity.

Where does this leave the concept of brand identity?

In spite of the indictments of concepts of identity in brand management, our analysis does not provide a conclusive answer. We offer instead four possible ways of rethinking identity (see Table 8.1), which each represent strategic approaches to brand identity:

1   Stick with brand identity
2   Modify brand identity
3   Bypass brand identity
4   Abandon brand identity.

In our analysis, we have noted that assumptions about identity – identities are essential, stable, enduring, innate – in brand management literature are at odds with notions of identity in much of current social thought. But perhaps for the very reason that contemporary identities are reflexive, dynamic, complicated and multifaceted, brands can best act as symbolic resources for consumer negotiation of their own identities if they come to represent relatively fixed or stable meanings. In other words, in a changing world in which selfhood is constantly threatened, brands can serve as anchors of meaning. So, according to this approach, existing brand identity models are almost right, although for the wrong reasons. So we stick with them and stop worrying about the way the metaphor of identity works.

Another approach is, if social identities are fluid and dynamic, brand identities must be flexible and adaptive. In order to stay relevant and connect with (post)modern

Table 8.1   *Four perspectives on brand identity*

	Stick with it	Modify	Sidestep	Abandon
Argument	Brand identity models have almost got it right. Brand identity works, but maybe for other reasons than brand management theory suggests.	Assumptions about identity in branding are flawed, but brand identity models can be adapted to more fluid contemporary social identities.	Brand relationships or other brand-as-person metaphors, not brand identity, should inform conceptions of brand meaning.	Identity is an inept metaphor in branding, an anthropomor-phism which confuses distinctions between subjects and objects in the branding process.
Implications	To act as resources in the construction of identity in an age of postmodern fragmentation, brands must represent stable meanings. Identity models are useful for this purpose.	In an age of fluid social identities, brand identities must also be flexible. Companies must engage with negotiations of individual and collective identity, and embrace diversity and polysemy.	Ignore identity in brand management. Consumers and their relationships with brands are vital in constructing brand meaning. Brand relationship should be in focus.	Explore other approaches to brand meaning. Seek new metaphors to understand brands and inform management.

consumers and other stakeholders, brands must be engaged in the negotiations of cultural identity in society. Companies that fail to relate brand identity management to wider debates of categories of identity might also find themselves under attack for reproducing outmoded, denigrating representations. And while it can be extremely difficult to avoid offending anybody and stirring controversy (as identities are constructed against 'the Other'), a strategic approach to brand communication and management informed by a deeper understanding of cultural symbols, tensions and debates will serve companies best.

Considering the limitations of the concept and metaphor of brand identity, we might argue that it is better to avoid it or outright reject it. If we believe that the anthropo-morphism implied in brand identity is useful in capturing brand meaning, we can avoid some of the confusions that the concept of identity presents us with by using other brand-as-person metaphors, such as brand personality or brand relationships. This does not mean that we deny that social identity issues play a strong role in brand management. But, as discussed, brand-as-person metaphors and their implied anthropomorphism have limitations. The final perspective on brand identity entails a rejection of this line of enquiry and a reliance on other metaphors and approaches to the research and management of brands.

CONCLUSION

The current approaches in cultural and social theory to identity challenge many of the central premises in the work we have reviewed on brand identity. It is striking that most strategic brand management theorists share the view that brands have intrinsic values that can be found in the brand itself rather than in relation to consumers. Terms such as core, essence, soul, DNA, genetic structure, innermost substance and essential qualities reflect an idea that there exists a single true representation of the brand's identity. Such assumptions are perplexing in work that prescribes how managers actively mould and remould brands and thus points to the malleable character of brand identity. Pointing to the dynamic nature of identity, Hall (1996) argues that the term of identification is more appropriate to identity. In organizational theory, processes of member identification have long been informed by studies of the dynamical relationship between how employees' self-concepts are related to organization image and identity (Dutton *et al.* 1994). So perhaps, branding is better understood as ongoing processes of identification of, on the one hand, brands with multiple, culturally significant, contested meanings and, on the other, identification of consumers and stakeholders with brands. If management theory is to assist in better understanding and developing brands in contemporary culture, it needs to reconsider current conceptualizations of identity.

KEY POINT

■ It is critically important for managers and brand researchers to understand and apply social and cultural identity theory in approaching brands.

QUESTIONS FOR DISCUSSION

1 How did the concept of brand identity emerge?
2 What is its usefulness and appeal as a brand management tool? Discuss the appropriateness of using the term 'identity' in brand management.
3 How can companies make use of knowledge of cultural identity in order to build strong brands? Give examples of companies that have been successful in this regard.
4 What relevance do cultural attributes (e.g. gender, race, sexual orientation, nationality, etc.) have for brand management? How far does existing work on brand identity address these cultural attributes?
5 Assess the four alternative perspectives on brand identity in Table 8.1. Which challenges do they pose for brand management practice?

NOTE

1 'A brand is a distinguishing name and/or symbol (such as logo, trademark or package design) intended to identify the goods or services of either one seller or a group of sellers, and to differentiate those goods or services from those of the competitors' (quoted in Hanby 1999: 7).

REFERENCES

Aaker, D. A. (1996) *Building Strong Brands*, New York: The Free Press.
Aaker, D. A. and Joachimsthaler, E. (2000) *Brand Leadership*, New York: The Free Press.
Aaker, J. L. (1997) 'Dimensions of brand personality', *Journal of Marketing Research* 34 (August): 347–357.
Balmer, J. M. T. (2001) 'Corporate identity, corporate branding and corporate marketing', *European Journal of Marketing* 35, 3/4: 248–291.
Batra, R., Lehmann, D. R. and Singh, D. (1993) 'The brand personality component of brand goodwill: some antecedents and consequences', in D. A. Aaker and A. L. Biel (eds) *Brand Equity and Advertising: Advertising's Role in Building Strong Brands*, Hillsdale, NJ: Lawrence Erlbaum: 83–96.
Belk, R. W. (1988) 'Possessions and the extended self', *Journal of Consumer Research* 15 (September): 139–168.
Castells, M. (1997) *The Power of Identity*, Malden, MA: Blackwell.
Christensen, L. T. and Askegaard, S. (2001) 'Corporate identity and corporate image revisited: a semiotic perspective', *European Journal of Marketing* 35, 3/4: 292–315.
Christensen, L. T. and Cheney, G. (2000) 'Self-absorption and self-seduction in the corporate identity game', in M. Schultz, M. J. Hatch and M.H. Larsen (eds) *The*

Expressive Organization: Linking Identity, Reputation, and the Corporate Brand, Oxford: Oxford University Press: 246–269.

Cornelissen, J. (2002) 'On the "organizational identity" metaphor', *British Journal of Management* 13: 259–268.

Czarniawska, B. (2000) 'Identity lost or identity found? Celebration and lamentation over the postmodern view of identity in social science and fiction', in M. Schultz, M. J. Hatch and M. H. Larsen (eds) *The Expressive Organization: Linking Identity, Reputation, and the Corporate Brand*, Oxford: Oxford University Press: 271–283.

Davies, G. and Chun, R. (2003) 'The use of metaphor in the exploration of the brand concept', *Journal of Marketing Management* 19: 45–71.

de Chernatony, L. (2001) *From Brand Vision to Brand Evaluation*, Oxford: Butterworth-Heinemann.

du Gay, P. (1996) *Consumption and Identity at Work*, London: Sage.

Dutton, J. E., Dukerich, J. M. and Harquail, C .V. (1994) 'Organizational images and member identification', *Administrative Science Quarterly* 39, 2: 239–263.

Elliott, R. and Wattanasuwan, K. (1998) 'Brands as symbolic resources for the construction of identity', *International Journal of Advertising* 17, 2: 131–144.

Ellwood, I. (2000) *The Essential Brand Book. Over 100 Techniques to Increase Brand Value*, London: Kogan Page.

Fournier, S. (1998) 'Consumers and their brands: developing relationship theory in consumer research', *Journal of Consumer Research* 24 (March): 343–373.

Gardner, B. B. and Levy, S. J. (1955) 'The product and the brand', *Harvard Business Review* (March–April): 53–59.

Giddens, A. (1991) *Modernity and Self-Identity: Self and Society in the Late Modern Age*, Stanford, CA: Stanford University Press.

Gioia, D. A. (1998) 'From individual to organizational identity', in D. A. Whetten and P. C. Godfrey (eds) *Identity in Organizations: Building Theory Through Conversations*, Thousand Oaks, CA: Sage: 17–31.

Gioia, D. A., Schultz, M. and Corley, K. G. (2000) 'Organizational identity, image, and adaptive instability', *Academy of Management Review* 25, 1: 63–81.

Goldman, R. and Papson, S. (1998) *Nike Culture*, London: Sage.

Grant, J. (1999) *The New Marketing Manifesto: The 12 Rules for Building Successful Brands in the 21st Century*, London: Texere.

Hall, S. (1996) 'Introduction: who needs "identity"?', in S. Hall and P. du Gay (eds) *Questions of Cultural Identity*, London: Sage: 1–17.

Hanby, T. (1999) 'Brands – dead or alive?', *Journal of the Market Research Society* 41, 1: 7–18.

Holt, D. B. (2002) 'Why do brands cause trouble? A dialectical theory of consumer culture and branding', *Journal of Consumer Research* 29, 1: 70–90.

Kapferer, J.-N. (1997) *Strategic Brand Management: Creating and Sustaining Brand Equity Long Term*, London: Kogan Page.

Kapferer, J.-N. (2001) *Reinventing the Brand. Can Top Brands Survive the New Market Realities?*, London: Kogan Page.

Kapferer, J.-N. (2004) *The New Strategic Brand Management: Creating and Sustaining Brand Equity Long Term*, London: Kogan Page.

Kates, S. M. (2002) 'The protean quality of subcultural consumption: an ethnographic account of gay consumers', *Journal of Consumer Research* 29 (December): 383–399.

Kern-Foxworth, M. (1994) *Aunt Jemima, Uncle Ben, and Rastus*, Westport, CT: Greenwood Press.

Klein, N. (1999) *No Logo: Taking Aim at the Brand Bullies*, New York: Picador.

Levitt, T. (1980) 'Marketing success through differentiation – of anything', *Harvard Business Review* 58, 1: 83–91.

McAlexander, J. H., Schouten, J. and Koenig, H. F. (2002) 'Building brand community', *Journal of Marketing* 66 (January): 38–54.

Miller, D., Jackson, P., Thrift, N., Holbrook, M. B. and Rowlands, M. (1998) *Shopping, Place and Identity*, London: Routledge.

Muñiz, A. M. J. and O'Guinn, T. C. (2001) 'Brand community', *Journal of Consumer Research* 27 (March): 412–432.

Olins, W. (1989) *Corporate Identity. Making Business Strategy Visible though Design*, London: Thames & Hudson.

Olins, W. (2003) *Wally Olins on Brand*, London: Thames & Hudson.

Park, C. W., Jaworski, B. J. and MacInnis, D. J. (1986) 'Strategic brand concept-image management', *Journal of Marketing* 50 (October): 135–145.

Perry, A. and Wisnom, D. (2003) *Before the Brand: Creating the Unique DNA of an Enduring Brand Identity*, New York: McGraw-Hill.

Reeves, R. (1961) *Reality in Advertising*, New York: Alfred A. Knopf.

Ries, A. and Trout, J. (1986) *Positioning: The Battle for Your Mind*, New York: McGraw-Hill.

Ryder, I. (2003) 'Anthropology and the brand', in N. Ind (ed.) *Beyond Branding: How the New Values of Transparency and Integrity are Changing the World of Brands*, London: Kogan Page: 139–160.

Smith, P. (1997) 'Tommy Hilfiger in the age of mass customization', in A. Ross (ed.) *No Sweat*, New York: Verso: 249–262.

Vargo, S. L. and Lusch, R. F. (2004) 'Evolving to a new dominant logic for marketing', *Journal of Marketing* 68 (January): 1–17.

Wilke, M. (1997) 'Big advertisers join move to embrace gay market', *Advertising Age* 68: 1–3.

Woodward, K. (1997) *Identity and Difference*, London: Sage.

Chapter 9

Brand management and design management

A nice couple or false friends?

Ulla Johansson and Lisbeth Svengren Holm

INTRODUCTION

The concept of 'brand management' has grown in popularity during the last decade, fostered by practitioners and researchers alike. Branding has become the overriding concern in marketing and strategic management. Moreover, a large share of today's consumption is regarded as 'brand consumption'. Design constitutes a parallel trend, and has become a cherished concept for strategic innovation and differentiation as well as for branding. However, before design reached this position, design management emerged as a concept for integrating design into a management context.

When comparing brand management (BM) and design management (DM) we noticed that they share a similar rhetoric. Both concepts claim to deal with the strategies of differentiation and positioning, the identity of the company and/or its products and to create values for both producer and customers. Despite the interest for design, design management as a concept did not grow out of its marginal role in management. Instead, brand management absorbed the interest that occurred for design (Walton 2002).

However, the complexity of design and the design process do not seem to be caught within the brand management concept. Rather, design as an aesthetic appeal is simplified and taken for granted. There seem to be differences between brand management and design management that need to be highlighted if we are to understand the role that design can play for the creation of brands. We therefore wanted to investigate how BM and DM relate to each other, how we can understand their differences and similarities. In this chapter, we will compare the roots and concepts of BM and DM. The aim is to create a better understanding of the complexities of design, as this could also be a contribution to the development of brand management. We will do this first by discussing the historical roots of each concept. We show how they are both similar and different at the same time and how the differences are related to different professional communities that they historically relate to.

136

Our method is built upon a combination of (1) active reading of the mainstream literature in the two research fields and (2) experiences from being active researchers in design management and part of the research community of brand management. The literature we have chosen is part of courses in BM and DM and is often referred to. The analysis is based on close reading of the books and articles. We focus particularly on similarities and differences in the way the different concepts craft arguments, and how they construct theories and claims.

DEVELOPMENT OF THE DESIGN MANAGEMENT CONCEPT

The concept of design is central to the understanding of design management. Design is both a noun, the outcome, and a verb, the process. The concept of design is broad and it is affected by the contexts in which it takes place. In this section we will start with a brief description of the design concept from an industrial perspective.

From design concept to industrial design cultures

The dictionary discusses design as 'making a plan or a mental scheme for something to be realized, a preliminary idea, and a project'. This meaning relates design to planning and organizing where organization design, research design and project design are common terms. This use of design is used in *management* but not in *design management*. Instead, design refers to the mental plan for and the process of making physical objects with the use of artistic methods, like sketching and craft modelling. This relates design management to the culture of the different design communities.

All kinds of designers, industrial, fashion designers, graphic, retail designers, etc., use sketching as a central work method – and the sketching method links design to art. But designers work in different contexts, with different constraints. Priorities and trade-offs between aesthetics, functionality, ergonomics, costs, etc. are driving forces for design development in both fashion and high-tech manufacturing. For fashion-driven products, the aesthetic appeal often supersedes the functional appeal, whereas for high-tech products both ease of use and ease of manufacturing often supersede aesthetic aspects. This creates different aesthetic philosophies that are constraints and challenges. The interplay between technical, material and design development has existed as long as people have made objects.

Designers need input from the market for their design. How designers get this input differs between design disciplines. The typical methods used by industrial designers are based on observations of users in action, focusing on the actual behaviour. This is combined with a sensitive interpretation of trends in the market. The research methods could be described as ethnographically and anthropologically inspired. The methods used by all designers are based on a notion that users do not know what they want in the future because they often have a conservative view on what is good design as they are fixed on what exists today. Therefore many designers reject traditional market research methods based on questionnaire and surveys. A new design concept is based on an empathic understanding of users as well as of current forms and trends. Designers are trained in form languages and in visionary thinking about future design. This links designers to the art world, also supported by the fact that designers are mostly educated at art schools. Design is however separated from art by its link to industrial process and its economic constraints.

Another aspect not often discussed outside the design literature is the influence of the national context for the development of design. Industrial designers as a profession emerged in the USA in the 1920s and mainly after the Second World War in Europe. Whereas the American designers had diverse backgrounds from advertising to stage decorators and entrepreneurship, European designers often had a background in arts, crafts and engineering. The pioneering American industrial designers had a clear commercial attitude which is still valid. Many European industrial designers worked for industry on commercial conditions, of course, but were also engaged in building the modern society after the Second World War. This social approach was supported politically through national design councils, more or less governmentally supported (Sparke 1988). Even if the argument that industries need better designed products has been important, the societal aspect is still part of the design discourse. In Japan the government supported the foundation of industrial design education to help restore its industry and become more competitive. In the USA there was never this kind of governmental support for design.

If there are differences between the American and the European industrial designers, there are of course also differences between designers from different European countries. Italian designers have been more aesthetically and artistically driven than, for instance, German and Scandinavian designers. The latter countries have a strong engineering culture that has had a great influence on the development of industrial design.

The design philosophy in different countries and communities changes over time and is a reflection of the societal values at large. However, even if the aesthetic philosophies change over time, the principal artistic methods and judgements are similar. There are, of course, differences between individual designers but there are also deep cultural influences from the contexts where the designers come from.

The struggle within the industrial design community to define design as an equal part of the product development process – next to the engineers and marketing – made the industrial designers less 'styling' oriented but more anonymous (Forty 1986). To understand industrial design and its relation to industry and fully appreciate the design management concept we have to look at this cultural diversity as well. A summary of the factors influencing the character of the development of design objects is shown in Figure 9.1.

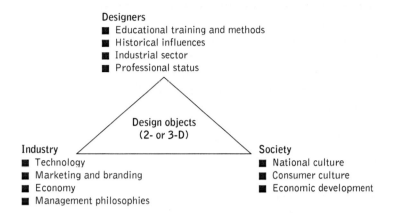

Figure 9.1   *Factors influencing the character of the design process and design approaches.*

Design as a management subject

The development of management in general did not take much notice of whether design was a special function, another way of working and seeing the products and its users, nor whether it had diversified aesthetic philosophies. The development of design management was therefore an answer to the need to make management aware of the potential to explore design methods and perspectives. The argument for the development of design management was that design would create better, more attractive and distinguished products (Lorenz 1986). Design was a hidden treasure that companies had not discovered yet (Jevnaker 2000).

When design management became an issue in the wake of the increasing interest for design in the 1980s, it consisted of two major themes: first, the integration of design into product development as mentioned above (e.g. Oakley 1990), and second, the coordination of design elements to create a coherent visual identity (Olins 1989). A third one was added due to companies' lack of knowledge about design, namely the organization of design as a function (Oakley 1990; Dumas and Whitfield 1990). Companies should integrate designers at an early stage of the process and make design investment an issue for top management. These arguments were important as many companies saw design only as a 'cosmetic' tool to make products 'look nice and different' *or* as a tool for designing the logotype (cf. Walsh *et al*. 1988; Cooper and Press 1995; Walker 1990).

This lack of notice bothered many designers. Companies missed a potential for strengthening their competitive edge. In the mid-1970s, the London Business School pioneered as a business school teaching design in the management curriculum (Gorb 1988). Despite a growing interest in the beginning of the 1990s, these attempts to combine design and management remained marginal events both in design schools and in management education. The two worlds of design and management lacked a common way of communicating and those people involved in design management teaching lacked a theoretical ground.

Management's understanding of design was a crucial factor for the degree of design's contribution to product development and a company's performance according to research (e.g. Walsh *et al*. 1988; Jevnaker 2000; Svengren 1995). The topics for research in design management that developed in the 1980s were hence to define what constitutes the value of design (Potter *et al*. 1991; Walsh *et al*. 1988).

A more theoretical relation between the discourses of design management and strategy was made by some researchers who interpreted their research findings with theories of competitive advantages (Borja de Mozota 1998), resource-based perspectives on strategic management (Kristensen 1998; Svengren 1995), organizational learning (Dumas 1994; Svengren 1995) and innovation and/or technology management (Ulrich and Eppinger 2000; Walsh *et al*. 1988). These researchers often focused on the prerequisites of management for the strategic use of design and the organization of the design function within manufacturing companies. A common line in the reasoning of these researchers was to argue for a competence to work efficiently with design competence, to know which designers to work with, i.e. design management alliances (Bruce and Jevnaker 1998). From a design management perspective the link between competence in the organization and the successful integration of design was quite obvious (e.g. Svengren 1995; Jevnaker 2000; Ulrich and Eppinger 2000).

Many publications on design management at the end of the 1980s had a focus on design rather as a communication tool for strategies and identity (cf. Olins 1989; Lawrence 1987; Pilditch 1987). The design perspective on communication was based on the notion that every company has a personality that develops over time. This in turn is the most important fundament for differentiation. Olins's book *Corporate Personality* (1978) discussed how companies developed a personality that reflected that of the founder which in turn created a unique identity that was reflected in the companies' design. This unique identity remained long after the founder was gone. Many companies, however, were ignorant about design – which created a gap between the true identity, 'who the company is' and what the design communicated, i.e. the image of the company. The company lost in credibility and image. The design should reflect the 'true' reality of the company, or at least a credible visual statement of company's strategies (Olins 1989). A logical deduction from this is that if you analyse a company's design you can also trace its identity, personality and (real) strategies or the gap between these. Design management therefore had to be concerned with the identity of the company.

Design companies who worked with the concept of corporate identity developed methods to investigate and visually analyse the identity of a company. Especially Olins (1989) argued for the need to develop the whole organization according to the identity in order to be credible and he therefore extended the concept of corporate identity to embrace also the behaviour of the people in the organization. This extension, however logical, made the concept of design management and corporate identity very complex

140

as it touched the domain of organizational behaviour and human resource, large fields in their own right.

In praxis, the argument for a credible identity led to the development of guidelines for the look of the logotype and its application on different items – letterheads, brochures, vehicles, buildings, etc. Corporate identity became very synonymous with graphic design programmes and the use of logotypes only. It is therefore not a surprise that this type of consulting came very close to the branding concept, which is also noted by Olins in a 2000 chapter entitled 'How brands are taking over the corporation'.

Parallel to this development is the outsourcing of manufacturing. When manufacturers discovered the value of the brand they logically focused their activities on how to build the brand, an aspect critically discussed for instance by Naomi Klein (2000). It was difficult to create better margins with in-house production, compared to outsourcing it to low-wage countries. The companies kept product development in-house to have control over design and the product as an expression of the brand. It therefore became obvious for industrial designers to incorporate the brand concept as the basis for their work. They no longer talk about the 'corporate identity' but rather 'the brand values' as a guide for their design work.

DEVELOPMENT OF THE BRAND MANAGEMENT CONCEPT

When brand became a strategic marketing issue in the 1980s, one of the arguments was often related to the minimal difference among products (Urde 1997). The diffusion of new technology at a high speed globally increased competition. Followers used the same technology as the leader and launched products with minor differences in design. Some companies' products were so similar that they challenged the patent rights. Many companies were eager to find other ways to protect their competitive advantages. One strategy was the emphasis on the brand name.

In the wake of increasing competition, it not only became necessary to communicate the brand name but to know how the brands were different. Due to the technological development with similar quality and standards, the image of the difference was of greater importance than the real difference. This was captured in the concept of positioning launched by advertising executives Al Ries and Jack Trout in 1982. In the highly competitive market there was certainly a need to position the company in the minds of the customers and to communicate this position with a strong and clear voice. In the marketing communication literature there was a frequent use of titles related to total and integrated communication (Holm 2002).

The brand was an obvious part of product augmentation (Keller 1998). Products were the physical solution for a functional problem as well as the status of the brand name. Marketing researchers often refer to the classical article 'Marketing myopia' by Theodore Levitt published in 1960 (1960/1975). From the 1980s, the interpretation of the 'marketing myopia', especially in the consumer market, was not only a focus on the product as a provider for a certain functional benefit but as an emotional experience. This has become stronger in the experience economy that was conceptualized in the 1990s (Pine and Gilmore 1999). The emotional associations consumers experience when buying and using the product became essential. In the marketing literature 'building the brand' was about building emotional associations (Aaker 1996) related to this experience. Functional issues just seemed out of date in the marketing literature. Increased competition on a global level as well as the development of the consumer society based on image and experience consumption brought many different complex situations that were new for companies.

Despite the development of experiences as products there is no lack of physical goods. Companies need to renew their product range quite frequently to remain attractive for a demanding consumer market. The question was if a company could use the same brand name for new products or not (Aaker 1996). To use the old, well-known brand name is a risk if the associations for the new product are not the same. One solution to this dilemma was that the link between the brand and the physical product became an issue of associations and values. According to Kapferer, the classical brand concept, where the brand is equal to the product, which in turn is equal to the promise or customer benefit, is no longer valid. Instead, the brand is endowed with features, images and perceptions (Kapferer 1992: 86). The brand receives a personality and creates a meaning where the product is just one expression of this meaning. The creation of meaning was often mentioned in the literature as the essentials of marketing and brand management (Salzer-Mörling and Strannegård 2004). As long as the meaning is coherent the company can launch quite different products, for instance Caterpillar when it launched boots.

Management models about brand management therefore focused to a high degree on how to analyse the brand's associations, the brand identity, and how to categorize and organize the brand structure for a company with a portfolio of different brand names (Aaker 1996; Kapferer 1992; Keller 1998; de Chernatony 2001). Basically these models combined marketing management models, especially marketing communication, and strategic management with the discussion about vision and mission.

The arguments for managing brands in professional and determined ways were that companies could capitalize on 'branding' from two perspectives: one was that brands could create value in the eyes of customers, which supported sales; another was that a strong brand could enhance the value of the company on the stock market. The last issue was argued for either as a protection against hostile takeover, or as creating a valuable asset when due for takeover. At a time when mergers and acquisitions increased at a high rate, branding became a valuable focus for management. The route for commercial success is to be found in the creation of brand images (cf. de Chernatony 2001). A logical consequence of this is that BM is the core in business and not only a function within marketing (Salzer-Mörling and Strannegård 2004).

The brand became regarded not only as a symbolic expression of the product, but also a symbol for the promise of certain performances of the company. The brand can be seen as an umbrella where sometimes the whole company turns into the body underneath it. Some companies, for instance Nike, went as far as to redefine itself into a 'branding-company' and as a consequence outsourced production. Even old manufacturing companies outsource, like Ford outsourced its car assembly.[1] Many companies will follow the route of Nike and Ford and become 'branding-companies' without any of the old core functions related to manufacturing or assembling.

If the notion of brand is as symbols and tools for creating a meaning to the consumption as already discussed by Baudrillard in the 1960s, the then development of brand management has taken a further leap into the heart of organizational development and strategic management (Baudrillard 1996/1968). Companies focusing on the promises of the brand will also develop an organization that can deliver these promises to ensure an adequate image. Integration between business, brand management and human resource management is therefore a necessity. 'Living the Brand is about how organizations empower and enthuse their employees' (Ind 2001: 1). The brand, hence, becomes an instrument for internal communication about the mission and the vision of the company (de Chernatony 2001). In this sense, Schultz and Hatch (Chapter 1 in this volume) identify corporate brand management as a dynamic process that includes a model for continuous adjustments of vision, culture and image. Christensen and Cheney (2000) reflect upon this as the self-autonomy of all the external communication companies do, the communication acts, advertising, etc. which reaches their own employees in the first place and is therefore an efficient tool for management.

The understanding of brand values has to be part of the culture of the organization, i.e. deeply rooted in how the organization as a collective behaves and acts. Hence, an organizational and cultural perspective on the brand management issues is a rather new topic with references to organizational identity. The concept of identity used in this discussion resembles the discussion of corporate identity in DM. Few authors have addressed both concepts simultaneously (cf. Hatch and Schultz 1997; Svengren 1995). Balmer (2001) uses the term business identity to cover all those concepts of identity that have been discussed in the last decade: corporate identity, organizational identity and visual identity.

ANALYSIS OF THE TWO CONCEPTS

When analysing the text we have used an inductive contrasting method, in order to come up with different themes where similarities or differences can be seen. We have listed these different themes that we have traced while reading and discussing the two fields. We found four main themes: (1) relation to the designed product; (2) relation to identity; (3) relation to value creation; and (4) relation to professional groups and management. This will be discussed below.

Brand management and design management in relation to the product

In brand management, the focus quite obviously has drifted away from the product as such and BM accordingly has become more loosely coupled to the product. Brands had a strong relation to physical products, especially in the field of fast-moving consumer goods. Competition in this field created a strong need for differentiation. The main tool for establishing a difference was to position the brand on the market through advertising. When brand management moves on to the corporate level the main communication tool is still advertising. It is therefore of greater interest to be creative in developing communication tools rather than the product as such. The development of media and events has not removed the classical ad as a major communication tool. In the communication perspective the brand is constructed as an immaterial and conceptual asset, related to the whole value of the company.

Design management, on the other hand, has a strong and intimate relation to the product as such. One reason for this is probably that the DM area is tightly related to designers, whose work and focus *are* the products. Designers belong to those professional groups that do not drift away from the artefacts, but rather prefer to speak *through* the artefacts. Design management was developed to reinforce the position and status of design and the designers alike, often within manufacturing companies. Another reason may be that DM has become more related to innovation (cf. Cooper and Press 2003; Keller 1998) as brand management has absorbed the communication perspective on design. Also, DM is a small academic area, intimately related to practice, with a low level of theoretic conceptualization, which in turn is a prerequisite for such a drift that has happened to design management.

Another aspect on this difference it that 'branding' has become a more general management concept, regarded as a tool for visual communication of the company's overall business strategy both internally and externally. The brand as a concept therefore has come to develop as an umbrella concept for the company – and one that has become more and more separated from the actual product offered. The outsourcing of manufacturing has further influenced this trend.

DM also claims to be related to the overall strategy of the company (Svengren 1995). But here the value is primarily built through working with the specific products and offerings as such and the experiences they relate to – making the products themselves more valuable and indirectly thereby creating wealth for the company.

Brand management and design management in relation to identity

In DM, the concept 'corporate identity' was created to highlight the need to integrate different design elements – product, graphic and environmental design. Design management arose as a function that should make sure that companies did not send diverging messages to different stakeholders. Instead, different design elements should build an orchestra and strengthen each other through a coherent visual identity of the whole company. This integration of the message – or one corporate identity – was the aim.

The discussion of 'who the company really is' was seen as another aspect of corporate identity, an aspect that referred to what was going on in organization development theories rather than marketing (Olins 1989). 'Identity', in management and organization literature, was an analytic concept used to understand 'who the organization really is' (Albert and Whetten 1985). Not that design management literature actually referred to organization theories, but the historical approach and the link to actors in the organization when discussing identity made the discussion in DM similar to the one in organization development (cf. Normann 1977). Organizational identity, unlike corporate identity, did not deal with the customer perspective. 'Corporate identity', therefore, can be seen as a concept embracing both perspectives in order to have a larger credential in the design. Both employees and customers should perceive the design as 'a true visual reflection' of the company. The link between 'corporate identity' and 'design management' was obvious for everyone that dealt with design.

The use of the identity concept within brand management is similar but the reference to organizational identity is rather new. Identity has been more related to the communication and profiling of the company – what identity did the company wish to have? BM in this sense relates to the use of identity from a strategic management perspective. What is the mission of the company and what is its vision? How can we *create* an identity that reflects the vision of the company (Aaker 1996; Kapferer 1992)?

Wally Olins and his book about corporate personality (1978) and corporate identity (1989) are often referred to within the brand management literature. A difference though is that to a great extent brand management literature primarily used marketing management as a framework. The models for brand identity that were developed in the beginning of the 1990s rarely bear any reference to the development of organizational identity within the field of organization theory.

To sum up, although the word 'identity' was used both in the brand management and the design management literature, it was based on slightly different theories, spoken by different people and different professions and thereby creating slightly different concepts.

Brand management and design management in relation to value creating

Branding has become such a well-known concept, that both in the public discourse and academia most people are well aware of the business dynamic behind a good brand – and thereby the importance of managing the brand. The way that brands have been explicitly valued in mergers and acquisitions makes it obvious that brands can have values that overrun the value of the whole company. Hence it becomes a necessity for a company in the early twenty-first century to 'manage the brand' or be part of the 'brand management discourse'. Branding has, within a short period, become not only an umbrella concept within marketing but also a financial benefit, an asset to create and manage.

Contrary to this, the explicit financial values of design and DM are more hidden. The value of good design and design management has never reached the attention related to the whole company value in the way brand management has. This is not to say that design management does not *have* such a value, but that it has not been recognized in the same way.

Intentions to prove the value of design, and hence the attempt to see the value added, have been faced with the difficulty of separating design from other product development activities. Design is perceived, and probably should be perceived, as a part of the innovation process where technicians, marketers, designers, etc. jointly add values. This is, however, contrary to branding. Branding has come to define itself as handling the totality – and then design becomes just an inseparable part of this totality.

Another result of these differences is that work with design and DM has become primarily related to costs. Work with branding has become linked to the income side and regarded more as an investment. This construction is, of course, highly artificial and even ironic. Since the character of the work as such, as well as the aim and result, in many ways is rather similar.

Brand management's and design management's relations to professional groups

Brand management is strongly related to marketing. Marketing, including corporate communication and sales, are big professional areas where BM easily can be incorporated. They are professional fields that are established as subjects at business schools. Therefore, it is understandable that they rapidly embraced 'brand management' as an activity of their own professions, and nurtured the concept as a strategic concept, something in line with the development of marketing as such. Marketing and BM have become almost equal. The development of brand equity has made not only marketers but also top management interested in brand management. In turn this means that the BM concept has strengthened marketing's organizational platform.

The situation for the discourse of DM is almost the opposite. There is no self-evident single profession to relate to. Few companies have the integrated DM embracing all design elements of the company. Each design discipline is related to a different profession or function in the company (Gorb 1988). In manufacturing companies with a product development the relation between industrial design and the product development function is self-evident. In service companies marketers are often also in charge of design (Dumas and Whitfield 1990). As advertising remains the foremost used communication tool graphic for building brands, design is subordinated as a service and tool for communication.

Most design disciplines work as consultants, be it graphic designers, fashion designers or architects. Design managers are an even smaller group, almost non-existant as a homogenous professional group. In product-based companies, design managers are sometimes industrial designers or they have an engineering background. Industrial designers are a small professional group and most product design work is done by engineers. Technicians often have difficulties embracing and understanding the need of the aesthetic design work, which is often seen as 'something extra' that they can do themselves. Marketers might have more of an understanding for the need of designers. However, they mostly work with graphic designers and more rarely with product designers.

One of the issues of DM was to highlight design as a strategic resource. This should bring design to top management's agenda and clarify not only the position of design within the company but also clarify the relation between design and the different functions within the company. Indeed, one could say that due to the importance of brands design has become part of top management's agenda.

Summary of the analysis

As we stated in the introduction, BM and DM have a similar rhetoric and claims. But there are also differences that we have discussed in the text above. The similarities and differences between brand management and design management are summarized in Table 9.1.

Table 9.1 *Comparison between the brand management and design management concepts*

Issues	Design management	Brand management
Relation to the product	Both started with a strong relation to the physical product	
	Concrete product starting point for analysis and development	Abstract associations starting point for analysis and development
	Concrete product basis for brand and identity	Abstract associations basis for brand and identity
	Closely related	Loosely related
Relation to identity	Both influence and construct the identity	
	Related to the organizational and historical development of the company	Related to the offering and target groups/market segments
	Related to the competence of the organization	Related to the strategic vision of management
Relation to value creation	Both create emotional and symbolic values for the company and the customer	
	Value creating mainly noticed through the design of the product/offering	Value creating mainly noticed through the associations of the offering

147

Table 9.1 *continued*

Issues	Design management	Brand management
	The value is seldom accounted for separately	The value of the brand is often accounted for separately
	Regarded mainly as a cost	Regarded as an investment and an asset
Relation to professional groups	Both claim to be part of top management's agenda	
	Fragmented throughout the organization	Coherent within the organization
	Closely related to manufacturing companies	Closely related to fast-moving consumer goods and services

CONCLUSIONS

Our comparative analysis shows that brand management and design management have many similarities. In fact, there are so many similarities that they might be called 'twin discourses'. However, they come from different contextual roots, they relate to different theoretical frameworks, and to different professional communities. Whereas DM emerged in manufacturing companies, BM emerged in the fast-moving consumer goods sector. Hence there are differences both in the conceptual understanding as well as in the professional performances, tools and work processes. They simply are two different conversations held in parallel and in different sectors of industry.

The main focus of design management has been on integration – both a functional and a visual integration. Identity and strategies of the company, based on the history, the actors of the company and their visions, are implemented through the design process. This notion of identity in DM relates more to organizational and strategic development as discussed for instance within strategic management literature (Mintzberg 2003; Normann 1977). This differs from the notion of identity within BM that relates more to the identity concept discussed within the marketing literature (Keller 1998). The development of the two concepts BM and DM has, therefore, not been a twin process.

Branding, despite its complexity, is directly related to the brand and its values. It can also be argued that it primarily relates to one symbolic dimension – the perception. Even if BM has become an overriding concept, it is a rather coherent concept related to the brand as a sign or symbol and to the *experienced* value of the customer. This does not mean that the management activities are easy – just that there is a conceptual coherence.

With DM the situation is somewhat different. First of all, it relates both to the activities of branding and designing, and to management. Designers are indeed part of the branding culture that emerged in the 1990s, as design is related to fashion, aesthetic appeal and symbols of consumption. On the other hand, industrial designers for instance have to deal with the aesthetic and functional experiences of the product, and also with the manufacturing, the distribution, the customer and the user situation, where the customer and the user are not the same. And all these perspectives have to be creatively interrelated and integrated. To focus only on experiences and perceptions is like focusing on the foam on the waves rather than the sea as such.

There are many research projects on the integration between engineers and marketing but less on the integration between the marketing and design professionals. Because brand management and design management share the goal of 'adding value' there is sometimes a taken-for-granted assumption among both practitioners and researchers that the integration between the design and marketing is a smooth process. However, with the different roots, tools and theoretical relations that we have demonstrated in our analysis, this is not self-evident. An area for further research is to understand what makes design a dynamic, contributing process and how this dynamic can be understood and integrated within the brand management concept.

KEY POINT

■ Branding is focused on emotional values, while design management is concerned with the balance between functional, emotional and production aspects. In the best situation the integration between brand and design will be a dynamic process and fruitful for innovations. With branding as an umbrella approach, there is a risk in treating design as a more narrow or reduced activity, or as a service to brand management – and that the potential of the design process, its creativity and dynamic, will not be recognized.

QUESTIONS FOR DISCUSSION

1 How can the holistic approach of the design process be integrated within the branding strategy?
2 How can brand managers ensure a good balance between a functional and an emotional approach to the products that a company is offering?
3 Who should in the end make the design decisions in product design, and other visual identity elements? The design manager? The brand manager?
4 Is there a rivalry between designers and marketers within companies? If yes, is it different than any other rivalry or is it actually a fruitful competition? What should be done about it, or how can that be used?

5 Designers and marketers have different educational backgrounds. Designers are for instance focused on developing their personal skill and style. In the education of marketers there is not the same issue of personal styles. Does this affect the construction of their professional identity and does this affect their relation to their work?

NOTE

1 The *Financial Times* in 1999 stated that 'the manufacturing of cars will be a declining part of Ford's business. They will concentrate in the future on design, branding, marketing, sales, and service operations' (quoted in Olins 2000).

REFERENCES

Aaker, D. A. (1996) *Building Strong Brands*, New York: The Free Press.

Albert, S. and Whetten, D. (1985) 'Organizational identity', *Research in Organizational Behavior* 7: 263–295.

Balmer, J. M. T. (2001) 'Corporate identity, corporate branding and corporate marketing: seeing through the fog', *European Journal of Marketing* 35: 248–291.

Baudrillard, J. (1996) *System of Objects*, London: Verso.

Borja de Mozota, B. (1998) 'Structuring strategic design management: Michael Porter's value chain', *Design Management Journal* 9, 2: 26–31.

Bruce, M. and Jevnaker, B. (eds) (1998) *Management of Design Alliances. Sustaining Competitive Advantage*, Chichester: Wiley.

Christensen, L. T. and Cheney, g. (2000) 'Self-absorption and self-seduction in the corporate identity game', in M. Schultz, M. J. Hatch and M. H. Larsen (eds) *The Expressive Organization: Linking Identity, Reputation, and the Corporate Brand*, Oxford: Oxford University Press: 246–270.

Cooper, R. and Press, M. (1995) *The Design Agenda. A Guide to Successful Design Management*, Chichester: John Wiley.

Cooper, R. and Press, M. (2003) *The Design Experience: The Role of Design and Designers in the Twenty-First Century*, London: Ashgate.

de Chernatony, L. (2001) *From Brand Vision to Brand Evaluation. Strategically Building and Sustaining Brands*, Oxford: Butterworth-Heinemann.

Dumas, A. (1994) 'Building totems: metaphor-making in product development', *Design Management Journal* 5, 1: 71–82.

Dumas, A. and Whitfield, A. (1990) 'Why design is difficult to manage', in P. Gorb (ed.) *Design Management. Papers from the London Business School*, London: Architecture Design and Technology Press.

Forty, A. (1986) *Objects of Desire. Design and Society since 1750*, London: Thames & Hudson.

Gorb, P. (1988) 'Introduction: what is design management?', in P. Gorb (ed.) *Design Management. Papers from the London Business School*, London: Architecture Design and Technology Press.

Hatch, M. J. and Schultz, M. (1997) 'Relations between organizational culture, identity and image', *European Journal of Marketing* 31, 5/6: 356–365.

Holm, O. (2002) *Strategisk Marknadskommunikation – Teorier och Metoder* [Strategic Marketing Communication – Theory and Method], Malmö: Liber Ekonomi.

Ind, N. (2001) *Living the Brand. How to Transform Every Member of your Organization into a Brand Champion*, London: Kogan Page.

Jevnaker, B. (2000) 'How design becomes strategic', *Design Management Journal* 11, 1: 41–47.

Kapferer, J.-N. (1992) *Strategic Brand Management. Creating and Sustaining Brand Equity Long Term*, London: Kogan Page.

Keller, K. L. (1998) *Building, Measuring, and Managing Brand Equity*, Upper Saddle River, NJ: Pearson.

Klein, N. (2000) *No Logo. Taking Aim at the Brand Bullies*, London: Picador.

Kristenssen, T. (1998) 'The contribution of design to business: a competence-based perspectives', in M. Bruce and B. H. Jevnaker (eds) *Management of Design Alliances. Sustaining Competitive Advantage*, Chichester: John Wiley.

Lawrence, P. (1987) 'Design as corporate resource', in J. Bernsen (ed.) *Design Management in Practice*, Copenhagen: Danish Design Council and Swedish Industrial Design Foundation.

Levitt, T. (1960/1975) 'Marketing myopia', *Harvard Business Review* (September–October).

Lorenz, C. (1986) *The Design Dimension. Product Strategy and the Challenge of Global Marketing*, Oxford: Basil Blackwell.

Mintzberg, H. (2003) 'Opening up the definition of strategy', in H. Mintzberg, J. Lampel, J. B. Quinn and S. Ghoshal (eds) *The Strategy Process: Concepts, Context and Cases*, Englewood Cliffs, NJ: Prentice Hall.

Normann, R. (1977) *Management for Growth*, Chichester: Wiley.

Oakley, M. (1990) *Design Management. A Handbook of Issues and Methods*, Oxford: Basil Blackwell.

Olins, W. (1978) *The Corporate Personality. An Inquiry into the Nature of Corporate Identity*, London: Design Council

Olins, W. (1989) *Corporate Identity. Making Business Strategy Visible through Design*, London: Thames & Hudson.

Olins, W. (2000) 'How brands are taking over the corporation', in M. Schultz, M. J. Hatch and M. Holten Larsen (eds) *The Expressive Organization: Linking Identity, Reputation, and the Corporate Brand*, Oxford: Oxford University Press: 51–65.

Pilditch, J. (1987) *Winning Ways: How "Winning" Companies Create the Products We All Want to Buy*, London: Harper & Row.

Pine, B. J. II and Gilmore, J. (1999) *The Experience Economy: Work is a Theatre and Every Business a Stage*, Boston, MA: Harvard Business School Press.

Potter, S., Roy, R., Capon C. H., Bruce, M., Walsh, V. and Lewis, J. (1991) *The Benefits and Costs of Investment in Design: Report DIG-03*, Milton Keynes/Manchester: Design Innovation Group, Open University and UMIST.

Salzer-Mörling, M. and Strannegård, L. (2004) 'Silence of the brands', *European Journal of Marketing* 38, 1/2: 224–238.

Sparke, P. (1988) *Italian Design: 1870 to the Present*, London: Thames & Hudson.

Svengren, L. (1995) 'Industrial design as a strategic resource', *Design Journal* 10, 1.

Ulrich, K. and Eppinger, S. (2000) *Product Design and Development*, New York: McGraw-Hill.

Urde, M. (1997) 'Märkesorientering – Utveckling av varumärken som strategiska resurser och skydd mot varumärkesdegeneration' [Brand orientation – development of brands as strategic resources and protection of brand degeneration]. Disseration, Lund University School of Management.

Walker, D. (1990) 'Managers and designers: two tribes at war?', in M. Oakley (ed.) *Design Management. A Handbook of Issues and Methods,* Oxford: Basil Blackwell.

Walsh, V., Roy, R., and Bruce, M. (1988) 'Competitive by design,' *Journal of Marketing Management,* 4, 2: 201–216.

Walton, T. (2002) 'Editorial notes,' *Design Management Journal,* 13, 3.

Part III

Consuming brand culture

Chapter 10

Symbolic brands and authenticity of identity performance

Richard Elliott and Andrea Davies

In a consumer culture people no longer consume for merely functional satisfaction, but consumption becomes meaning-based, and brands are often used as symbolic resources for the construction and maintenance of identity (Elliott and Wattanasuwan 1998). The consumer is engaged on a *symbolic project*, where she/he must actively construct identity out of symbolic materials, and it is brands that carry much of the available cultural meanings. Recent social and cultural theory has paid much attention to the 'aestheticization of social life' because it is widely assumed that the techniques used by individuals to perform their identity concern aesthetic or cultural practices and, moreover, that these performative aspects of the self increasingly constitute cultural resources or cultural capital (Adkins and Lury 1999). Featherstone (1991: 187) maintains that within consumer culture a new conception of self has emerged: 'The Performing Self', which places greater emphasis on 'appearance, display and the management of impressions'.

This chapter explores authentic and inauthentic identity performance through an ethnographic and co-operative inquiry study of the dynamics of symbolic brand communities and their consumption of brands. Through a focus on style subcultures and the consumption of fashion brands and music we show how identity is performed, how authenticity is communicated and recognized and how consumers learn 'to get it right' as they move from novices to a respected member of the subculture.

BRAND COMMUNITIES

The seminal study of Muñiz and O'Guinn (2001) defined a brand community as a non-geographical community based on a set of structured relations between admirers of a brand. They demonstrated that three brands – Ford Bronco, Macintosh and Saab – had groups of consumers who shared not just ownership of the brand but three traditional markers of community: shared consciousness, rituals and traditions and a sense of moral responsibility. Shared consciousness relates to the perception that 'we sort of know one another' even if they have never actually met. This triangular relationship between consumer, consumer and the brand is a central facet of a brand community. There is also a sense of brand-users being different from other people, and this extends into the concept of legitimacy, which differentiates between true members of the community, and more marginal consumers who might buy the brand but for the 'wrong' reasons. In this sense, in-authenticity of group membership is defined by failing to truly appreciate the culture, history, rituals and traditions of the community.

NEO-TRIBES

A more temporary and fragmented form of social grouping is that based on the metaphor of tribal communities arranged around consumption. Cova and Cova (2001) argue that neo-tribes are inherently unstable, small scale and involve 'shared experience, the same emotion, a common passion', but unlike a brand community the tribe is characterized by a 'volatility of belonging' which means that homogeneity of behaviour and formal rules are eschewed. A tribe is defined as a network of heterogeneous persons, in terms of age, sex and income who are linked by a common emotion. In fact, individuals can belong to more than one neo-tribe and can vary dramatically in the extent of their tribal affiliation. Whatever the depth of their affiliation with the tribe, they still consume not only branded skates but also symbolic brands such as tribal magazines and tribal T-shirts. Authenticity amongst the neo-tribal members is about authoritative performances of significant cultural display (Arnould and Price 2000), where a key issue is to separate ritual from everyday life.

SUB-CULTURES

A more stable and structural social grouping is that of the subculture, predominantly based on geography, age, ethnicity and social class. Class-based subcultures have traditionally been located within a framework of social resistance and reaction against dominant hierarchies of control. Historically this perspective has been used to explain the emergence of such subcultures as the Teddy boys, Punk Rockers and Hippies. Most of the studies of subculture identify social class and particularly the powerlessness of the working class as the main catalyst for the developments of these subcultures (Goulding *et al.* 2002).

However, increasingly, subcultural spaces are becoming sites of creativity and self-expression for both male and female participants from all social backgrounds. Subcultural activity is important for the construction and expression of identity, rather than cells of resistance against dominant orders. It is also important to recognize that subcultural choices are also consumer choices involving brands of fashion, leisure and a wealth of accessories, which speak symbolically to members of the group. A key issue amongst these symbolic brand communities is the authentic performance of style.

THE EMBODIED SELF AND STYLE

Style is comprised of a combination of dress and the way in which it is worn, where the body has become the site for identity (Entwistle 2000). Studies of youth subculture have shown the importance of the body in defining membership of a group and communicating it both within and outside the group. Hebdige (1979) describes how the 'cool' body style of the Mods distanced them from their lower-class environment of high-rise flats and low-status jobs. Similarly, Willis (1975) describes how the identity of 'hard' masculinity sought after by motorbike Rockers was articulated not just by the display of tough leather clothes but by a body posture of 'toughness'. Thus, subcultures produce their own particular social and consumption practices.

AUTHENTICITY OF PERFORMANCE

Thornton (1995) draws attention to the importance of 'authenticity' in the performance of identity in what she calls 'taste cultures', where people can develop 'subcultural capital' through authentic displays of 'cool'. The vital role played by authentic performance was identified in Nancarrow and colleagues' (2002) study of 'style leaders' that drew on Pountain and Robins' (2000) analysis of cool as requiring the bodily expression of 'ironic detachment'.

Goffman (1969) uses a dramaturgical metaphor to discuss the performance of identity, what he calls 'face work'. The emphasis is on the body as a crucial part in a competent performance, constantly signalling to others and reading the signals of other subcultural members. Thus authentic performance is both transmission and reception of culturally appropriate actions.

AN ETHNOGRAPHIC AND CO-OPERATIVE INQUIRY STUDY OF STYLE SUBCULTURES

To explore the dynamics of symbolic brand communities and their consumption of fashion brands, we developed a research group of participants who agreed to work with us on a co-operative inquiry (Heron and Reason 2001). The participants are 16 to 21-year-old students at a college in a city in south-west England. The city supports a standard range of high street branded clothing stores, clothing boutiques, sports and surfing clothes shops, second-hand (retro) and charity clothing stores.

The eight-month ethnographic research centred on stylish individuals and their friendship networks and comprised of participant-observation, video diaries, individual interviews and focus groups. In addition, some informants captured real-time style performances on video and then explained their interpretations to us. Being stylish was self-defined. Our informants expressed their interest in fashion, clothing and style in response to posters and flyers. Each participant quoted below is described in the terms they used to locate themselves in the style subcultures.

The performance of style

All participants identify themselves as 'Alternative'. They explain that the alternative subcultural style is distinct and set apart from 'Normals' and 'Townies/Trendies'.

> There's really, like, a fine line between them [Gothic and Alternative]. They're not like two separate groups completely, they kind of merge as one. You know like Goth and Townie is completely different. Goth and Alternative are very, very similar, and so it's really, well almost as one. But there's a slight difference. If you took it to the extreme [extreme Goth] then they'd be completely different. But regular [Goth or Alternative] people, they're roughly the same.
>
> Chris, Gothy Skater

Within the alternative style subculture there are micro-groups of style distinction, notably Goth, Metaller, Mod, Punk, Grunger, Skater, Surfer, Stoner, Hippie and EMO-Indie. The alternative style is far from homogeneous and our participants found it easy to locate the differences or subcultural style distinctions.

> Sophie's quite Punky and Laura's quite Gothy, I suppose. Sophie's boyfriend's quite Punky. Jodie and everyone, they dress Indie just baggy jeans and jackets and stuff they don't really dress it up. A few of my friends are quite Gothic. Yes, although I have Townie friends, but I don't really go out with them . . . So Sophie's [is the one] with the pink hair . . . Colourful, it's like quite young like Powerpuff and Hello Kitty and stuff. Vibrant. I don't think, I don't know, I've never seen her wear black. Gothic's are obviously quite black. Indies always wear, like, baggy jeans and a jacket. Like Jodie and everyone in the house is quite Indie. Terry, [and] Dan, that's in the band Bratt, they're quite Punky. And Terry used to be in the band, and he was really Punky. Dino's quite, he's not into Drum and Bass anymore but he looks like a Drum and Bass skater boy like visors and baggy T-shirts.
>
> Kirsty, Grunger

Brake (1985) suggests that style — composed of possessions, postural expressions, and argot and its delivery — communicates the degree of commitment to the group and opposition to the dominant cultural values. We found that young people followed the logic of their style habitus by playing according to culturally determined style codes and it was through the repeated and routinized enactment of these style codes that identities were performed. The logic of 'collective individuality' was an overarching key theme for all alternative-style micro-groups, and style repertoires formed the material resources rich in these subcultural meanings or style codes.

Style repertoires and style codes

We found that knowledge and performance of a style repertoire increased subcultural capital and perceived authenticity. Competence in the style repertoire endowed legitimacy as a subculture member. Incompetence highlighted a fake (staged authenticity) and the inauthentic. We found that membership would remain marginal and could lead to exclusion if the style performances were not improved.

Clothing and store brands, music bands and leisure venues are the material bases for enacting style codes. They form a style repertoire, an assemblage of material resources, used as props to support actions and behaviours that communicate style identity and membership. Skaters, Punks, Goths, Metallers, EMO-Indie and Grungers have clothing brands that are distinctive to their style group. For the Skater it is baggy Bleublot branded-trousers, training/sport branded-shoes (Dc's, Vans or Raw) and baggy T-shirts or jumpers that are key to their clothing distinction. For Metallers, a clothing repertoire of a rock band's T-shirt and black leathers were standard. Children's cartoon-branded merchandise we were told enabled Punk distinction. Sophie (Girlie-Punk) and Pippa (Scruffy Punk) describe the variety of accessories and cartoon brands they use to perform their punk identities:

> That's the poster on my door, it's about the size of me. Do you recognize them? Yeah it's the Power Plus Girls, PPG. They're cartoon characters but I like them for like the merchandise and stuff, *its stuff that people like me just like*. I like little retro kind of things like that, like Hello Kitty, Upsadaisy, Emily Strange, heard of Emily Strange? I kind of like it. I'm kind of like girlie pop punky, you know. People who like that tend to be, you know. You see them all round college. They all have the bead bracelets, which they make themselves. They all tend to look like . . . Hello Kitty T-shirts and stuff.

> Sophie, Girlie-Punk

> . . . this girl last night was wearing a Flat Stanley T-shirt, do you remember the book? Its this guy called Stanley and he gets squashed in the night by a pin board and he's called flat Stanley and his brother makes him into a kite and stuff. It's really good. And like Danger Mouse and stuff like that, its just kind of funky. Oh and Ghostbusters, all that kind of stuff.

> Pippa, Scruffy Punk

159

Allegiance to, and being seen in, culturally accepted store brands enabled our participants to perform their style. Shops and shopping are indicators of belonging to a different habitus and are used as markers of subcultural boundaries. There were three independent retail brands that all our participants agreed conferred an alternative-style distinction. The three stores, the Real McCoy, Pete's Place and the Blue Banana, are given significant emphasis in their shopping repertoires. These store brands are not located on the main shopping thoroughfare and would be difficult for the uninitiated to geographically locate. We were told that to shop here you were showing your individuality (alternative-ness) by not shopping on the high street. You also had to compose your style from the merchandise available in these stores rather than take a given 'catwalk' or 'trendy fashion' look. The clothes were also described as 'real' and it was their style heritage as either second-hand clothes from an earlier style-era or their status of not being transient high-street fashion that was important. Interestingly, for all our participants shopping in these stores was an expression and recognition of social collectivity – we were told that these were the stores where people like them shopped.

> That [pointing to a photo of the Blue Banana Shop] is where I got these jeans from and that's where I got my eyebrows done. If I want something that's alternative I go in there . . . there are like fishnet tights and some socks and things. There were like funky belts. There were guy belts, I think that might be a guy belt [pointing to a retail display in the photograph] . . . it's like black with silver studs . . . and that's the place I got my leather jacket from. That's like where you can get 'real' clothes from. It's quite popular. If you want something that's a bit old fashioned or like that's a really old leather coat. That's what they do [pointing to a photograph of The Real McCoy shop], like second-hand leather clothes. That's where you go if you want a leather coat, really. Or, well they do sell some baggy jeans but not very many. If you wanted like suede trousers or something you would go there, you wouldn't get them in a normal shop.
>
> Chris, Gothy Skater

H&M, the popular discounter of trendy fashion in Europe, was the only high-street fashion brand considered to be acceptable and common to all alternative-style repertoires. Because H&M sells a very wide range of clothing and has a quick turnover of fashion lines it guaranteed to our participants that both the clothing items purchased and their shopping activities in the store would be accepted as 'individual' or 'original' rather than mass-produced or standardized. We were told that you have to seek out and find interesting items among the almost overwhelming variety of clothing available at H&M, and that, despite being a well-known high-street retailer, it was unlikely that you would see another person wearing the same clothing item as you.

Pubs and clubs are 'sites of social centrality' (Hetherington 1998) where competent performance in culturally specific behaviours and actions were tested and flaunted. The style repertoire for alternative groups included music gigs (live performances) or local pubs but did not include the city's nightclubs or café bars, which were identified as venues for Trendies and Townies.

> But I got a picture of this to show you what more Townie girls look like. They're . . . kind of like people that go clubbing and with tight jeans and tight tops on . . . and they like going clubbing a lot, they hang out in Yes bar and Metzo's, places like that. Do you know where Yes bar is? It's by the college, they hang out there, Metzo, Casbar, you know, fashionable places. Generally with wooden floor-type places, really sleek, places that are less pub-y and more café bar.
>
> Chris, Gothy Skater

Our participants emphasized that it is not enough just to know which clubs and music gigs were in the style repertoire. For a competent performance it is important to be seen at and talk about the right venues, music gigs and bands:

> There's people who say, 'Oh, yes, I love Slipknot' I find that, there's people that I see in Exeter that I've never ever seen at a gig, so I think 'well you dress like it, but do you actually like the music?' I suppose that the music does come with it, it's more so with this music. The music is a big part of it. You go to gigs and people associate you with doing that sort of thing.
>
> Kirsty, Grunger

Style codes and distinctions extend to the behaviours and actions appropriate for different meeting venues and music. Georgina, for example, describes the different types of dancing (Moshing) expected from style groups. She explains that Gothic dancing is 'Pogo-ing' or 'Pitting', Metallers tend to headbang and often fight, while Punks 'Skang':

> And they [the Cavern] have like a bar, but mostly it's like the Moshing area.
>
> *What's Moshing?*
>
> There are different types of Moshing. There's like Pogo-ing which is just kind of jumping up and down. There's Pitting which is like you get a circle first and then people kind of run at each other. Well the circle kind of opens up out of the ground and then people kind of run into it. You get that at a lot of [music] festivals. You get big fights pits going on, it's really scary, especially with the big guys. It's just like 'ahhh!!!' so when you do get like a couple of the old-style skinhead metallers and they're like well into fighting. Like I'd rather stay out of that if I can. It can get a little bit violent. And then there's Skanging which is what the punks do. It's, kind of, just like jumping around and kind of putting their arms up high and going like this with your arms [putting them up and then bring them down to your knees in a hammer-type action] which is bizarre as well. Yes people just have a dance as well but mostly it's Moshing, I think. Kind of like, kind of like a cross between jumping and

161

headbanging at the same time. And then you get a Mosh pit which is like really tight, big [groups of] people. It's kind of all jumping together and it's like the music and stuff.

Georgina, Smart/Casual Goth

Style repertoires as local systems of knowledge

Style codes are continuously made and re-made, and appropriate identity performances for each style subculture are re-negotiated and changed by members. Legitimacy and competence in identity performance comes from knowing and often directing the changing repertoire of cultural actions. For example, several of our participants told us how their meeting venues had changed. Sophie explains how a new pub, the Hole in the Wall, was added to the style repertoire:

> And, like, we've also tended to go, like, like, recently, like, in the last 6 months, we go to the Hole in the Wall. It's just a pub. You know, you go for a couple of drinks. But then we go to, like, the Cavern, or whatever. But the Hole in the Wall's a fantastic place just to socialise. I've met so many people from there. That's where I met Jodie and everyone. But you just go along. You just talk to everyone.

Sophie, Girlie-Punk

Sophie is a more marginal member of the alternative group compared to several of our other study participants. Kirsty, for example, also told us about the Hole in the Wall pub and the Cavern as venues in the style repertoire but she described to us how the repertoire has been more recently re-negotiated and that now a new bar had been added. Sophie, a more marginal member, is not aware of this change. This represents a micro-political act of status claiming where Kirsty has been able to negotiate and establish a reputational position greater than Sophie.

> Hole in the Wall [a bar]. It's very exciting. It's where we always go now. It's like, you don't say, 'I'll meet you at whatever time' because you know you'll go there and there'll be loads of people there so yeh go there and then we'll come here [The Cavern] . . . it's quite Alternative. It's not, like if you went to Mint [a Townie bar and club] or somewhere everyone will like look at you like. In there [the Hole in the Wall bar] everyone's casual and my friends that are Gothic can go there and not feel, like, people will shout at them . . . We always think that, we say to ourselves, 'Why do we come here? Why don't we go somewhere else?' And then we think things like, 'Not everyone will be there'. And so now it's, kind of Bar Bomba as well. Everyone's, kind of moved to Bar Bomba slowly but it has to get around for everyone to go there instead.

Kirsty, Grunger

Style group members once aware of the accepted repertoire never question or challenge its contents. Rather it is accepted as a matter of taste distinction. The repertoire as such is not linked or in touch with what is happening in other subcultural style groups who also situate themselves as alternative, Punk or Gothic for example. What became clear from our participants' stories is that the style repertoire only has meaning and subcultural capital in the local context. They are local systems of knowledge, and to recognize the dynamic and local bases of cultural codes further exposes the inadequacies and problems of traditional approaches to market segmentation.

Authenticity in style performance

'Wearing the style like a second skin' or being 'natural' with the style was a recurrent theme. Our participants explained to us that an authentic style performance is natural, obvious and ordinary. It is implicit and should go unnoticed. To wear a style effortlessly was one way in which 'naturalness' and authenticity are conferred on the wearer.

> I don't try, even though I'm alternative, I don't try and look really, really different. Like, Sophie, when she goes out she looks really different. She's like Punky and stuff but I think I just fit in [to the alternative scene], really . . . Like when I was in year 8 it was more trying to be it. So loads of bracelets and stuff. I suppose by year 11 and especially going college now, you just relax into it. So, we just throw on, like, whatever's in your wardrobe which is like old . . . I suppose it's grown up rather than all the bracelets which is trying to be so.
>
> Kirsty, Grunger

Kirsty's story emphasizes that to consciously construct a style worn day-to-day is artificial and contrived rather than natural and authentic. To be authentic a style should 'come naturally' rather than be worked at.

In becoming members of a subculture we need to develop competence in the performance of appropriate cultural codes. The boundaries of a subcultural world are 'transgressed and rendered visible through "overperformance" of appropriate behaviour' (Horton 2003). Over-performance was an experience shared by many study participants when they began dressing differently. As aspiring or would-be style-alternatives they were in an initially strange subcultural world and their transition from a peripheral or marginal member to full membership was a process of trial and error.

Errors in their style performances made the style codes and repertoire explicit. It helped them to learn about style codes but their errors also made their performance contrived and inauthentic. We were told that 'trying too hard' was a common type of over-performance. It made the performer appear obvious rather than going unnoticed. Too many or too obvious style symbols were common mistakes which resulted in an exaggerated style performance. Georgina and Pippa explain:

> Well when I came to college I kind of wore . . . I got into wearing skirts, and more Gothy stuff . . . What you might call mini mosher. And then I got into the more

163

romantic Goth, fishnet tights and skirts and corset tops and I've got this pair of tights which I've cut the crutch out of and the feet off and wore them as sleeves, which I kinda like . . . I kind of faded out of that into kind of more normal [Goth] clothing, more smart casual.

Georgina, Smart/Casual Goth

. . . people that try too hard don't look right either. Like Dave's walkie thing. If they do that but they're trying too hard, they just look really like a duck! Rather than doing it subconsciously.

Pippa, Scruffy Punk

The nuances of the style repertoire were made explicit to our participants when they realized that their style performance was not received as authentic. Our participants had to learn which clothes to buy for each subcultural style group. Often as a novice they mixed up clothing from one subcultural alternative style with another but the most extreme transgression of the clothing repertoire is to mix Townie or Trendie clothing brands with an alternative look:

why didn't someone say to me – 'Soph, you look like a muppet!'. 'Cos the whole of year 10, I walked round school in my Alesso jacket [Townie sports brand] and my trendy shoes and like those spiky bracelets. I was like – 'Oh yeah, everyone wears those spiky bracelets I have to go and get one of those'. How bad was that! Spiky bracelets are so punk and then I'm wearing like a sports jacket. My year was full on Trendy, like full on Townie. The year above us there was like a group of about ten Punks and Goths, like full on. I see them round college now and they're really nice to me and I'm like – 'Oh yeah, hiya!' And they must think – 'god you were a muppet!'

Sophie, Girlie-Punk

It is not just what clothes to wear. All these aspects of the style repertoire need to be performed naturally and with ease to be accepted as authentic. One mistake in any aspect of the style repertoire blows the performance. As Chris explains 'it's the whole package'. A common story our participants told us was about supporting the wrong band or not honing the correct dance/band combination. Sophie lied to her boyfriend when she realized that she is supporting the wrong band:

And it's really funny because when I was going out with my ex, who was friends with, like, Rose and all that lot, and I told him how I was going to see a Sun 41 gig and it's really sad, I know I shouldn't have done it. He was, like, 'Oh, my God!!', because he was into, like, really heavy bands like Marilyn Manson and all that. Really heavy metal bands. And I was like . . . And I lied. And I was, like, 'Well, I'm seeing a man there'. I suppose [it was] my best friend, and her little brother and his friends.

I said, 'Oh, yes, it's because we're taking my friend's brother along'. So, it was, like, they made me feel embarrassed because that's what, because I was going to see them.

Sophie, Girlie-Punk

But Sophie soon finds that she understands the style repertoire much better and is able to use her subcultural capital to establish the legitimacy of an outsider:

I said to Dan, 'She's such a wannabe!' He's like 'No she's not.' And, like, when Dan told her I liked No Doubt [a band] she was like, 'Oh yeah, I love No Doubt.' There was one day she came in and she was like, 'Oh Dan, I bought JLo's new album.' You so don't do that if you like No Doubt. JLo, you know? I mean God!

Sophie, Girlie-Punk

Transgressing the subcultural style repertoire positions individuals as a novice or an aspiring subcultural member. Their performances are not considered natural and obvious. They are noticed rather than unnoticed. Our participants' stories show that immersion over time in a shared subcultural space produces more appropriate forms of performance and competence. They are able to increase their subcultural capital and re-negotiate their reputational position within the subcultural world.

What was also very clear was that our study participants were not equal in their subcultural capital. Some of them belonged to one style subculture, such as Gothic or Skater or Punk, while others were affiliated to the alternative style generally but had not aligned themselves with a specific micro-style group. An initial reading may suggest that there are malleable boundaries among style groups and that it is acceptable or legitimate to perform style identities within the 'Alternative-style' as long as there is no transgression to a Townie or Trendie style repertoire. This is not the case. Authenticity requires a commitment to one micro-style. Individuals who mixed and merged micro-styles were tolerated but were seen as more marginal members or novices who were still learning the style habitus. For example, to regularly (daily) change subcultural style was seen as a superficial dress choice rather than a lived way of being. Pippa explains how Rachel changes her style but how her friend Sorrel is cool and authentic despite the fact that her dress is very different everyday. The key is that Sorrel's varied dress is within the Punk repertoire rather than across several alternative subcultural styles:

Is Rachel, like, the same?

Not really, I think she'd kind of like to be. She wears, like, some baggy stuff but then other times she has a complete change and wears, like, tight jeans and tight tops and stuff and I'm, like, 'That's completely different to what you were wearing yesterday!' She kind of likes everything. I don't know, she kind of doesn't have a particular style. She wears quite a lot of other things which is quite good.

Pippa, Scruffy Punk

165

In contrast her friend Sorrel is authentic:

> she changes her clothes quite a lot, they're all in the same type but she wears like big baggy trousers one day and then the next day she'll wear a little dress. But they all stay in the sort of punky area, she wears like stripy tights and stuff. She always manages to look really cool.
>
> Pippa, Scruffy Punk

Sophie, describes herself as Girlie-Punk, but explains some of her worries and concerns. She does not feel that she is really accepted by alternative people. She both refers to alternative style subcultures as 'us' and also 'them'. Her subcultural status is less than clear. She explains:

> Because you're like into Punky music and stuff everyone assumes that Punks have got to look a certain way. And because I sometimes wear that look and because I sometimes wear arty clothes, I think people think – 'Oh she must be like a wannabe because she wears all sorts' . . . I think people don't like how I am because I wear all sorts, clothes. Like today I'm surf, I can be Punky and I can be quite like arty, you know. I don't know why people have to stick to it, like a certain look. It's so cliquey.
>
> Sophie, Girlie-Punk

For these same reasons Trendies, who follow high-street fashion trends, are seen as inauthentic and described as 'wannabes'. Wannabes do not wear style naturally or as a second skin. They are considered to be trying to be a style rather than being it and a perceived commitment or permanence to a style is important for authenticity. Participants expressed their annoyance and anger with the recent appropriation of subcultural style by high-street fashion and music stores:

> But yeah, usually kids get into it for like six months and then . . . or it comes into fashion. It came into fashion last year to dress in black and be a bit gothy. But you can tell when they're not really [Goth] . . . 'cos they're like . . . I suppose a lot of the stuff last year which was a bit gothy was a bit more spangly than anyone would actually wear if they were a really Goth . . . I suppose it is quite easy to tell if they are. Usually it's whether they're into it for the long term or whether they're just like – I'm going with the fashion. So you can tell really.
>
> Georgina, Smart/Casual Goth

Goffman (1969) maintains that the performer must believe in the action, must believe in the part being played. Failure to believe in the performance is what Sartre (1956) meant by 'bad faith', a form of self-deception. Kirsty, a Grunger, explained to us what it felt like when she went to a Trendie bar and needed to moderate her style so she didn't stand out too much and her reflections on dressing like an alternative Goth.

Like, sometimes we go Townie clubbing . . . we go to, like, Jojo's in the Mint [a Townie nightclub and bar] and then we just go Rococcos [a Trendy nightclub], but I don't like it. I dress up a bit more. Not, like, trendy, just, like a skirt or something with a just a black top. Not that alternative, but they look alright . . . I think sometimes I should dress up but I just don't feel comfortable . . . But if I had sort of a Goth's clothes, I'd feel so embarrassed and like you'd walk differently wouldn't you. Like really inward, and your head down and stuff. Really scared and you'd probably see that it wasn't them. Same as if I put my cousin's like Townie clothes on and stuff, I'd feel really funny, I wouldn't want to go out anywhere!

Kirsty, Grunger

Kirsty feels uncomfortable in performing another style or transgressing her Grunger style code of scruffy often dirty-looking second-hand retro clothes. She finds it difficult if not impossible to pretend authenticity. She explains that she cannot believe herself as authentic and recognizes it as a form of self-deception. We were told that the style performances that our informants believed to be authentic and which were also reinforced by others as style authentic enables them to feel integrated with their style group. They felt that they belonged and described themselves as 'regular' and feeling 'comfortable' within their style.

DISCUSSION

Thompson (1995: 210) describes the self as a *symbolic project*, which the individual must actively construct out of the available symbolic materials, materials that 'the individual weaves into a coherent account of who he or she is, a narrative of self-identity'. Our participants emerge as creative consumers searching for identity through the consumption and utilization of fashion and music. We have only just begun to explore the complexity of the dynamics of the self, the extent to which the symbolic meaning of goods can be used as resources for the construction and communication of identity (Elliott and Wattanasuwan 1998) and the role played by brands in the process. The use of brands to cohere, manage and delimit social groupings and the processes involved in the negotiation and re-negotiation of brand meanings stresses that the symbolic project of self is contained and attempted within a cultural context.

Identities and style micro-cultures are not fixed entities but are observed by researchers as they are poised in transition between positions (Hall 1992). Our participants talk about learning to perform their style. They are aware of their novice position or staged authenticity and seek to become true or style authentic. Subcultural codes and style repertoires are also shown to be local and dynamic, constantly being formed and re-formed as taste distinctions, and to this extent for many participants authenticity is desired but almost always unachieved. The performed-self is poised between 'who I am' and 'who I want to be', it is neither one nor the other, and it is

167

never complete. We are beginning to recognize and elaborate a third position, a position in and between, the 'self in-between'. It is never fixed, it is always moving, always in the middle, always 'becoming' but never achieving totality or coherence (Deleuze and Parnet 1987). By attending to the authenticity of performance and focusing on recording changes and mutation in the subcultural codes and style repertoires of symbolic brand communities we have begun to observe identity construction as a process and have begun to appreciate the dynamics and tensions of self as 'becoming-being' (Hardt 1993). The performance of style repertoires as subcultural capital are immanent dimensions of becoming-being. It makes us sensitive to the fact that we so easily and readily view identity(ies) as in some way fixed, stable and coherent rather than recognize that what we view as the self is merely one moment in time in a dynamic process of always becoming. This has implications for our use of ethnographic and interpretive research methods to examine how individuals and groups use brands and symbolic resources for micro-cultural identity construction and maintenance.

CONCLUSION

In this chapter we have shown the construction of identity at the social level, shown it to be socially maintained and have identified the role and importance of fashion and music brands in these processes. We have demonstrated the role of authenticity of performance in building subcultural capital and facilitating membership of micro-cultures and their associated brand communities of music and fashion. We have demonstrated the use of style repertoires and shown how these are local and dynamic systems of knowledge.

The power and significance of cultural meanings and information are often left out of traditional measures of brand equity but our study has shown them to be a key dynamic of brand value. We should acknowledge and understand the importance of the local systems of cultural meaning that determine the acceptance of a brand and its place (priority or valence) in a cultural repertoire.

KEY POINT

■ Authenticity of performance plays a crucial role in building brand communities involving music and fashion.

QUESTIONS FOR DISCUSSION

1 To what extent do consumers *actively* engage in searching for brand meanings?
2 How do cultural meanings come to be invested in fashion brands?
3 How can novice members of a style subculture ensure their acceptance by other members?
4 What are 'style repertoires' and how can they be recognized?
5 Should measures of brand equity include the social and cultural aspects of brand symbolism? How might this be done?

REFERENCES

Adkins, L. and Lury, C. (1999) 'The labour of identity: performing identities, performing economies', *Economy and Society* 28, 4: 598–614.

Arnould, E. and Price, L. (2000) 'Authenticating acts and authoritative performances: questing for self and community', in S. Ratneshwar, D. Mick and C. Huffman (eds) *The Why of Consumption: Contemporary Perspectives on Consumer Motives, Goals and Desires*, London: Routledge: 140–163.

Brake, M. (1985) *Comparative Youth Culture*, London: Routledge & Kegan Paul.

Cova, B. and Cova, V. (2001) 'Tribal aspects of postmodern consumption: the case of French in-line roller skaters', *Journal of Consumer Behaviour* 1, 1: 67–76.

Deleuze, G. and Parnet, C. (1987) *Dialogues*, trans. H. Tomlinson and B. Habberjam, New York: Columbia University Press.

Elliott, R. and Wattanasuwan, K. (1998) 'Brands as resources for the symbolic construction of identity', *International Journal of Advertising* 17, 2: 131–144.

Entwistle, J. (2000) *The Fashioned Body*, Cambridge: Polity.

Featherstone, M. (1991) 'The body in consumer culture', in M. Featherstone, M. Hepworth and B. Turner (eds) *The Body: Social Process and Cultural Theory*, London: Sage: 170–196.

Goffman, E. (1969) *The Presentation of Self in Everyday Life*, London: Allen Lane.

Goulding, C., Shankar, A. and Elliott, R. (2002) 'Working weeks, rave weekends: identity fragmentation and the emergence of new communities', *Consumption, Markets and Culture* 5, 4: 261–284.

Hall, S. (1992) 'The question of cultural identity', in S. Hall, D. Held and T. McGrew (eds) *Modernity and Its Futures*, Cambridge: Open University Press: 273–325.

Hardt, M. (1993) *Gilles Deleuze: An Apprenticeship in Philosophy*, London: University College London Press.

Hebdige, D. (1979) *Subculture: The Meaning of Style*, London: Methuen.

Heron, J. and Reason, P. (2001) 'The practice of co-operative inquiry: research with rather than on people', in P. Reason and H. Bradbury (eds) *Handbook of Action Research: Participative Inquiry and Practice*, London: Sage 179–188.

Hetherington, K. (1998) *Expressions of Identity: Space, Performance, Politics*, London: Sage.

169

Horton, D. (2003) 'Green distinctions; the performance of identity among environmental activists', *Sociological Review* 53: 64–77.

Muñiz, A. and O'Guinn, T. (2001) 'Brand communities', *Journal of Consumer Research* 27 (March): 412–432.

Nancarrow, C., Nancarrow, P. and Page, J. (2002) 'An analysis of the concept of cool and its marketing implications', *Journal of Consumer Behaviour* 1, 4: 311–322.

Pountain, D. and Robins, D. (2000) *Cool Rules: Anatomy of an Attitude*, London: Reaktion Books.

Sartre, J.-P. (2003/1956) *Being and Nothingness: An Essay on Phenomenological Ontology*, London: Routledge.

Thompson, J. B. (1995) *The Media and Modernity: A Social Theory of the Media*, Cambridge: Polity.

Thornton, S. (1995) *Club Cultures: Music, Media and Subcultural Capital*, Cambridge: Polity.

Willis, P. (1975) 'The expressive style of a motor-bike culture', in J. Benthall and T. Polhemus (eds) *The Body as a Medium of Expression*, London: Allen Lane.

Chapter 11

Branding ethics

Negotiating Benetton's identity and image

Janet L. Borgerson, Martin Escudero Magnusson and Frank Magnusson

Companies market their identities as assets, leveraging their own personal uniqueness as strengths. To differentiate their brand identity, Benetton, the internationally renowned apparel manufacturer, has connected to global issues with ethical import, attempting to associate the company's business with ethical behaviour – or, at least, the concern of a global citizen – and project that responsible image to consumers. In this quest to convert identity into a recognizable and appealing image, Benetton has produced nonconforming and occasionally shocking advertising. Focus on ethical values or social responsibility, in one form or another, has become a significant part of the corporation's business strategy and corporate image creation.

What is the relationship between the ethical messages communicated by Benetton and the United Colors of Benetton brand, and the identity of the core company? How can we understand the infamous *gap* between brand identity and brand image, or between corporate intentions and consumer response? An interest in ethical issues inspired an investigation into how companies can communicate ethical values and views in order to add value for themselves, consumers and society. This chapter, intersecting as it does with branding and business ethics, begins with the notion of expanding the realm of social responsibility for companies and advocating companies' active participation in their own ethical development, enabling business and ethics to coexist and thrive together.

Our research included analyses of various Benetton advertising campaigns, webpages, retail environments and other strategic communication outlets – such as fashion shows – in conjunction with a consumer survey. Consumers indicated that they do value ethics and think that companies should communicate their ethical values in everything they do. However, there is a paradox in the data: consumers value ethics, but say they would not be affected if Benetton stopped promoting ethical values in their marketing campaigns. Apparently, these consumers do not attach purchase-influencing import to Benetton's ethical messages and activities.

Several possible explanations for such a paradox were considered, and none of these was ultimately dismissed completely. First, consumers may not care about ethics, even though they say they do. Second, perhaps iconic brands, such as Benetton, are so strong

171

and popular that altering the corporate image and identity will not affect popularity, nor perhaps, even scandals around misleading or non-genuine ethical messages (cf. Schroeder 2000). Third, what if Benetton's identity is hollow? When consumers seek and call out for an ethical response, they receive only an echo, provoking the impression that something is missing behind the brand image's ethical message. Is it possible that the brand, United Colors of Benetton, creates the company? Does United Colors of Benetton brand have a life of its own? Moreover, can Benetton, the company and site of identity, direct this brand? Or can it be seen as a Frankenstein, a creation no longer controlled by the forces that apparently created it?

After a discussion of our research on Benetton and Benetton's marketing communications, we consider the theoretical – ontological and semiotic – implications of our observations, particularly in relation to communicating ethical messages within brand strategy. We propose the term *motivated referent* to articulate a sign-site – in lieu of corporate being or identity – known in speech act theory as a 'performative', a 'discursive practice that enacts or produces that which it names' (Butler 1993: 13). A motivated referent, as distinct from notions of company as entity, may be necessary for the understanding of a genuine ethical message that maintains a semiotic sophistication and ontological intelligibility, yet offers a notion of 'identity' that still requires a consistency among coextensive signs. Drawing upon semiotic analysis and empirical data of actual outcomes in consumer and retail environments, we substantiate with theoretical clarification 'insights at the level of everyday actualized meanings' (Mick *et al.* 2004: 20).

BENETTON'S ETHICS: IDENTITY AND IMAGE

Managing corporate identity demands that companies define the distinctive idea of their organization and how this is represented and communicated to a variety of audiences (e.g. Margulies 1977; Olins 1995; Fombrun 1996). Carefully managing those distinct characteristics that make up the corporate identity affects the company's image, often via a brand. Corporate image can be broadly understood as the totality of a stakeholder's perceptions, including associations in memory, of the way an organization presents itself, either deliberately or accidentally (Keller 2000; Markwick and Fill 1997). Of course, consumers interpret the same objects, images and moments differently, thus, corporate images differ across consumer segments and stakeholder groups. Corporate image management, including mobilization of brands, must take into account the inevitable multiplicity of images (Dowling 1993) when hoping to create consumer value through corporate image.

However, a corporate identity aspiring to ethical characteristics or socially responsible image cannot simply be an isolated slogan, a collection of phrases; rather, such underlying identities are said to require tangibility, visibility, and perhaps consistency with other aspects of corporation. Everything the organization does should be an affirmation of its identity (Olins 1995). In other words, companies that express ethical standpoints regarding social issues should take into account the effect that such action has on the corporate identity and consumers' expectations.

Corporations' ethical views apparently communicate corporate values through various communication media, often incorporating strategic pursuit of brand identity. Focusing on the marketing communications utilized by a company helps to clarify what the corporation desires to project about itself. Communication processes inking a company's desired identity and the images consumers create and interpret become relevant; yet coordinating the different communication channels so that they project consistent and coherent ethical values and views can become problematic. Communication channels vary, including, for example, store layout, product design, advertising and brand related events. Moreover, the effectiveness of these processes, as indicated by consumer response, suggests how communication influences corporate identity and image. We have limited ourselves to a primary focus on Benetton's brand, United Colors of Benetton, since this brand has been one of the most active in communicating ethical values – not only for the brand, but also for the company behind the brand.

BENETTON: THE CASE STUDY

The Benetton Group spans 120 countries within the clothing sector with well-established United Colors of Benetton and Sisley brands; and in the sportswear and equipment sector through brands such as Playlife, Nordica, Prince, Rollerblade and Killer Loop. The Group's global commercial network of 5,000 retail outlets increasingly focuses on large floor-space mega-stores offering high-quality customer services, generating over 2 billion euros yearly. Benetton produces 90 per cent of its garments in Europe, including Eastern Europe, and the remaining 10 per cent is under licence in markets in India and Turkey, strictly for the local market.

Benetton created marketing communications campaigns that could be implemented globally, tapping into the kinds of issues that concern many people within Benetton's brand reach. Fabrica, located in Italy and formed in 1994, holds responsibility for the company's strategic communication, which developed into two distinct campaigns: an image campaign focusing on communicating who they are and what they stand for; and a product campaign communicating what Benetton makes, emphasizing product attributes and qualities.

Benetton has produced several distinct communications campaigns, some of which have proven quite controversial, for example showing AIDS victims, death row inmates and graphic war violence (cf. Borgerson and Schroeder 2002; Goldman and Papson 1996; cf. Schroeder 2000). We have looked to the communications campaigns for clues to Benetton's image, as well as a vision of its corporate identity. Some might say that Oliviero Toscani, the photographer behind Benetton's controversial ad campaigns during the 1990s, created Benetton's ethical associations without reference to Benetton's

173

corporate identity or intensions at the time; and when he left Benetton, so did the ethical values and views. The extent to which such a created image also creates the company will be discussed later. However, the ethical values linked to United Colors of Benetton continued after Toscani, both in consumers' minds and, for example, in the Volunteer campaign, produced in conjunction with a United Nations assistance programme. Ethical expectations for Benetton's identity would apparently extend throughout the organization, including continuous reaffirmation through various communication channels.

The study was divided into two parts, an examination of Benetton's communication strategy at retail outlets in Stockholm, Sweden, including a Benetton fashion show, and a survey of young Swedish consumers' responses to Benetton's image. We were interested in Benetton's expression of its ethical values and views in these outlets, and, also, in documenting the value of Benetton's ethical commitments for consumers, particularly in their purchase behaviour.

Retailer viewpoints

Several Benetton managers, employees and consultants were interviewed on videotape about ethical values and retailer practice. The Benetton shop managers we interviewed claimed to experience a certain pride and generally to share in Benetton's apparent values. However, in the Benetton stores we observed, few visual, textual or behavioural artefacts represented the ethical connection to the company, nor, we found, did a store-sponsored fashion show reaffirm Benetton's ethical identity or values. Thus, Stockholm stores provide primarily product-oriented information, with social or ethical issues incorporated indirectly via the brand logo. Most of the communications exist in the form of Benetton company-provided product-oriented posters that project United Colors of Benetton's multicultural, multi-coloured associations. These retail environments reaffirm company strategy to keep image and product apart.

When asked how they applied Benetton's ethically conscious image in the shop design, shop managers seemed unenthusiastic, reporting: 'well, we receive pictures that constitute a basic foundation for Benetton's ethical points of view' or 'we receive some pictures that we put up'. Similarly, the public relations consultant for Benetton's fashion show seemed unconcerned with any ethical value relevance: 'They are similar [Benetton's fashion shows] in most countries. [The goal of the fashion is] To present Benetton's clothing collections in an appealing manner.'

However, in spite of the fact that this fashion show was a new product campaign, an attempt to incorporate Benetton's ethical values and views emerged in the casting of 'everyday people' of different racial backgrounds as models, a typical Benetton strategy. As our public relations informant revealed:

We never use professional models for Benetton shows. They [the models] have to be natural everyday people. We wanted people with different racial backgrounds [something that Benetton, Italy always wants]. Well, the multi-cultural backgrounds of the models is pretty much how we communicated Benetton's ethical values, but we did not work so much with that when putting this fashion show together.

Eschewing professional models might be seen as an attempt to express Benetton's uniqueness and connection to real people.

Our research reveals that Benetton Italy exerts a high degree of influence, which may be connected to Benetton's strategy of creating image campaigns with ethical values and views that are globally applicable. However, the PR agency's ability to adapt Benetton's ethical values and views to Swedish society seems restricted. An exchange with a DJ at the fashion show reveals further gaps between corporate goals and local practice:

> Interviewer: Is this Benetton's music that you are playing here today? [Benetton/ Fabrica produce their own music.]
> DJ: No. It's my own.
> Interviewer: Did you receive directives for the choice of music?
> DJ: Yes, they picked out a couple of songs [shakes his head], but I prefer my own music [smiles].
> Interviewer: Have you listened to Benetton's own music?
> DJ: No!

Thus, although Fabrica specifically makes music for Benetton fashion shows, no doubt considering particular sounds a part of Benetton's image, the DJ plays his own music.

Benetton's ethical values and views do not permeate its different communication channels; its social and ethical image fails to be coherently and consistently communicated. We asked how shop managers are informed about Benetton's work with ethical values and how they are motivated to express these values in their own communication medium. A third shop manager admitted:

> In the stores we probably don't work so much with that, but when Benetton promotes their national campaigns then it comes out. Probably a lot of people do not know where the money goes to, social causes that they support.

These shop managers appear not to feel part of the image campaign created by Benetton, hence, they do not concentrate on this area and leave it up to the company to express who they are.

For example, none of the shop managers were informed of, or invited to, the fashion show – a food and drinks included, staged in a hip underground cave affair – and they expressed confusion at having been left out of such a Benetton event. These situations seem strange. The retail stores are outlets for communication: the way the stores present Benetton affects the image that consumers have of the company. Image, and reputation, as well, are not based solely on advertising and website representations. We believe that Benetton has not used the communicative tools of shop design, including the way values are expressed there by employees – nor an event, such as, the fashion show – to communicate image-related values, and this surely impacts consumers.

CONSUMER PERSPECTIVES

How do consumers value and react to companies communicating ethical values and views? Our consumer study investigates how ethics affects the purchase behaviour of consumers with regard to Benetton's ethical communication. Smith (1990) considers consumer boycotts as examples of ethics as a consumer value and defines ethical purchase behaviour as an expression of the individual's moral judgement in his or her purchasing behaviour. Social outrage manifested in boycotts illustrates that ethics can matter to consumers – moreover, this social phenomenon marks ethics as a factor affecting purchase behaviour. Of course, there are varying levels of involvement open to the consumer, as buying ecological milk at a grocery chain may demand less effort then seeking out and buying directly from a small, local organic dairy. To investigate how consumers value branded ethics this study focused on consumer reactions to Benetton's ethical image, which we discuss below.

Seventy-six business students at Stockholm University participated in a survey about ethics and consumer behaviour. The survey, which includes a mix of Swedish students and international exchange students, indicates a positive response to ethical messages connected to a brand image. About half said that a company communicating an ethical message is more likely to capture their attention. A majority (71 per cent) of the consumers experience added value if a product is tied to an ethical standpoint. However, half of the respondents claimed that they would not be affected if Benetton discontinued its ethical communication, and about a third did not know if they would be affected. This apparent paradox suggests that consumers think that ethics is valuable in a brand, but at the same time they do not attach a significance to this that would affect their purchase behaviour. Interesting, specifically in relation to our discussion of Benetton's lack of image communication in product-focused environments, is the response that 55 per cent of respondents think it important for a company to communicate its ethical message in everything it does, that is, in advertising, stores, at sponsored events and on websites. Why does there seem to be a gap between Benetton's identity and image in relation to ethical values and views? Does the paradox in our consumers' responses demonstrate ambivalence around this gap? Should identity and image be aligned and the gap closed for added value?

The consumer does not have to consume a company's product(s) in order to consume and relate in various ways to the brand image. Reaction to ethical messages affects the process of consumption. Even if a consumer has no current interaction with Benetton's products, the brand image he or she carries has the potential to influence purchase behaviour in the future. Has Benetton handled this complex of considerations well? Does it make sense to promote a corporate identity that creates an ethics-tinged brand image and rely on this to push image-carrying consumers into ethics-less product-related outlets? To illuminate the significance of our research from a wider philosophical perspective, we discuss how ethical values and views, communicated via brands, illuminate the relationship between corporations and consumers from an ontological point of view. We believe there is a problem with the status of the company, Benetton, as a referent (Floch 2001).

ONTOLOGIES OF BRANDING – CAN IDENTITY INFLUENCE BRAND MEANING?

To understand brands, we need to recognize how meaning and identity interact – in other words, how semiotics works together with ontology (Butler 1997). Our utilization of ontology, or considerations around questions of being, grounds our desire to uncover how companies' ethical viewpoints are manifested through the different communication channels at hand, including the brand. Ontology develops understandings of what exists and, furthermore, in what *being* consists. Moreover, recent work in ontology includes consideration of how meaning and being are created, interrelated and represented in ethics (Borgerson 2001) and marketing contexts (Borgerson and Schroeder 2002, 2005). Ontology often focuses on the relationships between forms of being, for example how the self and others form relationships. A being's 'meaning' may be seen as arising out of these relationships, forming a basis for further interaction. We draw out these ontological aspects, observing brands and the relationships they create, including effects on the identity of the company. Once we recognize that assumptions and expectations regarding the form in which things exist affect the way we understand relationships and interaction – for example, between corporations and their images – notions around ontology and the brand demand exploration.

Research has addressed how corporations construct themselves as *entities* (Balmer 2001; van Riel and Balmer 1997), *identities* (Rindova and Schultz 1998) or *expressive* organizations (Hatch and Schultz 2000). Whereas brands have been understood to occupy marketing communications in the form of representations, images, pictures or signs, companies have been perceived as *real* objects in the world with solid qualities existing over time and, often, but not always, in an apparently identifiable space. In other words, relationships between companies and brands have been shaped by perceptions of what exists, for example real objects versus images. Moreover, research into consistency between a company's corporate identity and its corporate image is, also, often based upon assumptions of what exists, for example the identity is the 'real' corporation whereas the image only represents, and commonly misrepresents, this identity (see Christensen and Askegaard 2001; Chapter 5 in this volume). When the possibility of communicating genuine ethical values and views – generated by a corporate identity, corporate image and brand strategy – is the focus, proclamations about the ontological status of these become more complicated. Whose ethical message is it, after all?

177

Companies communicate via brands; and from an ontological perspective, the brand plays a significant role in conveying a meaningful ethical (or otherwise) message. If the brand forms relationships between consumers and companies (Fournier 1998; Fournier and Aaker 1995), then what is the 'being' of the brand in relation to corporate identity and image? Where in these relationships is meaning and ethical value created? Researchers concerned with brands and their significance have focused on human-like qualities of brands – personality, relationships, identity, and so forth (see Chapter 8 in this volume). The personification of brands, as characters and partners, has had significant implications, for example the development of a brand personality can be explained in terms of the brand as a relationship partner (Fournier 1998). Thus, meanings seem to arise, constructed by consumers, based on behaviours exhibited by personified brands or brand characters (Allen and Olson 1995). Of course, the 'behaviours' consist in marketing mix activities and brand management decisions that trigger attitudinal, cognitive and/or behaviour responses on the consumer's part, leading to the pointed desire to know the company behind the brand (i.e. Kapferer 2001). Balmer (2001) suggests a corporate brand requires making known the 'attributes of the organization's identity' and the communication of this identity and its meanings throughout the entire organization. Brands are being used to direct attention to the identity of the corporation behind the brand.

REVISITING THE GAP: CORPORATION, IDENTITY AND IMAGE

A company that hopes to send a message through its communications may fail to do so because of a gap between the impressions consumers receive and the preferred message. This might be thought of as a gap between corporate image – or interpretant – and corporate identity. This gap is usually thought to relate to miscommunication and misrepresentation; and recommendations to solve such problems often call for bringing image into line with the real company. Notice that this distinction between the corporation, corporate image and the corporate identity may appear to be a distinction between an image or representation and a 'real' object, that is, the 'real' corporation (Christensen and Askegaard 2001: 299). Such an assumption might lead us to describe the problem as one of bringing a marketing communications-based message into line with the preferred identity of the corporation, for example around communicating genuine ethical messages (Escudero Magnusson and Magnusson 2002). That is, the real corporation has an ethical commitment and related message, but this fails to be transmitted through marketing communications. Such an understanding has resulted in the following situation:

> identity and image management has become a fast-growing industry in which the justification of new image and identity programs relies on the ability to claim a better

understanding of the organization as it 'really is' and to 'sell' some symbolic constructions as being more true representation than others.

(Christensen and Askegaard 2001: 299–300)

Following Christensen and Askegaard, we turned to semiotics to explore the issue as a
question about ontological status of the company or organization: What kind of being
does it have?

To what do we look when we seek the entity to which the images – for example of a
genuine ethical message – must adhere? What happens if we look 'behind' the brand and
to our amazement there is nothing there? What if there does not exist a *core* or *essential*
company behind the brand, and *corporate being* is merely a useful construction (cf.
Coupland and Brown 2004)? This is not to argue that there is no company, or that its
buildings, products and personnel do not exist. Rather, we point to the ephemeral nature
of identity, and the difficulty in establishing the one true nature of a corporate brand.
What, then, does the brand reflect? Do companies, then, really have the power or control
to create ethical meaning?

THE COMPANY IS AS THE BRAND MAKES IT

The Peircian semiotic system (see e.g. Christensen and Askegaard 2001) can help us
explicate and better understand the flaws in our original evaluation of Benetton's
situation: Benetton was assumed to be an object, or referent, of some ontological solidity.
Apparently, the representation of Benetton and Benetton's ethical message in marketing
communications required realignment to close the 'gap' between corporate image and
Benetton's corporate identity. This gap, we assumed, undermined Benetton's efforts to
promote itself and its product and brands in relation to its corporate ethical identity and
gain added value through its communication channels. Yet, if we assume for a moment
that Benetton itself is not a referent in the object sense, but simply a collection of pre-
existing signs and codes, then our earlier recommendations express a misunderstanding
of the nature of the identity/image problem and the presence of the 'gap'.

Following upon Peircian logic, the corporation, or organization, becomes as much
a sign as the sign of this sign, supporting the claim that there is no company or – after
the demise of the referent – referent motivated corporate identity behind the brand.
Moreover, we might say that the company is as the sign makes it. All aspects of the
corporation are as much signs as the brand or logo. The troublesome hypothesized 'real'
object or corporate being, including some renditions of 'identity,' often results from the
desire for, or commonsense habit of invoking, an object or referent to 'motivate' the sign,
in the sense that if there is a sign, it must be the sign of *something*.

Christensen and Askegaard's concern around these issues is that if the arbitrariness
of the 'real object', or company, is not recognized and taken into account, this solid-
seeming 'reality' will resist criticism and change, as 'Reality is the phantasm by means

179

of which the sign is indefinitely preserved from the symbolic deconstruction that haunts it' (Baudrillard quoted in Christensen and Askegaard 2001: 309). Ability to change and innovate may be compromised if the 'real' status of the company as pre-existing and somewhat static overshadows the assumed flexible nature of signs. That is, if the referent, source or real company is understood as a sign, flexibility increases. In conclusion, then, identity managers make an error in suggesting the corporate image must be brought into line with this *something* of a corporation – the real object or referent. Such an error, conceptual or otherwise, is not necessary, however. A *motivated sign* refers to a sign resulting from an object or referent. A corporate image could be understood as a motivated sign, but a sign motivated by corporate identity, understood as sign.

Whereas we understood semiotically the disappearance of the referent, we felt diminishing that position of the semiotic triad to a simple sign threatened the ability to ground a genuine ethical message, which we considered crucial for reasons mentioned earlier, including increased value for Benetton, consumers and society. We developed the notion of the *motivated referent* to mirror the motivated sign, but to designate solidity capable of grounding ethical values and views.

MOTIVATING A REFERENT TO ELIMINATE A GAP

We propose the term motivated referent to articulate a kind of condensed collection of signs and codes that takes on the status of a referent. For example McDonald's corporate designs – arches, red and yellow graphics, Ronald McDonald – have taken on more meaning than a mere fast-food restaurant, they refer to concepts such as American success (and excess), globalization and McDonaldization. A motivated referent can take on solidity beyond a simple sign, perhaps as 'social historical simulations of organized realities' (Christensen and Askegaard 2001: 311). A motivated referent announces its status as motivated, not by some 'real' beyond signs, but as a sign of a sign. Thus, the relation between the 'real' of a referent and the unreliability, or flexibility, of the sign displays an exchange in which the inferred reliability of a referent confesses its place among signs, yet upon which we confer a conventional stability capable of holding down ethical commitments and developing plans through time. A company or corporation in trying to bring its corporate image into line with its corporate identity attempts to align or make consistent marketing communications with the motivated referent of the corporation.

Clearly, it is both performative and purposive that some signs motivate a referent. This consideration of the motivated referent is particularly important in terms of an ethical message. An ethical message – of values and views – must be seen as related to something beyond a simple transient sign. Commitment to ethical values, in particular, requires the notion of an agent, or collection of agents, that – with intention – follow through on a set of beliefs, or programme of action, that they believe will bring about a desired, and apparently ethical, situation in a way that other sets of beliefs or plans of actions would not. A sign, conventionally portrayed, then, is not a particularly satisfactory site of such commitment. (If all agents are understood to be signs, the inability to distinguish among signs carries the entire sign versus referent debate into irrelevance.) Rather, a motivated referent can focus ethical concern and commitment, even when this is understood to be conventional, rather than universal, or true and right in all circumstances.

BENETTON'S ETHICAL MESSAGE: SOME INSIGHTS

At this point, we can understand Benetton's problem of making its ethical message genuine in several ways. We could attend to Benetton as something real, a collection of people, buildings, factories united by the ideals and intentions of owners and managers, for example. This real, continuously existing and existentially consistent entity forms the referent to which the sign, or brand, United Colors of Benetton refers. Because of a gap in the marketing communications, the corporation's attempt to make its ethical message genuine among consumers in terms of its corporate image has failed. The job at hand is to make the vision available via marketing communications consistent with the intended ethical message of the corporation, presumably stemming from the corporate identity.

This version of the problem's solution ignores the question of the company or corporation 'behind' the brand. As we have suggested, perhaps there is not one. Perhaps when we look to the corporation to reassert its ethical commitments so that we can articulate and communicate them in a more effective and accurate manner, we will find emptiness where we expected to find real people, ideas and intentions. Consider the following very concrete sense of searching for real people: a person whose brother is diagnosed with AIDS remembers Benetton's advertising campaigns picturing AIDS patients. Perhaps Benetton has someone working at their company who knows something about AIDS and where one can go for help and information about medicines. She calls Benetton and asks if she can speak to the person who knows about the AIDS epidemic and the people who are suffering from it. *No one at Benetton can take her call*, not even someone who advises the corporation on the ethics of its ad campaigns.

This can also be understood in a semiotic sense: the interpretant, or image, 'asks' for a response or genuine message to communicate but receives only more signs, not a response to previous enquiries. This emptiness behind the interpretant, and, in turn, corporate identity, provokes a situation in which the 'asking' creates the referent itself – the process behind the 'motivated referent' – that is, in the 'asking' a referent is created (Derrida 1984). As in many existentially uneasy situations, the response to this echo and sense of the abyss into which questions fly is often to hypothesize an object, the 'real' referent.

Rather than simply assert theoretical insight into the importance of a motivated referent in creating a genuine ethical message – and using Benetton as a jumping-off point related to identity analysis – we believe that Benetton serves as an illustrative

181

example of the weakening of the object referent relation both to the sign and the interpretant. We would argue that Benetton has strengthened the relationship between the
interpretant, or image, and the sign of corporate identity, allowing the object referent
to lose status as the underpinning basis of the identity sign and the interpretant. This
is exactly what we expect to see, given a semiotic analysis, and can be understood as a
disruption of the equilibrium of the semiosis triangle (see Christensen and Askegaard
2001). Data gathered on Benetton help illuminate the semiotic and ontological phenomena of the disappearance, or banishing, of the object referent and points to the elusive
nature of corporate identity.

RECONCEPTUALIZING THE BENETTON 'GAP'

In the initial stages of our research, we assumed a *corporate being* did indeed exist
behind this iconic brand – with recognizable, even human qualities. The existence of an
identity, that is, corporate being, was not questioned or doubted. In contrast, the brand
was treated as an abstract extension of the company: the brand's 'being' seemed clearly
intangible. Furthermore, the brand was depicted as a spokesperson speaking on
behalf of the company, presenting the identity of the company and, thus, communicating
ethical messages from the company. The brand in this view is a reflection or messenger
of the company or corporation and, consequently, features such as culture, values and
visions end up being transmitted via the brand. Because of these perceptions of the
company–brand relationship, typical managerially relevant recommendations focused
upon coordinating the 'real' company's communications, in order to voice the company's
genuine ethical message through all channels.

A provocative and challenging alternative viewpoint began to emerge during the
investigation, however. Perhaps our initial point of focus was insubstantial. Or perhaps
Benetton has failed in communicating a consistent and coherent message because *there
is no corporate being* behind United Colors of Benetton. Concerning this emergent absence,
one could argue that our initial insights for companies wanting to communicate an ethical
message have no real relevance: if the company lacks corporate being, a real identity, it
would be difficult to implement such recommendations.

CONCLUSION

We have suggested that a semiotically sophisticated way to understand the Benetton
problem, and one more in tune with Baudrillard's motivation of Peircian semiotics,
would be to regard as an illusion the solid 'real' supposedly at the core, or soul, of
Benetton's corporate identity. We can develop insights, discussed earlier, further. One
way to explain and work with this illusion without betraying co-extensiveness of signs is
to see the corporate identity as a motivated referent, a sign-object created, as it were,

in the wake of Benetton's brand. There has been no suggestion that a sign, and in this case a motivated referent, is *incapable* of constructing a coherent identity with the resulting communication of this identity as corporate image. Work in this vein that brings signs into coherence, or consistency, does not fall into the illusory task of claiming 'to have access to a world behind and beyond those symbols, a world behind appearances or beyond representations' (Christensen and Askegaard 2001: 308). Rather, the task of the identity manager is to bring all signs into coherence in a way that best approximates an image that the corporate identity, understood as motivated referent, requires. The work, then, remains in the reading of cultural signs, making them as consistent as possible in a way that best communicates the desired image without reference to some mistakenly ontologized referent.

KEY POINT

■ The way to understand and manage the gap between corporate identity and corporate image may be to realize that both are constructions: identity is difficult to pin down, and one cannot speak of a single, solid identity.

QUESTIONS FOR DISCUSSION

1 Is it important for corporate identity to be genuine? How does this chapter's ideas influence your answer?
2 Is it possible to create a consistent brand or corporate identity by coordinating the communication channels in a coherent way?
3 What are some of the dangers of the gap between brand or corporate identity and image?
4 Should companies like Benetton try to control their image?
5 How can understanding how identity works illuminate brand thinking?

REFERENCES

Allen, D. E. and Olsen, J. (1995) 'Conceptualizing and creating brand personality: a narrative theory approach', in F. Kardes and M. Sujan (eds) *Advances in Consumer Research* 22: 392–393.

Balmer, J. M. T. (2001) 'Corporate identity, corporate branding and corporate marketing: seeing through the fog', *European Journal of Marketing* 35: 248–291.

Borgerson, J. L. (2001) 'Feminist ethical ontology: contesting "the bare givenness of intersubjectivity"', *Feminist Theory* 2, 2: 173–187.

Borgerson, J. L. and Schroeder, J. E. (2002) 'Ethical issues of global marketing: avoiding bad faith in visual representation', *European Journal of Marketing* 36, 5/6: 570–594.

Borgerson, J. L. and Schroeder, J. E. (2005) 'Identity in marketing communications: an ethics of visual representation', in A. J. Kimmel (ed.) *Marketing Communication: New Approaches, Technologies, and Styles*, Oxford: Oxford University Press.

Butler, J. (1993) *Bodies that Matter: On the Discursive Limits of 'Sex'*, New York: Routledge.

Butler, J. (1997) *The Psychic Life of Power*, Stanford, CA: Stanford University Press.

Christensen, L. T. and Askegaard, S. (2001) 'Corporate identity and corporate image revisited: a semiotic perspective', *European Journal of Marketing* 35, 3/4: 292–315.

Coupland, C. and Brown, A. D. (2004) 'Constructing organizational identities on the Web: a case study of Royal Dutch/Shell', *Journal of Management Studies* 41, 8: 1325–1347.

Derrida, J. (1984) 'Devant la loi', in A. P. Griffiths (ed.) *Philosophy and Literature*, Cambridge: Cambridge University Press.

Dowling, G. R. (1993) 'Developing your image into a corporate asset', *Long Range Planning* 26, 2: 101–109.

Escudero Magnusson, M. and Magnusson, F. (2002) 'Making your ethical message genuine', Master's thesis, Stockholm University School of Business.

Floch, J.-M. (2001) *Semiotics, Marketing and Communication: Beneath the Signs, the Strategies*, trans. R. O. Bodkin, New York: Palgrave.

Fombrun, C. (1996) *Reputation: Realizing Value from the Corporate Image*, Boston, MA: Harvard Business School Press.

Fournier, S. (1998) 'Consumers and their brands: developing relationship theory in consumer research', *Journal of Consumer Research* 24 (March): 343–373.

Fournier, S. and Aaker, J. (1995) 'The brand as a character, partner, and person: three perspectives on the question of brand personality', in F. Kardes and M. Sujan (eds) *Advances in Consumer Research* 22: 391–395.

Goldman, R. and Papson, R. (1996) *Sign Wars: The Cluttered Landscape of Advertising*, New York: Guilford.

Hatch, M. J. and Schultz, M. (2000) 'Scaling the Tower of Babel: relational differences between identity, image, and culture in organizations', in M. Schultz, M. J. Hatch and M. H. Larsen (eds) *The Expressive Organization: Linking Identity, Reputation, and the Corporate Brand*, Oxford: Oxford University Press: 1–35.

Kapferer, J. N. (2001) *[Re]inventing the Brand: Can Top Brands Survive the New Market Realities?*, London: Kogan Page.

Keller, K. L. (2000) 'Building and managing corporate brand equity', in M. Schultz, M. J. Hatch and M. H. Larsen (eds) *The Expressive Organization: Linking Identity, Reputation, and the Corporate Brand*, Oxford: Oxford University Press: 115–137.

Margulies, W. (1977) 'Make the most of your corporate identity', *Harvard Business Review* 55 (July–August): 66–74.

Markwick, N. and Fill, C. (1997) 'Towards a framework for managing corporate identity', *European Journal of Marketing* 31, 5/6: 340–355.

Mick, D. G., Burroughs, J., Hetzel, P. and Brannen, M. Y. (2004) 'Pursuing the meaning of meaning in the commercial world: an international view of marketing and consumer research founded on semiotics', *Semiotica* 152, 1/4: 1–74.

Olins, W. (1995) *The New Guide to Identity: How to Create and Sustain Change through Managing Identity*, Hampshire: Gower.

Rindova, V. and Schultz, M. (1998) 'Identity within and identity without: lessons from corporate and organizational identity', in D. A. Whetten and P. Godfrey (eds) *Identity in Organizations: Developing Theory through Conversations*, Thousand Oaks, CA: Sage: 6–51.

Schroeder, J. E. (2000) 'Édouard Manet, Calvin Klein and the strategic use of scandal', in S. Brown and A. Patterson (eds) *Imagining Marketing: Art, Aesthetics, and the Avant-Garde*, London: Routledge: 36–51.

Smith, C. M. (1990) *Morality and the Market: Consumer Pressure for Corporate Accountability*, London: Routledge.

van Riel, C. B. M. (1995) *Principles of Corporate Communications*, London: Prentice Hall.

van Riel, C. B. M. and Balmer, J. M. T. (1997) 'Corporate identity: the concept, its measurement and management', *European Journal of Marketing* 31, 5/6: 340–355.

Chapter 12

Brand ecosystems

Multilevel brand interaction

Sven Bergvall

Consumers come in contact with hundreds of brands every day, in advertisements, retail environments, work places and websites – deeply embedding brands into culture. Traditional marketing research, however, has viewed brand management mostly as a production issue, focusing on how companies create strong brands. Recent research has turned to the interaction between producers and consumers of brands in a brand meaning creation process. In this chapter, I broaden this notion further by introducing the concept *brand ecosystems*, acknowledging that brands are cultural as much as managerial concepts, and pointing to the myriad influences on brand production and consumption. Three empirical levels of analysis are developed – governmental, technology and company – with several examples drawn from the ICT sector to illuminate how brands interact within ecosystems.

The current movement in brand research has created powerful tools for exploring the brand creation process as a dyadic relationship between producer and consumer, but largely missing from these theoretical insights is a deeper awareness of basic cultural processes that affect contemporary brands, including historical context, governmental support, institutional actors and consumer perception. In other words, *neither managers nor consumers have total control over brand meanings* – cultural codes constrain how brands work to produce meaning. Brand ecosystems fit into this cultural context to understand how seemingly disconnected phenomenon, like a governmental initiative and product launch, profoundly influence and control each other as they assert and depend on the existing cultural interrelation.

After a brief dip into current brand research, let us go to the pond to see why brands in brand ecosystems are not that unlike frogs burping away at night. The themes presented here centre around the notion that brand interaction is deeply interwoven into culture – like all text, and here trying to develop the understanding of how brands and culture fit together. What I add to this mix is a mesh of actors, an ecosystem if you will, resisting and responding to both internal and external forces. Just like a rabbit can't easily turn into a fierce predator, brands – when established – are constrained within a cultural context, in symbiosis with other actors. The case of Swedish–Japanese mobile phone company Sony Ericsson and the Swedish ICT sector is used throughout the chapter as an example of the multilevel cultural forces affecting and being affected by the brand creation process.

BRANDING

Brand research has been generally involved in developing theories that explain how to create, manage and understand successful brands from a strategic, or producer, point of view. While these issues are of great importance for understanding some aspects of the brand creation process, such research has a tendency to assume a rather static and controllable brand environment. Recently, a research stream has taken a radically different approach by focusing on consumers and their relationships with brands (e.g. Fournier 1998; Kates 2000). This work has shown that brands and brand communication are interpreted or read in multiple ways, often not at all in line with the intended meaning of the brand manager, prompting an important and illuminating reconsideration of brand management and shifting attention from brand producers toward consumer response to understand how branding creates meaning (e.g. Elliott 1994; Hirschman and Thompson 1997; Johar et al. 2001). Cultural codes, ideological discourse, consumer's background knowledge and rhetorical processes have been cited as influences in brand interpretation and consumers' relationships to advertising and mass media. Consumers are seen to construct and perform identities and self-concepts, trying out new roles and creating their self-image within and in collaboration with consumer culture (cf. Fournier 1998). While not fully accepted by mainstream brand research, these concepts have found their way into contemporary consumer behaviour textbooks (cf. Solomon et al. 2002).

There are several reasons why brands have become such important meaning systems in the current society and market. Branding seems to have become an imperative, and building strong brand identity along with strong relationships with customers have become increasingly important, or at least increasingly emphasized in the brand management literature (e.g. Keller 2003). The premises for using brands in society are changing as consumers become more reflexive of their own and the brands' roles in consumer culture, as indicated by the No Logo movement (Klein 2000) and other issue management problems (Holt 2004). In the same tradition, consumers are starting to organize around brands in similar ways to past times tribes, but with brands as 'chief' and uniting power, with the creation of brand communities (e.g. McAlexander et al. 2002; Muñiz and O'Guinn 2001), even stretching to media 'brands', such as Star Trek (Kozinets 2001). Parallel to these new community forms, consumer identities seem to be increasingly unstable (Featherstone 1991). As consumers, we are able to show more flexibility and freedom in our choice of life path and lifestyle than ever before. Consumers can be described as seeking to create a self-image by combining a 'unique' consumption pattern, using the brands that best fit current lifestyles (Schroeder 2002). This way, brands may play a stabilizing role as a fix-point for consumers in search of an identity, but the change in consumer lifestyles in itself may obviously also engender the opposite

187

effect: an increasing brand disloyalty. This is both because the meaning of brands and brand categories shift when entering a hyper-affluent society, where buying a watch can stand against a car or a vacation, and changes in cultural tensions that suddenly make previously important identity building brands totally irrelevant (Holt 2004).

At the same time, the interest for and application of various kinds of alliances has increased greatly, going from the enormous bank and pharmaceutical company fusions to a supermarket chain (ICA) opening small stores in gas stations (Statoil) in Sweden. These methods seem to have become more of a rule than exception in business (Bengtsson 2002). The same is true regarding brand strategy, with its surge in co-branding, ingredient branding, mixed brands and other forms of brand cooperation (cf. Aaker and Joachimsthaler 2000; Apéria 2001; Kapferer 1997). The forms are of course variable, but the general notion is that in order to counter consumer eclecticism no one company or institution is able to offer a complete solution, but has to rely on others to satisfy consumer need for both variety and continuity, thus creating a more compelling offer, in a way, by covering more meaning, or identity, creation material. In this muddle of brands and brand interpretations and meanings there exists a certain element of chance as well – a well-executed plan is by no means a guarantee for success – or, as related to one of contemporary philosopher Odo Marquard's (1991) central concept of 'the accidental': chance occurrences, including one's birthplace, home and parents that profoundly influence one's life chances. At this level, one can connect the accidental to contemporary brand research – brand managers must acknowledge that brand meaning is not completely purposeful, that is accidents, such as consumer resistance, misunderstanding, appropriation or indifference, exert a marked influence on brand communication.

These phenomena are especially visible in the information and communication technology (ICT) sector. This sector received a lot of attention during the 1990s all over the world, and Sweden was no exception, which resulted in a surge of new companies, many becoming international or even global in just a couple of years. The amazing growth attracted interest from other parties as well, at the municipal and state level, including non-governmental organizations. Inspired by the highly successful Silicon Valley in California, a number of 'Valleys' sprung up around the world. In Sweden, the 'Mobile Valley' in Kista, a suburb of Stockholm, gained most attention. At the end of 2000, however, gloom hit the fast-growing industry. A large number of companies went bankrupt and almost all had to downsize to survive. Both in boom and gloom, the ICT sector has been forced into new ways of thinking and acting, with companies relying more and more on system interaction involving several different actor levels in brand creation rather than standing on their own. In a way they create a sense of belonging both for themselves and in their interaction with consumers.

BRAND ECOSYSTEMS

This shift toward a more networked society opens up new possibilities to reflect on the interaction between different actors in the brand creation process, without limiting the analysis to inter-company relations or even company–consumer–brand relations. One approach to this complex issue is through the use of brand ecosystems, an inter-disciplinary framework that draws on three empirical levels of analysis. As brands act within a cultural context there is a mesh of moulding and controlling links to other brands and actors that brands have a hard, if not impossible, time breaking loose from. In nature an ecosystem is really an 'arbitrarily' chosen area with similar or uniform conditions. Ecosystems are generally seen as being fragile and sensitive to interference from the outside, with friends of the planet almost constantly (perhaps correctly) being concerned with the destruction of valuable ecosystems, like the Everglades in Florida. Without doubt, some areas are worth preserving, but ecosystems are often quite versatile and robust with change as a rule rather than exception; without it we (as humans) would never have had a chance to get to the position we have today (cf. Hedrén 2002). Let's look at the pond, with its myriad species, ranging from the lowly shore grass to the proud heron spreading its wings. All these together define the ecosystem, none of them really more important than the other, and one species' presence is enough to exert influence on everyone else, and a change of habits affects the whole system. If the fox (yes, I have a romantic view of ponds) suddenly started eating grass instead of rabbits, the existing balance would change and soon enough the whole ecosystem would be different – not worse, but definitely different.

I am not the first to use the term brand ecosystem; Agnieszka Winkler (1999), in the midst of the 'warp-speed' economy, used it to describe the different stakeholders in a brand in a time of immense changes to brands and branding logic that was happening with the disappearance of packaged goods – all with the help of technology. Without judging the validity of her claims, this approach is, while in spirit the same, quite different and very much a company-centric view in line with classic brand management. To her credit, the notion that not only the brand manager controls the branding process, but that more people are involved, is important. However, while true, it is in my view too limited as it only concerns the brand production side. Another closely related term is 'brand ecology', coined by Larry Percy and colleagues (Percy et al. 2001), to describe a way of going beyond demographics to understand the relationships smaller groups have with wider aspects of brand consumption, including social and cultural issues. This approach has many touching points with brand ecosystems, with its interest in a larger involvement in the environment around brands and an interest in understanding not only what is consumed, but also why. It is, however, more focused on a consumer perspective, and 'explores how this brand-related behaviour integrates with wider social and cultural experience in the life-world of the active consumer' (Elliott and Jankel-Elliott 2002: 2). While the search for an increased understanding of the drivers of consumption is not new, to say the least, the combination of ethnography and brand ecology is promising

– even if the most apparent goal is to gain more finely tuned demographical data. The view of the consumer is, however, limiting in the sense that it gives just that, often hiding other interesting, and powerful, interactions on other levels – in other words, brand ecosystems.

By applying the brand ecosystem lens one can see that governmental efforts, including cities, regions, states, nations, as well as non-governmental organizations and international associations, can be noted to control branding. For example, the city of Stockholm heavily promotes concepts like 'information technology', 'broadband', and 'wireless', and civic leaders actively encourage technological development, application and infrastructure (cf. Dobers 2003), even owning a company (Stokab), making sure there is an optical fibre network spanning each and every street of the city. Furthermore, industrial centres, such as Kista Science City, a Stockholm suburb, accelerate this boosterism by regionally consolidating commercial and technological resources, including the recent creation of the Royal Institute of Technology (KTH)-Information Technology University, a joint venture between a number of Stockholm's universities to create an ICT education powerhouse. All these efforts were made possible and viable only by the existence of companies like Ericsson in the area, yet they now act as a reciprocal agent both by attracting new ICT companies and students and in a broader sense framing Swedish high-tech brands.

At the technological level, branded product development platforms such as wireless, 3G and Bluetooth illustrate a mid-point between governmental action and firm-level branding; these efforts often consist of industry (and state) consortiums joined together to promote broad technological adoption and change. The importance of co-owned or 'standard' technologies has increased in recent years as both technologies and market conditions have become more complex, while the ICT sector is at the same time more and more turning towards consumer space.

Most typical for brand research is, the firm level, that is, company brands, brand families, corporate brands, and so on, where brand management challenges product management for strategic superiority. Here, changes involve the increasing complexity of branding due to the blurring relationship between products and services. While this by no means is an exhaustive selection, it gives a sketch toward an understanding of the multilevel interaction in the meaning creation process.

The company level

Companies are to an increasing extent interacting with each other as well as with actors on different levels. The way mergers and joint ventures have exploded in the last decade is a good example of companies using other brands to create a more complete image, touching aspects of the experience sphere not attainable by themselves. An example of this is the mobile phone company Sony Ericsson, a combination of both Sony's and Ericsson's failing mobile phone divisions, each on their own unable to create enough market attention. The combined company has inherited meaning from both mother companies, among other aspects using the 'business' image of Ericsson and the 'play' image of Sony, but also cultural aspects from their respective national 'brands'. Sony Ericsson, being formed from a Japanese and a Swedish company, stems from two distinct cultures, both however strangely alike – Sweden often being called the Japan of Europe – both countries generally are seen as preferring the austere and clean to the more outspokenness of southern Europe. This heritage can be seen in product design, advertisements and promotional websites like the one for their top-of-the-line model P800. The site (www.sonyericsson.com) opens up to an arid, modern, 'Nordic light' landscape only constrained by a mirrored floor and an 'office building' to the left, as well as with mirrored windows – the modern city combined with the vast expanses of the wilderness present in both Swedish and Japanese cultural mythology.

The tension between the company's parents continues with a falling-down phone, presenting a car racing game on its screen, combined with an office building, representing 'play' and 'work' respectively. As the scene turns, the screen of the phone turns into a bar chart, while the building in the background turns into floor – and a GO table, a traditional Japanese board game. It is easy to see that Sony Ericsson is using cultural values not only from its parent companies, but also their countries of origin. This re-creation of culture in the brand creation process has effects on the image of Japan and Sweden as well, in this case reinforcing the already strong image of the simple yet high technology of both countries.

Another aspect of this interaction is the increased use of co-branding, ingredient branding and such. An interesting example of Sony Ericsson's use of co-branding comes with the T310 phone, targeted to the youth segment. The main feature of the phone is the fact that you can play the game *Tony Hawk's ProSkater 4*, a popular PlayStation 2 title, on it. But it doesn't end there; by successfully skating through levels on the phone, previously inaccessible levels are unlocked on the PlayStation version. Sony Ericsson is thus co-branding with one of its parents, Sony, influencing the image of them both. In terms of brand ecosystems, Sony Ericsson is increasing its cultural space by including the cultural connotations of Sony and PlayStation while at the same time nudging them towards the cultural brand ecosystem of mobile communications.

Sony Ericsson is, like most other mobile phone manufacturers, highly dependent on different kinds of co-owned and standard technologies. As Ericsson originally was behind the short-range wireless technology Bluetooth, it is integrated into most phones, and as a part of the mobile phone operating system company Symbian, the user interface on their prestige phones is 'standard' as well. They are even offering their own technical platform, the 'heart' of the phone, to other companies, the only remaining differences to them really being the outer shell. By using 'standard' technology, Sony Ericsson is not only recreating the brands of the technologies, but also of how technology in a more general sense is perceived in a cultural context as standardized technology is reinforcing the image of what technology is. Why Sony Ericsson needs to use standardized technology will be developed further in the next section.

191

The technological level

The increased reliance on technological standards – such as the previously mentioned Bluetooth, UMTS, also known as third generation mobile phone technology, or 3G, and GSM, the currently most used mobile phone communication platform – is not only a result of the ever-increasing complexity and enormous costs involved in new technology development, but also signify an increased dependence for companies on others to create credibility and a sense of continuity – or anchoring themselves in an existing brand ecosystem. The technologies mentioned above are not only technological platforms that deliver value to consumers, but also create a brand image that is used by the participating companies, thus entering them into the brand ecosystem. The trend toward standardized technologies can be seen as a sign of companies lacking the maturity to deliver their own technologies and having to create a mesh of interoperable devices to satisfy customer demand, as can be seen in text from the official Bluetooth website:

> A core value of the Bluetooth SIG Mission Statement is 'interoperability'. One factor in a positive user experience for consumers of wireless technologies is knowing when two or more products are likely to work with one another. The most efficient and effective means to assist customers in identifying both product capabilities and the source of a technology is through branding and trademarks. When used consistently, trade names become a valuable resource in the consumer purchase making decision.
> (www.bluetooth.com)

One could claim that in the networked or communication society it is impossible not to have standards because of the demands for interoperability, but just a look at the personal computer industry, with its standard PC (most likely a Dell) running some flavour of Windows (even more likely), is required to realize that the situation there is probably more than most companies can even dream about. Yet most industries do not have these strong players – even though Nokia, in the mobile phone sector, for a while seemed on the verge of gaining this position – forcing them to cluster together to thrive. These technology clusters are, because they are seldom true global standards, subject to the same competitive environment as regular brands, just involving more actors, including government and non-governmental actors. This special situation seems, however, to make competition particularly fierce, possibly because there can be governmental prestige, to say nothing of job opportunities, vested in the outcomes. The mobile phone industry has had many of these standard 'wars', such as the one about communication protocols, which European and US-backed interests have been fighting off ever since the first-generation analogue phones came out in the 1970s. The cultural importance of being part of the winning standard cannot be understated, as it represents a radical shift in the brand ecosystem not unlike the introduction of a new dominant species.

Interestingly enough, the standard clustering is not limited to branded communication protocols, but a number of manufacturers have created a jointly owned operating system – Symbian. While the argument that it is a good idea to make different devices talk to each other is plausible, there is no doubt that other reasons are behind a 'standardized' user interface. One important factor in this case is quite obviously that the personal computer operating system near-monopolist Microsoft is trying to enter the fast-growing mobile phone market with a flavour of Windows. Simultaneous to the creation of a strong standard is the cultural embedding of how the particular service should work. Who wins the standard is highly dependent on what allies either side has. In the classic VHS vs. Beta struggle, the tide was turned in favour of VHS when the pornographic industry adopted its format for the distribution of their content, even though Beta provided superior picture quality. Chance is simply a factor that has to be in the equation. Moreover, even being on the winning team in a fight for a standard, there are not that many reasons to celebrate. Companies using standardized technologies are still me-too players without any distinctive competitive advantages – they are just using the standard.

The strategic weakness that results from companies using standardized technology also propagates to the technology level, as a co-owned technology has no way to manifest itself except in participating company products. An unused or weak standard is as valuable as an unsold product, ignored by the marketplace and without any impact on the brand ecosystem, weakening rather than strengthening the participating companies. The creation of a strong co-owned brand affects the branded products using it, in a sense levelling the field as all involved organizations become more dependent on the same brand, as was seen, for example, when IBM opened up its PC architecture. It did not take long for IBM to lose its market dominance to more-or-less generic 'IBM PC compatible' competitors – the standard 'IBM PC' brand became strong at the company brand IBM's expense. There is thus a reciprocal dependence between companies and their shared technologies that creates a more compelling image of themselves while at the same time affecting internal brand power relations (cf. Balmer and Greyser 2003).

Brands acting on the technological level are probably the most active members of brand ecosystems, as they only live through others. They are important bearers of cultural values to companies, but also to governmental and non-governmental actors because of their ability to define broader brand cultural segments.

The (non-)governmental level

Government and non-governmental organizations are highly dependent on both company and technology brands as they have to manifest many of the desired cultural aspects unattainable by themselves. In city management there is an obvious interaction between institutional and private enterprises (cf. Czarniawska 2000; Dobers 2003) became a major part of a city's image is based on the actions of private enterprises in the area, while its main effects are felt by municipal actors. A classic example of this is the 'rust belt' in the US Midwest, which suffered from massive manufacturing plant shut downs in the 1970s, and is still unable to attract talent and new enterprises like other named areas such as 'Silicon Valley', resulting in an almost uncontrollable downward spiral. It is therefore important for both municipalities and countries to work long term and of course also to bet on the right horse – it doesn't matter if you are a world leader at something if the industry suddenly disappears.

While there are not that many in marketing focusing on the branding of countries and municipalities, it is possibly the most important area as it in many ways sets the stage for interaction in the brand ecosystems. I 'know', for example, that Japanese small electronics are the best in the world, while Japanese cars are unsafe and rust. Looking at these two product categories more closely probably proves both claims more-or-less false, yet they still exist. Interestingly enough, this is probably not the image Japanese consumers have, at least when it comes to their cars. The interaction is thus not only internal, but possibly more important is the way it is appropriated by outside actors; city and country brands are often as global as Coca-Cola (if perhaps not as well known).

Stockholm has at least since the turn of last century, from the Stockholm Exhibition, a predecessor to the World Fair, in 1897, had the image of being modern and progressive (Czarniawska 2002), adopting the latest and greatest, all in order to at least be comparable to the world metropolises, even though it is situated at the rim of the world. Almost as a precursor for what was to come, Stockholm built the Globe arena in 1989, to signal that the city was ready to grow in importance, because it 'was not simply an imposing edifice, but also a massive monument to consumption – "The Globe", at one and the same time an ever-presence like global forms of capital, a structure in which to consume global entertainment commodities, and a device for marketing Stockholm as an international centre for investment opportunities, corporate capital, banking and tourism' (Pred 1995: 16), to which one can add information technology. With the start of the boom in the ICT sector in the mid-1990s, Stockholm created several concurrent initiatives promoting the city as at the frontier of ICT, ranging from the Stockholm Challenge Award, a world's best ICT city challenge, to mCity, a project organized by the city that enables mobile access to municipal services, and of course the efforts to brand the suburb Kista (incidentally close to Swedish for silicon) as the Silicon Valley of Europe, with the company Ericsson as its powerhouse. All these activities were of course carried out to increase the city's service to its citizens, but also to build Stockholm's image as modern and progressive (Czarniawska 2000). None of these activities would have been set in motion without having something to build on, and supporting the claims were not only the embedded cultural notion of modernity, but also successful companies and technologies.

City and state level actors can to some extent influence their own image, but in fact they rely heavily on other actors, as can be seen in Invest in Sweden's (ISA 2002) report on the current state of the Swedish ICT sector. The report is filled with quotes from major corporations praising Sweden and its business climate. The report thus provides Sweden with a borrowed image by the inclusion of global corporations whose centre of activity is definitely not placed in Sweden, but yet creates the sense that Sweden is almost like home because the global (and easily recognized) brands exist there, and think it's a good place to be. In the same spirit, the Swedish Export Council sponsors trips and exhibition space every year to high-tech shows like CeBIT in Hamburg and E3 in Las Vegas, partly to help struggling companies, but also for the obvious reason to show that Sweden is on the cutting edge of technology. The promotion is not limited to these kinds of openly sponsored marketing channels, and a lot of work is done behind the scenes, such as the struggle for the location of the European Union's joint information technology department, the location of which to some extent signifies the leading ICT nation in Europe. While the ball is still up in the air all interested parties have used the process to beef up their ICT image.

Stockholm has also used the power of the media. The most eye-popping piece came in *Newsweek* (McGuire 2000), with a front-page headline 'Stockholm: Hot IPOs and Cool Clubs in Europe's Internet Capital' – ironically this appeared merely weeks before the start of the global downturn of the ICT-sector which hit Stockholm particularly hard – a situation the city is still struggling with.

CONCLUSION

Brands, through their ever-presence in contemporary society, are deeply embedded in culture, making them important actors and building blocks in identity creation processes. While consumers have been quite invisible in the description of brand ecosystems, they are of course ever-present and important drivers of the whole system in their appropriation of brands. In this time, there is still a need for continuity and brands have, to a large extent, in western society, taken the place of what in past times religion had as a fixing point in people's lives. With brands' increased importance it becomes interesting to explore in what ways brands interact with other cultural cornerstones. The interaction is not static and fixed, but rather fluid and continuous, where any action affects the whole (not that unlike life at the pond).

By using ecosystems and the connection to the intricately intertwined relations in nature, one can understand that brands' relations to each other are not simply linear or easily dissectible. Whereas ecosystems focus on the relationships between different species in nature, brand ecosystems do the same with culture. Where most have interested themselves in company brands, it is worthwhile to expand the scope and include, at least, technology and governmental 'brand' aspects as it gives a broader understanding of the cultural underpinnings and drivers in the brand creation process. The importance of country and city brands cannot be overestimated, as could be seen in the heyday of Nokia, when it was almost enough to be Finnish to get money from US investors. While the situation for technology and company brands are slightly different, they are both highly dependent on each other as can be seen with the virtual explosion in co-branding, ingredient branding and other forms of brand cooperation.

KEY POINT

- Brand creation is not only an internal process, but rather a moulding inter-action with a mesh of multiple cultural levels, forming a brand ecosystem.

QUESTIONS FOR DISCUSSION

1 How does the brand ecosystem model differ from traditional brand management?
2 Choose a well-known brand and try to map its ecosystem: what are the governmental, technological and cultural influences that affect the brand?
3 How can brand ecosystems contribute to the understanding of the brand creation process?
4 Discuss the statement neither managers nor consumers fully control the branding processes.
5 What different roles do companies play in brand ecosystems?

REFERENCES

Aaker, D. A. and Joachimsthaler, E. (2000) *Brand Leadership*, New York: The Free Press.

Apéria, T. (2001) *Brand Relationship Management: Den Varumärkesbyggande Processen*, Stockholm: University School of Business.

Balmer, J. M. T. and Greyser, S. A. (2003) *Revealing the Corporation: Perspectives on Identity, Image, Reputation, Corporate Branding, and Corporate-level Marketing*, London: Routledge.

Bengtsson, A. (2002) *Consumers and Mixed-Brands: On the Polysemy of Brand Meaning*, Lund: Lund Business Press.

Czarniawska, B. (2000) 'The European capital of the 2000s: on image construction and modelling', *Corporate Reputation Review* 3, 3: 202–217.

Czarniawska, B. (2002) *A Tale of Three Cities: Or the Glocalization of City Management*, Oxford: Oxford University Press.

Dobers, P. (2003) 'Image of Stockholm as an IT city: emerging urban entrepreneurship', in B. Bjerke (ed.) *Entrepreneurship: New Movements*, Aldershot: Edgar Elgar.

Elliott, R. (1994) 'Exploring the symbolic meaning of brands', *British Journal of Management* 5: 13–19.

Elliott, R. and Jankel-Elliott, N. (2002) 'Using ethnography in strategic consumer research', *Discussion Papers in Management* 2, 2: 2–22.

Featherstone, M. (1991) *Consumer Culture and Postmodernism*, London: Sage.

Fournier, S. (1998) 'Consumers and their brands: developing relationship theory in consumer research', *Journal of Consumer Research* 24, 4: 343–373.

Hedrén, J. (2002) *Naturen som Brytpunkt: om Miljöfrågans Mystifieringar, Konflikter och Motsägelser (Nature as Dividing Line: the Mystification, Conflict and Contradictions of Environmental Questions)*, Eslöv: B. Östlings bokförl. Symposion.

Hirschman, E. C. and Thompson, C. J. (1997) 'Why media matter: advertising and consumers in contemporary communication', *Journal of Advertising* 26, 1: 43–60.

Holt, D. B. (2004) *How Brands Become Icons: The Principles of Cultural Branding*, Boston, MA: Harvard Business School Press.

ISA (2002) 'ICT – information & communications technologies,' http://www.isa.se

Johar, G. V., Holbrook, M. B. and Stern, B. B. (2001) 'The role of myth in creative advertising design: theory, process and outcome', *Journal of Advertising* 30, 2: 1–26.

Kapferer, J.-N. (1997) *Strategic Brand Management: Creating and Sustaining Brand Equity Long Term*, London: Kogan Page.

Kates, S. M. (2000) 'Out of the closet and out on the street! Gay men and their brand relationships', *Psychology and Marketing* 17: 493–513.

Keller, K. L. (2003) *Strategic Brand Management: Building, Measuring, and Managing Brand Equity*, Upper Saddle River, NJ: Prentice Hall.

Klein, N. (2000) *No Logo*, London: Picador.

Kozinets, R. V. (2001) 'Utopian enterprise: articulating the meanings of Star Trek's culture of consumption', *Journal of Consumer Research* 28 (June): 67–88.

McAlexander, J. H., Schouten, J. W. and Koenig, H. F. (2002) 'Building brand community', *Journal of Marketing* 66, 1: 15–37.

McGuire, S. (2000) 'Shining Stockholm', *Newsweek* 7 February.

Marquard, O. (1991) *In Defense of the Accidental: Philosophical Studies*, New York: Oxford University Press.

Muñiz, A. M. and O' Guinn, T. C. (2001) 'Brand community', *Journal of Consumer Research* 27, 4: 412–432.

Percy, L., Rossiter, J. R. and Elliott, R. (2001) *Strategic Advertising Management*, Oxford: Oxford University Press.

Pred, A. (1995) *Recognizing European Modernities: A Montage of the Present*, London: Routledge.

Schroeder, J. E. (2002) *Visual Consumption*, London: Routledge.

Solomon, M., Bamossy, G. and Askegaard, S. (2002) *Consumer Behaviour: A European Perspective*, Harlow: Prentice Hall.

Winkler, A. (1999) *Warp-Speed Branding: The Impact of Technology on Marketing*, New York: John Wiley.

Chapter 13

Selling dreams

The role of advertising in shaping luxury brand meaning

Arianna Brioschi

In this chapter, I present recent research on how advertising helps build luxury brands and develop a model of the two-way value creating relationship that links the firm and the consumer. The conceptual framework construction for luxury goods is based on the assumption that the firm-designed brand identity is linked to the consumer-read brand image, via brand meaning creation and interpretation, driven by the cultural codes of luxury branding. I identify consumer-related luxury brand meanings (brand values from the firm's point of view) that can be effectively incorporated into luxury brand communication strategies to shorten the gap between brand identity and brand image.

Brand equity is recognized to be among the most important assets of the firm (e.g. Kapferer 2004). From a firm's point of view, brand equity concerns itself with issues that make a particular brand recognizable and favourable over other alternatives. In short, brand equity creates cues to memory, and the brands provide a summary of information for consumers; they are used as a form of 'mental shorthand' (Aaker 1997). However, a brand does not only signal a product's value – it can also have a particular resonance, which makes the product personally meaningful and intrinsically relevant for the consumer. Consumers look to the meanings created in both the marketing and social environments to assist with this individual meaning construction.

Moreover, consumers are creative meaning constructors – interpreting marketer-derived meanings of the brand (transmitted through various aspects of the cultural system) and actively adopting or changing these meanings through a kind of discourse between the 'accepted' meaning and their personal life situation (e.g. Holt 1997; Thompson and Haytko 1997). Consumers make use of the information in the marketing environment and cultural environment, and combine this information with their own goals and history to make sense of the brand and to create an individualized meaning of the brand. Therefore, from the marketer's perspective, it is extremely important to understand how meaning can be constructed in the marketing environment. Meanings are communicated via marketing initiatives – distribution channel choices, pricing; advertising in particular helps transfer meanings to brands. Luxury brands provide a rich arena to investigate branding processes – an arena in which image and symbol drive brand value, largely via advertising campaigns (see Chapter 4 in this volume). This chapter reports results from an analysis of about 200 contemporary advertising campaigns from the culture of luxury brands, that help map the luxury brand universe, and which elicit a number of theoretical and practical applications.

LUXURY MEANINGS

Communication strategies play decisive roles in building consumer's perception of luxury. For example, visual and textual descriptions in advertisements help the viewer to infer the luxurious properties associated with products, services and brands, infusing them with desired symbolic images by emphasizing elements such as exclusivity and scarcity that support a luxury attribution and aura. Vigneron and Johnson (2004) propose a theoretical framework of the brand–luxury construct, based on the early work of social theorist Thorstein Veblen (1899), as updated by Leibenstein's classic luxury brand research (1950). Leibenstein suggested that the utility derived from a product might be enhanced by external effects, such as the quantity of goods consumed by other persons, or relating to the fact that the product bears a higher rather than a lower price tag. Leibenstein emphasized the role of interpersonal relations in the luxury brand consumption, and derived three main effects, which he called Veblen, snob and bandwagon. Vigneron and Johnson proposed two additional luxury effects: personal pleasure and emotional experience, both linked to the consumer's *personal* reactions to luxury consumption. These self-referential aspects of consumption, which regard the private and personal sphere of an individual, can be associated to literature on the experiential and emotional aspects of consumption and to the personal pleasure derived by possessing and using luxuries.

I propose that two further consumption characteristics coexist in today's luxury goods market. First, what I call fashionable consumers are motivated by the search for fashion, style or trends – they let themselves be swayed by trends, fads and the 'latest'. In this realm, manufacturers actively seek to shorten the 'life' of their products via planned obsolescence to secure a repurchase rate. Advertising helps convince people that the 'new' or 'improved' version of the same product is not just functional, but 'socially superior' to the old (Mason 1981). At the opposite side of the consumption continuum, we find conservative consumers that are fond of traditions who seek goods that relate to the past, or that exhibit classic taste or heritage. Authenticity and the quest for perfection and timelessness typify this consumption attitude.

EMPIRICAL ANALYSIS AND METHODOLOGICAL APPROACH

To investigate the luxury communication terrain, I adopted a multi-method study to maximize analysis potentials and enhance research results. First, content analysis in the chosen empirical field of luxury goods advertisements will permit an understanding of the meanings given to luxury via advertising. The content analysis was complemented by a statistical clustering technique applied to the sample to identify themes and patterns in luxury branding.

Which products and brands should be regarded as luxuries? If we take a broad definition as a starting point, there is no fixed ground to select a luxury product since any product and any brand may be transformed into a luxury. Furthermore, luxury often refers to an immaterial state of mind or existential condition. For this study, I narrow the scope to material luxury objects. In the three-tiered division of luxury, we refer to the lower and intermediate levels of the luxury market: these are the most profitable segments for the luxury industry (Kapferer 2004). Moreover, highly exclusive luxury goods are inherently rare, and not as commonly promoted via traditional communication strategies such as print advertisements.

The selection process resulted in a sample of 198 magazine advertisements, which were collected from eight popular consumer magazines, such as *Elle*, *Marie Claire*, *Vogue*, *Architectural Digest* and *Elle Décor* in the year 2000. The selected advertisements include 10 product categories and 112 well-known and recognized brands, which were reported to be luxury brands by a pre-test sample of consumers. Generally speaking, the relatively small number of advertisements in the sample is indicative of the investigated consumption domain – luxury brands are subject to a communication paradox, and must balance their exposure ratio with the awareness needs.

I first classified the products' category and brand, then coded each advertisement's objective and subjective content within the luxury branding framework. Each thematic code was described using terms and ideas pertaining to the implied brand meaning. Judges used these descriptions to identify themes in each analysed advertisement. We also added the country of origin code and devoted a code to both aesthetic and artistic elements of the advertisement.

Where applicable I used a dichotomous scale to indicate whether the advertisement presented or not a certain property. In the other cases I qualitatively recorded the ad's characteristics and subsequently moved on to a reclassification in broader categories. The coding of the ads involved both visual illustrations and the themes conveyed by the combination of copy and illustration. Visual codes were simple counts (e.g. the presence of men or women), while the thematic codes were much more judgemental (e.g. the snob code). The following definitions informed the content analysis' subjective aspect:

- *Veblen code* (conspicuous, display, showing off, comparisons, status, jewellery, gems, gold, wealth, richness, abundance)

- *Snob code* (scarcity, exclusivity, few distribution points, limited edition, different from the masses, standing out, distinction, dandy, aristocratic, elite sports, refinement, black tie)
- *Quality/functionality code* (manufacturing, utility, functions, applications, workings, handmade, raw materials)
- *Emotion/hedonism/experiential code* (feelings, pleasure, enjoyment, desire, satisfaction, relaxation, excitement, sentiments, love, magic, the five senses – taste, sight, smell, listening, touching)
- *Aesthetic/artistic code* (elegance, attractiveness, beauty, refinement, harmony, design, artistic disciplines, show-biz, museums, paintings, art)
- *Tradition code* (tradition, old times, mature men/women, time passing, history, classic, discretion, father and son)
- *Modern/fashion Code* (contemporary, up to date, trendy)
- *Country-of origin code* (made in, use of foreign languages).

From this analysis, several themes in contemporary luxury advertising emerged.

EMERGENT THEMES IN LUXURY BRAND ADVERTISING

Setting

The centrality of the product in luxury advertisements represents a large portion of our entire sample without models, including cases in which the advertisement shows only a part of the product. If additional objects are present within the advertisement, the overall look does not strongly change. The product still usually gets the central position in the overall visual design. The only difference is that other elements are placed in a marginal position to complete the image. These objects are largely classifiable in a few groups:

- *Status* references (caviar, cigar, swimming pool, tuxedo, Martini cocktail, cigar, chaise longue, pool table, coupé sportscar, sailing boats, finely dressed table, precious earrings, gala evening in the background, Sony Aibo, exotic landscape, oil paintings);
- *Quality* references (mechanisms, craftsman in his workshop) that are almost exclusively used in watches advertisements;
- *Art* references (Tamara Lempicka painting, Japanese garden background, Duca d'Urbino etching, Botticelli's *Primavera* painting, Japanese dress, Art Deco interior);
- *Famous cities* (Venice canal, New York skyline, Ville de Paris, Paris boulevard);
- *Gift-giving* references (Christmas tree, gift box, perfume box);
- *Racing/freedom* references (vintage racing car, F1 racing cars, Mille Miglia racing car, Biplane, navigation map, albatross, America's Cup).

201

Interpersonal relationships

The relationship between persons and the product remains one of the most crucial signifiers within advertisements. Persons in advertisements supply the consumer with a certain identification frame – whether the person is presented as a user or is presented within a lifestyle setting, the viewer is invited to identify him/herself with the presented person. Only 36 per cent of the advertisements for luxury products use persons in their campaigns, except for perfume advertisements of which instead more than half uses one or more persons in the visual. This is somewhat surprising, since of the total sample, the ads that were less likely to depict persons were those related to luxury goods that can be worn or used as ornaments (jewellery and watches). One explanation could be related to the importance of 'relevance' (Aaker 1992) in the creation of meaningful advertisements. Since in creating advertisements some images are more relevant than others, whether an advertisement or other media image influences our expectation of what ought to be depends on the relevance of the characters portrayed in that image. It is in the advertiser's interest to make those characters seem relevant to as many viewers as possible in the hope that viewers will also see the featured product as relevant. For this reason, most characters or models in advertising are decontextualized or are contextualized only loosely, in that aside from such cues such as gender and age, we have little objective information about what kind of person this is in an advertisement and his/her similarity to us. Since luxury ads could engender a refusal reaction if proposing aspirational levels of attractiveness, popularity and wealth that consumers couldn't easily reach if they 'only' used the same product the model used, cues that might indicate the model is not like the viewer are removed or minimized.

Product

When models are not present, the product captures a central position in the imagery of luxury advertisements. Nearly half of the advertisements for luxury goods without persons concentrate on the product standing alone. In many advertisements that employ limited visual or verbal material to create their message – often showing only the product or the brand name – empty space contributes to the product's luxurious and exclusive image. Thus, empty or white space, rather than imparting no information, as might be inferred from a strictly information-processing view of adverting, imbues luxury products with meaning.

The link between emptiness and luxury can be traced within sociology studies. Although quantity remains a sign of power and wealth, austerity penetrates in several domains as a sign of distinction. Abstinence and understatement becomes a sign of cultivation and good taste (Bourdieu 1984). Soberness as such, restraining oneself and especially the aesthetical appreciation of emptiness makes the principle of what Bourdieu (1984) defines as *amor vacui* – a mark of excellence.

Stuart Ewen (1988) has furthermore pointed out that ads for luxury goods often adopt a style that could be called classical. Traditionally, art historians have tended to discuss classicism as the first phase in a recurring stylistic cycle that begins with simplicity, symmetry and order and moves toward increasing elaboration and extravagance. The artistic movements with which the label classicism is most closely associated have tended to coincide with historical periods defined by the consolidation of wealth and power (e.g. Schroeder and Borgerson 2002). It has been a style of exclusion and containment, and it is these aspects that appear to be most relevant to its current position as a status indicator in advertising. Classicism, originally a fairly austere style, represents power, wealth and taste, 'visually reinforcing the power structure in any period, today and yesterday' (Conway and Roenisch 1994: 16). The ad's simple composition and lack of props are ingredients of a reactive classicism, a style that implicitly rejects outspoken conspicuous consumption.

Colours

Colour often is invoked as a primary influence in the brand evaluation process. The affective response to colours (Wagner 1990) can directly control emotions and to a certain extent the behavioural and cognitive sphere of individuals since it is capable of attracting/distracting, transmitting happiness or sadness, tranquillity or anxiety (Wagner 1990). In my sample, I found the most prevalent colours clustered toward neutral shades, white, black, and black and white together. Monotonous backgrounds in neutral colours, such as black and white, let the product stand out in all its glory. Black and white moreover suggests refinement and understatement, which can effectively contrast with the Veblen connotations of luxury. Eschewing colour connotes classicism.

Veblen code

If products are to be transformed into luxury objects, adding the wealth connotation can transfunctionalize them into expressions of richness and affluence. When we look at ads for luxury products, whether cars, clothes or gadgets, we find that explicit mentions of status appeal are the exceptional not the rule. This does not mean that social status is entirely absent from these ads. But its presence is signalled indirectly, through more elliptical language and, essentially, through images.

Veblenian consumption meaning is epitomized by the desire for, acquisition and/or display of valued objects calculated to increase social honour in a community. It is interesting to note that Veblen connotations recur in less than 20 per cent of my sample, which may be interpreted as the manifest consequence of luxury companies' understanding of the contrast between the desire to show off that drives some consumers of luxury goods and the pressure for reticence that comes from part of today's society. Luxury brands rarely play on such elements as conspicuous display, showy comparisons, status appreciation, display of jewellery, gems or gold, wealth, richness and abundance references.

Snob codes

Uniqueness and social status lead consumers to desire and seek consumer goods, services and experiences that few others possess (Blumberg 1974; Snyder and Fromkin 1980). This tendency to seek unique consumer products is of superior importance in marketing luxury brands marketing. Advertising is not the only means that marketers use to appeal to uniqueness motives. Product differentiation, prestige pricing and exclusive distribution are also components of marketers' appeals to consumers' desires for unique products.

Strategies conceived to enhance the scarcity and exclusivity value of the luxury brand can thus promote it as part of a limited series, numbering the product or presenting it as a special edition. In this way the scarcity code works via a real limited production. Another way to reach the same result is restraining distribution, setting up an exclusive outlet network in which to offer the goods. This last tactic is very common for luxury goods and frequently underlined in the related advertisements. About two out of three of the brands in the sample indicated one way or another that the products could be bought only at selected or exclusive boutiques, or were a sign of distinction, signalling refinement and connoisseurship. Some brands go as far as listing the cities (mostly international capitals or elite holiday resorts) and retail addresses that carry their goods.

One of the employed symbols of snobbishness is a nineteenth-century figure with an extreme concern for refined elegance and clothing: the dandy. Today the dandy aristocratic figure refers, in luxury advertisements, to the fact that the product is intended for someone who knows perfectly where to go in life. In their article on luxury possessions and practices, Dubois and Laurent (1995) define 'having put on a tuxedo or evening dress' as being related to luxury behaviour. Someone, frequently a man, marked by a charismatic aura, is presented within the advertisement with the figure of a distinguished gentleman, perfectly costumed, generally with white shirt and black tie – the James Bond look to make a case. The dandy-aristocrat looks self-confidently at the camera, exudes style and perfectly controls his appearance. The code shows a role model of exclusive and self-assured lifestyle, which makes it perfect for a luxury goods advertisement.

Country of origin code

Research in sociology, anthropology and cross-cultural psychology has provided ample evidence for the existence of national and cultural stereotypes (see Peabody 1985, for a review). National and cultural stereotypes may be defined as beliefs that various traits are predominantly present and therefore characteristic of a particular nation or culture. The stereotype of the French, for example, includes, among other things, the belief that French people are distinguished from many other nations by their aesthetic sensibility and good taste, whereas practicality and a utilitarian orientation, on the other hand, are commonly associated with American culture (Peabody 1985). Two comprehensive reviews of country-of-origin effects (Bilkey and Nes 1982; Ozsomer and Cavusgil 1991) have consistently concluded that a favourable country-of-origin image has a positive effect on perceived quality. Even though printed in Italian magazines, about 15 per cent of the sampled advertisements use French or English.

Aesthetic code

Aesthetics is closely identified with the fine arts: painting, poetry, architecture, sculpture, dance and music. That is why we have identified references to these dominions as indicative of an association of aesthetics to the luxury object. Our sample presents a large proportion of advertisements of the sample total that employ aesthetics (28.7 per cent). Including aesthetic suggestions in the advertisement is particularly meaningful for luxury brands since one of the necessary abilities to discern aesthetic qualities is taste (Bourdieu 1984). The individual with taste is thus able to interpret an image and associate it with other experiences, giving it meaning. Consumers learn to recognize aesthetic value through repeated exposure to the style dictates proposed in media communications.

Beauty interacts with other types of values to enhance the consumption experience, for example aesthetic value may blend with practical value: utility. Aesthetics refers to the benefit acquired from a product's capacity to present a sense of beauty or to enhance personal expression. Style demands, product-appearance demands, art purchases and fashion following are examples of consumers' pursuing aesthetic needs.

Art critic John Berger draws fascinating parallels between the history of art and advertising, pointing out that advertising depends heavily on the techniques, symbols and history of paintings. Direct references to painting, such as reproducing well-known images, framing products like pictures and quoting of art historical sources, lend cultural authority to an ad and links it to taste, prestige and affluence (cf. Schroeder and Borgerson 2002). The typical role of art is not to represent costliness, which, after all, could be symbolized equally well by other means, but to suggest that the consumer is a person of discriminating taste and, therefore, of status (Bourdieu 1984). As an index of social position, leisure is most effective not when it is dissipated fruitlessly but when it serves as the opportunity for personal cultivation and refinement. Cultivation and refinement persist after the leisure time has been expended; therefore, their value as social markers is more permanent. Accordingly, it is to these after-effects of leisure, which could be termed 'secondary' indicators of status, that Veblen ultimately refers to. Consequently, art itself is often represented in luxury product advertising, implying that the viewer possesses the superior connoisseurship needed to decipher such a representation.

Quality

Olson (1972) proposed the quality perception process to have two stages in which consumers first choose surrogate indicators of product quality (i.e. quality cues) from an array of product-related attributes, and then combine their evaluations of these individual cues into an overall judgement of product quality. Quality cues can be ascertained by the senses prior to consumption. Quality cues are categorized as either intrinsic or extrinsic. Intrinsic cues are part of the physical product. Extrinsic cues are related to the product, but are physically not part of it. A distinction is further made between experience quality attributes and credence quality attributes. Experience attributes can be ascertained on the basis of actual experience of the product, whereas credence attributes could not be determined even after normal use for a long time.

This model of perceived quality also fits into means-end chain theory, which states that consumers have organized their product knowledge in hierarchical knowledge structures or schemata (e.g. Peter and Olson 1993). Perceived quality is a fairly abstract global concept (end), which is based on rather concrete product characteristics (means). Quality in luxury goods advertisements is usually ascribed to intrinsic cues such as manufacturing and raw material. In our sample the code has been evoked in about a third of the cases.

LUXURY BRAND CLUSTERS

To classify these codes, cluster analysis was undertaken to ascertain if any patterns were present in luxury advertising. Variables for the cluster analysis were the same used for the content analysis except for background colours which, for statistical purposes, were reclassified in compact categories: white, black, black and white, dark colours, light colours and a category for backgrounds which were unclassifiable by the presence of a specified hue (such as natural surroundings). The sample has also been reclassified to include one single observation for each brand. Where data of several advertisements for the same brand had been collected, I have summarized the findings using a simple 'preponderance rule', the brand would be classified by the presence of those codes, which appeared in the majority of the single ads. In this way, some conventions of luxury ads emerge.

Four clusters emerged. The first group, which I call 'Mechanical', includes mostly mechanical products, with automobiles and watches prevailing. The second consists of mainly champagnes and jewellery, 'Sparkle'; fashion brands dominate group three, 'Fashion'. The last cluster shows no common thread, but includes mostly European brands associated with particular founders, designers or artisans, so it is termed 'European style'.

Some initial interesting considerations can be presented on the differentiating codes that emerged within this typology. The cars and watches cluster generally features both with a headline caption and body copy in their ads. Most of the ads for brands in cluster one also use a white background on which to present product images. The most relevant categories for brands in cluster one are cars and watches, products that usually possess a higher degree of functional attributes that could justify an advertisement's use of

Table 13.1 Luxury brand advertising cluster analysis

Cluster	Mechanical	Sparkle	Fashion	European style
Brands	A. Lange & Sohne	A.G. Spalding	Baccarat	Audemars Piguet
	Alfa Romeo	Barthelay	Brioni	Balenciaga
	Aurora	Baume & Mercier	Burberry	Berlucchi
	Bang & Olufsen	Berluti	Celine	Chanel
	Bentley	Boucheron	Damiani	Chopard
	Blancpain	Bulgari	Daum	Dior
	BMW	Calvin Klein	Dolce & Gabbana	Etro
	Breguet	Cartier	Ermenegildo Zegna	Hermès
	Bulova	Chaumet	Fratelli Rossetti	Land Rover
	Eberhard	Cristal Saint-Louis	Frette	Longines
	Gianmaria Buccellat	De Beers	Giorgio Armani	Loro Piana
	Girard-Perregaux	de Grisogono	Gucci	Omega
	Hublot	Dom Pérignon	Hogan	Patek Philippe
	Jaeger leCoultre	Franck Muller	Kenzo	Pierre Cardin
	Jaguar	Georg Jensen	Lacoste	Remy Martin
	Louis Roederer	Laurent-Perrier	Louis Vuitton	Roger Dubuis
	Maserati	Piper-Heidsieck	Mauboussin	Salvini
	Mercedes	Raymond Weil	Moet & Chandon	Sergio Rossi
	Mont Blanc	Rolex	Omas	Smythson
	Paul Picot	Ruinart	Pollini	Versace
	Perrier Jouet	S.T. Dupont	Pomellato	Wyler Vetta
	Piaget	TAG Heuer	Prada	
	Porsche	Taittinger	Scavia	
	Rado	Valextra	Tod's	
	Tiffany	Veuve Cliquot Ponsardin	Trussardi	
	Ulysse Nardin	Waterman	Van Cleef & Arpels	
	Vacheron Constantin		Venini	
	Volvo		Yves Saint Laurent	
	Zenith			

an informative frame. These are brands that also imply tradition undertones, such as qualitative supremacy, aesthetic touches and that draw on emotional suggestions.

Brand advertising in the second group is characterized by a black backdrop on which products can stand out as if they were placed in a velvet case. Many jewellery brands use black to highlight the sparkle and shine of stones and gems. Furthermore, this group emphasizes nationality to typify brands as luxuries. One explanation could derive from the indication that many brands in this cluster are champagne. Champagne is, as a rule, typified as a French product and using French in the ads' text can emphasize its country of provenance.

The third group has the peculiarity of not being characterized by almost any of the codes we identified as typically pertaining to luxury goods. These brands often employ a very simple ad format – no headline or body copy – only the brand's name or logo is mentioned, in a typical fashion industry convention (Codeluppi 1989). Black and white photography dominates in the fourth group. This artifice is used to allude to the brand's refinement, taste and finesse qualities. Most of the companies that advertise in this cluster complement their message format with additional objects. These are also brands that, together with those in cluster one, use the snob code to enhance their luxury value.

It seems that some brand categories, such as cars, watches, champagne and jewellery have common traits that have been used to communicate the brand's luxury status. Cluster results show that different brands build luxury meanings in different ways. Whereas luxury connotations that stem from the research framework have been identified as pertaining to luxury goods overall, particular product categories often highlight distinctive codes.

CONCLUSION

Broadly generalizing, there are two ways in which brand meaning can be seen as internalized by consumers. One approach argues that marketers create symbolic meaning for a product or brand and inject it into a 'culturally constituted world' – products acquire a stable meaning, and that consumers accept this meaning 'provided' for them (McCracken 1987), and choose products and brands that suit their identity or values (Aaker 1997; Fournier 1998; for a review see Holt 1997). Another approach contends that consumers use creative ways to combine and adapt meanings to fit their own lives. From this perspective, the meanings of products, brands and advertisements are not perceived similarly by all consumers, but are interpreted in accordance with an individual's life. Individual preferences are a mix of interpretations, discourses or frameworks used by consumers to link together the brand, the social situation and the individual (Holt 1997; Thompson and Haytko 1997).

My perspective assumes that marketers attempt to instil meaning into products and brands via cultural codes such as aesthetics, luxury and quality. I do not deny that consumers creatively interpret and construct individual meanings based on their life tasks and life goals. This study shows how the cultural codes of branding interact with brand identity and consumer response within luxury brand advertising. In this way, brand meaning develops from the interchange among three environments: the marketing, the individual and the cultural, as each environment contributes to a uniform way for consumers to identify and interact with a branded product. This research started from semiotics and viewed the product as a sign for consumers' needs. However, only the sign-object relation, or semantics, was taken into account. Given that content analysis typically limits itself to the signs and symbols within the message, the interpretant of the sign, or consumer response, is neglected.

Luxury brands must construct luxury in their communication strategies, by signalling, for example, scarcity, quality, value, selective distribution and high prices. Understanding the cultural codes of branding through advertising research can help firms identify which luxury codes work for their brands or the most appropriate cultural 'language' of luxury – verbal, visual, design or artistic cues. Content and interpretive research can reveal how advertising language evolves and the current pace and direction of change in communicating luxury status to brands, since advertising imparts information but does much more in communicating to consumers what products and brands mean. Brands express who and what customers are and these identities are shaped by transferred cultural codes. Consumers use advertising to learn new meanings and to confirm/ reinforce those they already know. In an ongoing and largely unobtrusive way, then, people 'read' advertising as a cultural text, and advertisers who understand this meaning-based model can create powerful and intriguing campaigns.

KEY POINT

- Luxury brand advertising depends on a set of cultural codes to communicate luxury effects, including the snob effect, the bandwagon effect, exclusivity, aesthetics and tradition, and can be grouped into four main types, largely according to product class.

QUESTIONS FOR DISCUSSION

1 What are the underlying features of luxury brand campaigns as found in this chapter?
2 Find some luxury brand advertisements and apply the codes discussed here. Are they present in your sample? What do they suggest about the brand strategy?
3 How are luxury brands distinct from other brands? Why do consumers pay for luxury?
4 How do the conventions of luxury branding influence advertising strategy?
5 Compare and contrast this chapter's ideas about luxury branding to Kapferer's approach in Chapter 4 this volume.

REFERENCES

Aaker, D. A. (1992) *Managing Brand Equity: Capitalizing on the Value of a Brand Name*, New York: The Free Press.

Aaker, J. (1997) 'Dimensions of brand personality', *Journal of Marketing Research* 34: 347–357.

Bilkey, W. J. and Nes, E. (1982) 'Country-of-origin effects on product evaluation', *Journal of International Business Studies* 13: 89–99.

Blumberg, P. (1974) 'The decline and fall of the status symbol: some thoughts on status in the post-industrial society', *Social Problems* 21 (April): 480–498.

Bourdieu, P. (1984) *Distinction: A Social Critique of the Judgement of Taste*, Cambridge, MA: Harvard University Press.

Codeluppi, V. (1989) *Consumo e comunicazione*, Milano: FrancoAngeli.

Conway, H. and Roenisch, R. (1994) *Understanding Architecture*, London: Routledge.

Dubois, B. and Laurent, G. (1995) 'Luxury possessions and practices: an empirical scale', *European Advances in Consumer Research* 2: 69–77.

Ewen, S. (1988) *All Consuming Images*, New York: Basic Books.

Fournier, S. (1998) 'Consumers and their brands: developing relationship theory in consumer research', *Journal of Consumer Research* 24 (September): 343–373.

Holt, D. B. (1997) 'Poststructuralist lifestyle analysis: conceptualizing the social patterning of consumption in postmodernity', *Journal of Consumer Research* 23 (March): 326–350.

Kapferer, J.-N. (2004) *The New Strategic Brand Management: Creating and Sustaining Brand Equity Long Term*, London: Kogan Page.

Leibenstein, H. (1950) 'Bandwagon, snob, and Veblen effects in the theory of consumer's demand', *Quarterly Journal of Economics* 64 (May): 183–207.

McCracken, G. (1987) *Culture and Consumption*, Bloomington: Indiana University Press.

Mason, R. S. (1981) *Conspicuous Consumption: A Study of Exceptional Consumer Behaviour*, Farnborough, Hants; Gower.

Olson, J. C. (1972) 'Cue utilization of the quality perception process: a cognitive model and an empirical test'. Unpublished doctoral dissertation, Purdue University.

Ozsomer, A. and Cavusgil, S. T. (1991) 'Country-of-origin effects on product evaluations: a sequel to Bilkey and Nes review', in M. Gilly (ed.) *AMA Educators' Proceedings: Enhancing Knowledge Development in Marketing*: 261–277.

Peabody, D. (1985) *National Characteristics*, Cambridge: Cambridge University Press.

Peter, J. P. and Olson, J. C. (1993) *Consumer Behaviour and Marketing Strategy*, New York: Irwin.

Schroeder, J. E. and Borgerson, J. L. (2002) 'Innovations in information technology: insights into consumer culture from Italian Renaissance Art', *Consumption, Markets, and Culture* 5, 2: 154–169.

Snyder, C. R. and Fromkin, H. L. (1980) *Uniqueness. The Human Pursuit of Difference*, New York: Plenum.

Thompson, C. J. and Haytko, D. L. (1997) 'Speaking of fashion: consumers' uses of fashion discourses and the appropriation of countervailing cultural meanings' *Journal of Consumer Research* 24, 2: 15–42.

Veblen, T. B. (1899) *The Theory of the Leisure Class*, Boston, MA: Houghton Mifflin.

Vigneron, F. and Johnson, L. W. (2004) 'Measuring perceptions of brand luxury', *Journal of Brand Management* 11, 6: 484–506.

Wagner, C. (1990) 'Color cues', *Marketing Insights* (Spring): 42–46.

Index of companies

General index

eBooks

eBooks – at www.eBookstore.tandf.co.uk

A library at your fingertips!

eBooks are electronic versions of printed books. You can store them on your PC/laptop or browse them online.

They have advantages for anyone needing rapid access to a wide variety of published, copyright information.

eBooks can help your research by enabling you to bookmark chapters, annotate text and use instant searches to find specific words or phrases. Several eBook files would fit on even a small laptop or PDA.

NEW: Save money by eSubscribing: cheap, online access to any eBook for as long as you need it.

Annual subscription packages

We now offer special low-cost bulk subscriptions to packages of eBooks in certain subject areas. These are available to libraries or to individuals.

For more information please contact webmaster.ebooks@tandf.co.uk

We're continually developing the eBook concept, so keep up to date by visiting the website.

www.eBookstore.tandf.co.uk